## RECIPES THAT CAPTURE THE FLAVORS OF LA DOLCE VITA, FROM BOLOGNA TO BROOKLYN—ITALIAN AND ITALIAN AMERICAN–ISH CAKES, COOKIES, PIES, AND PASTRIES, FROM THE JAMES BEARD AWARD–NOMINATED BRAINS BEHIND ONE OF AMERICA'S BEST BAKERIES

A joyous celebration of Italian, American, and Italian American tastes and traditions, *Dolci!* is a compendium of molto delizioso baked goods from both sides of the Atlantic. Baker Renato Poliafito pays homage to pastries of the Old World and the New—with perfected versions of classics like Pastiera and Torta Caprese, Honey-Ricotta Black and Whites, and Butter Cookies.

Poliafito puts his own unique spin on the baking traditions of both countries with recipes of his own invention that are a mash-up of Italian flavors and American innovation. Think Aperol Spritz Cake, Italian Krispie Treats, Malted Tiramisù, Panettone Bread Pudding, and Mocha Orange Whoopie Pies. In addition to the many cakes, pies, tarts, and cookies, he also shares a host of savory recipes—Sourdough Focaccia Three Ways, Perfect Grissini, Cacio e Pepe Arancini—and, for good measure, Italian-inflected cocktails (Amaro Root Beer Float!). A vibrant comingling of two great culinary cultures filtered through the mind of an American with the heart of an Italian, *Dolci!* hits the sweet spot between Italian and American baking.

# DOLCI!

Catania, Sicily, Italy

# DOLCI!

American Baking with an Italian Accent

## RENATO POLIAFITO

with Casey Elsass

*Photographs by Kevin Miyazaki*

ALFRED A. KNOPF   NEW YORK   2024

## THIS IS A BORZOI BOOK PUBLISHED BY ALFRED A. KNOPF

Copyright © 2024 by Renato Poliafito
Photographs copyright © 2024 by Kevin Miyazaki

All rights reserved. Published in the United States by Alfred A. Knopf,
a division of Penguin Random House LLC, New York, and distributed in
Canada by Penguin Random House Canada Limited, Toronto.

www.aaknopf.com

Knopf, Borzoi Books, and the colophon are registered
trademarks of Penguin Random House LLC.

Library of Congress Cataloging-in-Publication Data
Names: Poliafito, Renato, author. | Elsass, Casey, author. |
  Miyazaki, Kevin J., photographer.
Title: Dolci! : American baking with an Italian accent / Renato Poliafito
  with Casey Elsass ; photographs by Kevin Miyazaki.
Description: First edition. | New York : Alfred A. Knopf, 2024. | Includes index.
Identifiers: LCCN 2023013872 (print) | LCCN 2023013873 (ebook) |
  ISBN 9780593537183 (hardcover) | ISBN 9780593537190 (ebook)
Subjects: LCSH: Baking. | Desserts. | Cooking, Italian. | Cooking, American. |
  Baked (Bakery) | LCGFT: Cookbooks.
Classification: LCC TX765 .P65 2024 (print) | LCC TX765 (ebook) |
  DDC 641.81/5—dc23/eng/20230404
LC record available at https://lccn.loc.gov/2023013872
LC ebook record available at https://lccn.loc.gov/2023013873

Some of the recipes in this book may include raw eggs, meat, or fish. When
these foods are consumed raw, there is always the risk that bacteria, which is
killed by proper cooking, may be present. For this reason, when serving these
foods raw, always buy certified salmonella-free eggs and the freshest meat and
fish available from a reliable grocer, storing them in the refrigerator until they
are served. Because of the health risks associated with the consumption of
bacteria that can be present in raw eggs, meat, and fish, these foods should not
be consumed by infants, small children, pregnant women, the elderly, or any
persons who may be immunocompromised. The author and publisher expressly
disclaim responsibility for any adverse effects that may result from the use or
application of the recipes and information contained in this book.

Cover illustrations by Phillip Pascuzzo
Cover design by Kelly Blair
Interior illustrations © Adobe Stock

Manufactured in China

First Edition

Capri, Campania, Italy

AGAIN,
FOR MY MOM.

Naples, Campania, Italy

# CONTENTS

Taormina, Sicily, Italy

# INTRODUCTION

In the summer of 1957, Antonio Poliafito left Sicily by boat and arrived in New York harbor with only a few lira in his pocket. He spent his first few nights in the city sleeping on a park bench until he eventually connected with other Sicilian immigrants, packed into a few square blocks in Bushwick, Brooklyn.

Once my father, a tailor by trade, found a steady job and a suitable place to live, he sent for my mother and newborn sister. They arrived in Brooklyn the week before Thanksgiving, a uniquely American time of the year.

By the time I burst onto the scene in the mid-70s, my parents were the owners of a dry cleaning business and living in Middle Village, Queens. I was the youngest of three, and the most Americanized of the family. I wasn't expected to speak Italian like my brother and sister were; my parents would speak to me in Italian and I would answer in English. But outside of my home, I was nothing but Italian. My name was the butt of jokes, my relatives lived thousands of miles away, and my parents' thick accents and dysfunctional English was a constant reminder that I was different.

Every few years, my parents would take me to Sicily under the guise of a summer vacation. It was always exciting, seeing family, eating great food, and experiencing a slower way of life. But often summer vacation extended from weeks into months and, on a few occasions, well into fall, when I would be enrolled, against my wishes, in a local school. Suddenly, I was nothing but American, my cultural references and limited Italian useless in the classroom, all my video games, TV shows, and friends an ocean away. Acclimating to this new life was almost a form of torture for me. And eventually, to my complete elation, my parents would decide to head back to New York and I'd quietly settle back into the familiar.

But even in New York, I couldn't escape Italy. Italian American culture makes up so much of the fabric of the city, from annual festivals that crowd the streets to pastry shops shilling cannoli to full neighborhoods in all five boroughs that feel like you've stepped into an episode of *The Sopranos*. When it came time to choose a college, I enrolled at Skidmore College in Saratoga Springs, New York, safely nestled way upstate and at arm's length from anything remotely Italian.

The joke was on me because, as an art student, my focus became Italian art. Through the Renaissance painters I began to understand a culture I had so quickly dismissed. I did a semester abroad in Florence, about as culturally different from our small Sicilian village as you can get. Suddenly a whole new world opened up to me, an entire country I had never experienced. Every turn revealed something new: food, art, architecture, music, and people. I started thinking about who I was, culturally, and finding a new appreciation. Much to the surprise of my parents, my pilgrimages to Italy become more frequent, more expansive, more exploratory, and, most important, on my own terms.

Over the years I've covered most of the country, discovering the cultures and traditions that make every region unique. Although I love Italy with all my heart, I'll always be an American looking in. And although New York will always be home, there's a small piece of me that knows I'm from someplace else. My Italian identity lives alongside my American one, and in a weird twist of fate, I'll never fully be either.

Two decades ago, I decided to leave my advertising career and go into the bakery business, opening Baked, a small café in Red Hook, Brooklyn, paying homage to classic American pastries. I had very little experience beyond my occasional homemade treats, so I had to learn on the job how to be a baker and run a business.

American baking is an amalgam of influences from different cultures, often digested into something brand new. It was a perfect starting point to learn a wide variety of techniques and flavors. But privately, in my own baking, I had already started exploring Italian flavors and time-tested recipes that were approachable, simple, and rustic.

As I learned more about both Italian and Italian American desserts, I began to find the pastry discoveries I made in Brooklyn as thrilling as those I made in Rome. Shining cases in both cities were packed with baked goods I had never tried or even heard of. Seeing how immigration both preserves and evolves traditions, especially in the U.S. where so many other immigrants have shared and melded their experiences together, was fascinating. I felt like I was getting in touch with my heritage, understanding more about who I am, where I come from, and how that culture evolved in the city I call home. It dawned on me that my next endeavor should echo that part of me that lives in the in-between.

Ciao, Gloria opened its doors on October 1, 2019. I finally had a bakery that was not only a reflection of who I am, that fully represents my point of view, but also a space to play, explore, and expand my understanding of what Italian and Italian American pastry can be. We are a place that feels Italian, like a beachside resort in the summer, but also a modern American daytime café, where you can come for breakfast, lunch, or a slice of cake over coffee. It's a marriage of my two cultures, through food that's uniquely me. After a childhood of trying to avoid it, I'm leaning into my Italian American heritage. Hey, better late than never!

This book sits at the intersection between Italian, American, and Italian American baked goods. It's packed with the flavors I grew up with, the techniques I acquired later in life, the shared traditions of nonnas from Bensonhurst to Bologna, and the collective hearts and imaginations of Italians in two countries. I explore Old World Italian classics like Cassata (page 218), Pastiera (page 91), and Crostata Classica (page 77), while also respecting newer innovations like Cannoli Croccante (page 169) and Delizia al Limone e Basilico (page 256). Some of the recipes rely heavily on Italian American traditions like Honey-Ricotta Black and Whites (page 63), New York Cheesecake with Berry Topping (page 188), and Butter Cookies (page 57). But many of the recipes sit in the in-between, inventions that are a mash-up of Italian flavors and American innovation, like the Aperol Spritz Cake (page 209), Spumoni Loaf (page 191), Malted Tiramisù (page 243), Panettone Bread Pudding (page 255), and Chocolate Amaro Pecan Pie (page 93). I hope this book inspires you, educates you, and encourages you to explore finding your voice within time-honored traditions. These recipes bring me so much joy and I hope they spark the same feeling as you start baking with an Italian accent.

Grazie mille,

*Renato*

Taormina, Sicily, Italy

# A QUICK HISTORY OF ITALY

A perfectly placed peninsula in the middle of the Mediterranean Sea, Italy has been a crucial piece of land throughout recorded history. During Roman times, it was the center of the Western world (as far west as the known world extended at that point). It was at the center of the Renaissance, a hotbed of science, art, and culture. For better or for worse, Italian explorers like Christopher Columbus and Marco Polo ushered in the Age of Discovery. It was the historical birthplace of ballet and opera, and today holds a global influence on fashion, design, and cuisine.

But Italy as we know it didn't exist until 1861, when several separate regions, kingdoms, small states, and islands decided to unify in an event dubbed the Risorgimento, or rebirth, under the new Kingdom of Italy. (The unification was completed in 1870 when Rome officially incorporated.) Until that point, each region had its own language, laws, customs, food, and traditions.

Sicily, where my parents were born, was both blessed and cursed for its ideal location as a giant, fertile island in the middle of the Mediterranean. It was first colonized by the Ancient Greeks, then came under the control of the Roman Empire. After the fall of Rome, it was host to a who's who of invaders—including the Vandals, Ostrogoths, Byzantines, Islamic Moors, Normans—then back to the Holy Roman Empire, then under Spanish rule, before being united with Italy in the Risorgimento. All those occupiers brought with them distinct influences on the culture of the island, and Sicily is just one of twenty regions in Italy that all underwent drastic changes as wars were fought, kingdoms fell, and modern borders were established.

Even though the country is unified today, these distinct regional histories can still be seen in many aspects of Italian life, most of all the food. Things that we consider inherent to "Italian cuisine" actually come from distinctly different regions: risotto, panettone, osso buco (Lombardy); tortellini, balsamic vinegar, Parmigiano (Emilia-Romagna); biscotti, pecorino, panzanella (Tuscany); carbonara, bruschetta, porchetta (Lazio); pizza, mozzarella, limoncello (Campania); caponata, cannoli, granita (Sicily).

Mass emigration from the late-1800s on, especially from Southern Italy, to American cities like New York, Philadelphia, and Boston introduced a wider population to the traditional Italian foods, cultures, and stories. Many of those stories, including mine, began in Brooklyn, where the impact of Italian culture can be seen on almost every block. From the bakeries and restaurants to the last names listed on the mailboxes of the apartment buildings, there are parts of this borough that feel like you could be in Italy, where customers interact with their butchers in Sicilian dialects, or hundreds gather for annual street fairs to celebrate San Gennaro and bite into a freshly fried zeppole.

Over the last century, Italian food and culture have become so interwoven into the fabric of American culture, that the line where one begins and the other ends has become blurred. I guess that's the goal of every group of people who have come to the U.S.: never to assimilate, but to enhance, and in some way, improve upon what they find here. As the son of immigrants, this is something I have understood from a very young age. In my own way, through my food, I try to share this with my customers: to remember where we came from and, more importantly, where we are going, together.

# IN DEFENSE OF THE SCALE

As you flip through the recipes in these pages, you'll notice something different: every ingredient is listed, first, in grams. Not by volume—tablespoons and cups—but by weight.

A lot of cookbooks use this space to list the pros, cons, and preferred brands for an army of kitchen equipment. Besides the typical cake pans, baking sheets, and piping bags that most people who are casual-to-obsessive bakers probably already have, there's not a lot of specialty equipment in this book and, where there is, I make sure that it's clearly noted.

So instead, I want to focus on the *most* important piece of equipment any baker, at any level, should own: a kitchen scale. No other tool will improve your baking more drastically than the switch from measuring to weighing.

Every ingredient in this book is listed in grams first (with volume measurements beside) because I really want to encourage you to make the switch, for a few simple reasons:

1. **ACCURACY**: Dry ingredients, like flour or sugar, are notoriously variable when measuring by the cup. Even liquid ingredients, like water or milk, can be hard to get 100 percent right in a measuring cup, especially if you have to bend down to read the side. Weighing out the exact amount will be accurate every time.
2. **EASE**: Sometimes measuring oddly shaped things like nuts, or tedious things like herbs, or sticky things like honey is more trouble than it's worth. Weighing frees you from the hassle.
3. **DIVISION**: When dividing dough, portioning batter, or splitting pastry cream, it's usually easier, and less messy, to weigh out the portions rather than trying to use a volume measure, or worse, eyeballing it.
4. **CONSISTENCY**: If you've ever nailed a batch of cookies the first time, then bombed them the second time, you've probably said, "I'm just not good at baking." If you're sticking to grams, you'll have a consistent texture, portion, and bake every time, guaranteed.

The transition to weighing takes a little getting used to, but most of that work is buddying up to the "tare" button on your scale. This button automatically sets the scale back to zero. So every time you're weighing an ingredient for prep or measuring directly into a bowl, remember to hit the tare button. For example, if a recipe says to combine 100 grams of flour and 50 grams of cocoa powder, you'll want to set your bowl on the scale and press tare. Then spoon flour into the bowl until the scale says 100 grams. Hit tare again and spoon in 50 grams of cocoa powder. (I like to make little pockets of ingredients in the bowl, just in case I need to scoop some back out.)

The only exception is for small amounts of ingredients, usually 1 tablespoon or less. Some scales have trouble registering such minute amounts, so go ahead and measure by volume if you're struggling. (And in these cases, being off by a gram or two isn't going to derail anything.) But the weights are still listed for the purists out there who don't even remember where their measuring spoons are!

Ultimately, my aim in championing weight is simple: I want to set you up for success. I've been baking for decades. I've made the recipes in this book over and over again—as have my friends and recipe testers—to make sure that they're perfect. So why would I give you second-rate instructions? If you prefer to work by volume, I've included those measurements throughout. But for me, weight is the way to go. I know it's a big step putting your measuring tools—the training wheels of baking—away, but graduating to the scale is a guaranteed way to bake better. You can trust me, I'm a professional.

# 1

# BUONGIORNO!

Catania, Sicily, Italy

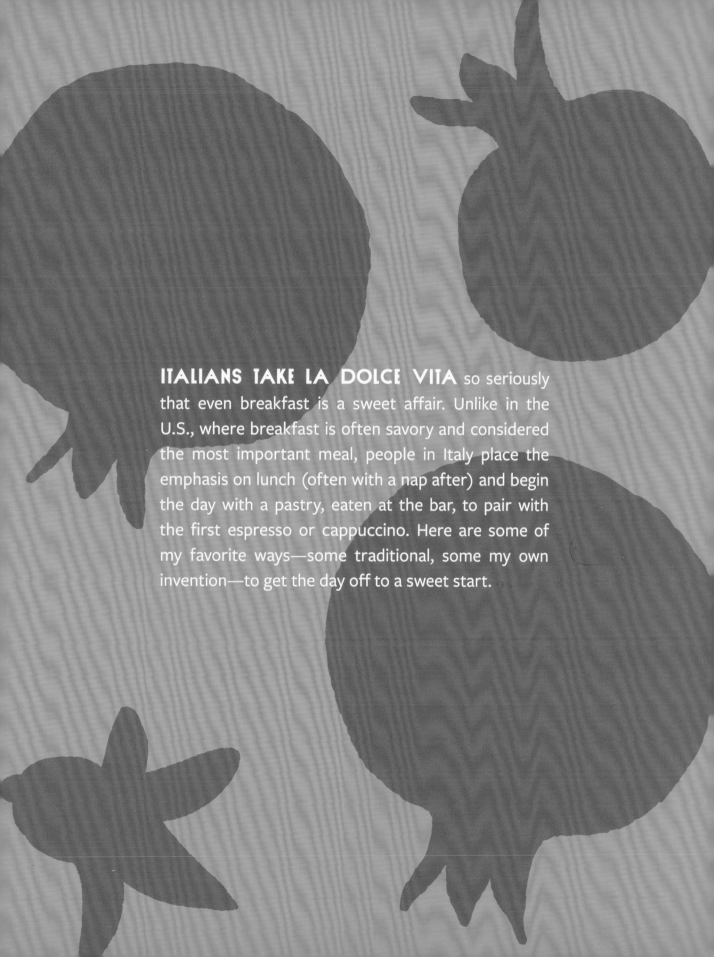

**ITALIANS TAKE LA DOLCE VITA** so seriously that even breakfast is a sweet affair. Unlike in the U.S., where breakfast is often savory and considered the most important meal, people in Italy place the emphasis on lunch (often with a nap after) and begin the day with a pastry, eaten at the bar, to pair with the first espresso or cappuccino. Here are some of my favorite ways—some traditional, some my own invention—to get the day off to a sweet start.

Capri, Campania, Italy

Ciao, Gloria,
Prospect Heights, Brooklyn

Fortunato Brothers,
Williamsburg, Brooklyn

Catania, Sicily, Italy

# HIT THE BAR

The cappuccino e cornetto is to Italians what bacon, egg, and cheese with a cup of coffee is to New Yorkers. But instead of a diner or street cart, Italians flock to their local bar for breakfast on the go. Unlike our alcohol-focused bars in the U.S., the main feature here is the espresso machine, which is running constantly. Italians will pop into the bar throughout the day for a shot of caffeine, but they're most popular in the morning for a quick pastry with coffee. Breakfast is a time for something sweet, and common items include a cornetto (a much sweeter, softer version of a croissant), brioche, or sometimes a piece of crostata or torta. After eyeing the selection, you first pay at the cassa (register) before finding a spot to stand at the bar and handing your receipt across the counter. For a few minutes, you pause and relax. Then with a quick wave, a grazie, and a buona giornata, you're out the door and back onto the street, ready to start your day.

# CIAMBELLA DELLA MATTINA

**MAKES 1 BUNDT CAKE**

*The ciambella is a typical citrus-based breakfast cake served in the morning in bars across the country. It's pleasantly simple, both in flavor and in effort. Because I couldn't resist adding some American touches here, blueberries and a wildflower honey glaze bring a little extra sweet zing, making this a breakfast that straddles the best of both worlds.*

### FOR THE CAKE

| | | |
|---|---|---|
| All-purpose flour, plus more as needed | 390 grams | 2¾ cups |
| Baking powder | 13 grams | 2½ teaspoons |
| Fine sea salt | 4 grams | 1 teaspoon |
| Granulated sugar | 400 grams | 2 cups |
| Grated lemon zest (from about 2 lemons) | 10 grams | 2 tablespoons |
| Olive oil | 245 grams | 1¼ cups |
| Sour cream | 230 grams | 1 cup |
| Mascarpone | 110 grams | ½ cup |
| Large eggs, at room temperature | 4 | |
| Fresh or frozen blueberries | 280 grams | 2 cups |

### FOR THE GLAZE

| | | |
|---|---|---|
| Powdered sugar | 240 grams | 2 cups |
| Wildflower honey | 40 grams | 2 tablespoons |
| Fresh lemon juice (from 1 large lemon) | 45 grams | 3 tablespoons |
| Pinch of salt | | |

**NOTE**

If you have a regular-sized tube pan in your possession instead of a Bundt, go ahead and use it! Just adjust your bake time accordingly. We used a standard 12-cup Bundt pan for this recipe, which works in the same fashion, and gives this ciambellone a nicer visual. I also recommend using a simply shaped Bundt pan. The less indentations and curves it has, the better your chances for a flawless knockout!

Preheat the oven to 350°F (180°C) and set a rack in the center. Coat a 12-cup (2.8 liters) Bundt or 10-inch (25 cm) tube pan with nonstick spray and lightly dust with flour.

**Make the cake ▶** In a medium bowl, sift the flour, baking powder, and salt. In the bowl of a stand mixer, combine the granulated sugar and lemon zest. Massage the zest into the sugar using a pinching motion, evenly incorporating and releasing the oils. Add the olive oil, sour cream, and mascarpone. Snap on the whisk attachment and beat on medium-low speed until well combined, about 2 minutes. With the mixer running on low speed, add the eggs one at a time. Add the flour mixture in two parts and beat until fully combined, about 2 minutes, stopping to scrape the sides as needed. Remove the bowl from the mixer and use a rubber spatula to gently fold in the blueberries. Pour the batter into the prepared pan. Bake until a cake tester comes out clean, 1 hour to 1 hour 25 minutes. Let the cake cool in the pan for about 30 minutes before turning out onto a wire rack to cool completely, about 1 hour.

**Once the cake is cool, make the glaze ▶** In a medium bowl, whisk the powdered sugar, honey, lemon juice, and salt to make a thick glaze. Spoon the glaze over the top of the cake, letting it slowly fall down the sides. Let the glaze set for about 20 minutes before slicing and serving.

The ciambellone can be covered and stored at room temperature for up to 3 days.

# COFFEE-COFFEE CAKE

**MAKES 1 TUBE CAKE**

*Anyone who has been to my home can tell you that I have a mild coffee addiction. There are no fewer than six different kinds of coffee makers on my kitchen counter and in my cabinets. So, it's no surprise that I love to infuse the flavor of coffee into most of my baked goods. One obvious vehicle is this cake. A coffee cake blanketed in crumbs is such a classic New York institution, a gift from central European and Jewish immigrants. This version, shot through with a very Italian touch—an espresso-infused ripple of streusel through the center plus more espresso in the chunky, sugary crumbs piled on top—feels like a perfect reflection of the intermingling that happened in lower Manhattan at the turn of the twentieth century. If all that espresso doesn't put a pep in your step, nothing will.*

### FOR THE FILLING

| | | |
|---|---|---|
| All-purpose flour | 20 grams | 2 tablespoons |
| Granulated sugar | 40 grams | 3 tablespoons |
| Dark brown sugar | 25 grams | 2 packed tablespoons |
| Ground cinnamon | 5 grams | 1½ teaspoons |
| Instant espresso powder | 1 gram | 1 teaspoon |

### FOR THE CRUMB TOPPING

| | | |
|---|---|---|
| Cake flour | 120 grams | 1 cup |
| Granulated sugar | 50 grams | ¼ cup |
| Dark brown sugar | 50 grams | ¼ cup packed |
| Instant espresso powder | 2 grams | 2 teaspoons |
| Ground cinnamon | 6 grams | 2 teaspoons |
| Fine sea salt | 2 grams | ½ teaspoon |
| Unsalted butter, melted and cooled | 85 grams | 6 tablespoons |

### FOR THE CAKE

| | | |
|---|---|---|
| All-purpose flour, plus more as needed | 250 grams | 1¾ cups |
| Granulated sugar | 200 grams | 1 cup |
| Baking powder | 10 grams | 2 teaspoons |
| Baking soda | 3 grams | ½ teaspoon |
| Fine sea salt | 2 grams | ½ teaspoon |
| Unsalted butter, cubed, at room temperature | 125 grams | 9 tablespoons |
| Sour cream | 290 grams | 1¼ cups |
| Large eggs, at room temperature | 3 | |
| Pure vanilla extract | 15 grams | 1 tablespoon |

**Make the filling** ▶ In a medium bowl, whisk together the flour, granulated sugar, brown sugar, cinnamon, and espresso powder.

**Make the crumb topping** ▶ In a medium bowl, whisk together the cake flour, granulated sugar, brown sugar, espresso powder, cinnamon, and salt.  ▶▶▶

Drizzle in the melted butter in two parts, mixing with your hands to evenly moisten and form large crumbs.

**Make the cake** ▶ Preheat the oven to 325°F (160°C) and set a rack in the center. Coat a 10-inch (25 cm) tube pan with a removable bottom with cooking spray and lightly dust with flour.

In a stand mixer fitted with the paddle, mix the flour, granulated sugar, baking powder, baking soda, and salt on low speed until combined. Add the cubed butter and mix on low until the dry ingredients form a sandy, coarse crumb, about 2 minutes. In a medium bowl, whisk the sour cream, eggs, and vanilla. With the mixer running on low, add the sour cream mixture in two parts, stopping to scrape down the sides after each addition. Increase the speed to medium-high and beat until the batter is light and fluffy, about 1 minute.

Scoop half of the batter into the prepared pan, then sprinkle the filling evenly over the top. Add the remaining half of the batter and smooth into an even layer. Scatter the crumbs over the top of the cake.

Bake until the cake feels firm and a tester comes out clean, 60 to 65 minutes. Cool completely in the pan, about 1 hour, before unmolding. Dust lightly with powdered sugar before slicing and serving.

The coffee cake can be covered and stored at room temperature for up to 2 days.

Manhattan Bridge, Dumbo, Brooklyn

Court Pastry Shop, Cobble Hill, Brooklyn

My parents' first apartment, Bushwick, Brooklyn

Carroll Gardens, Brooklyn, New York

# CUCCIDATI SCONES

**MAKES 8 LARGE SCONES**

*Long before the Fig Newton, there were cuccidati. Also known as buccellati and probably a dozen other names, these are a classic shortbread cookie with a rich, boozy, fig and fruit filling, traditionally served around the holidays. It's a recipe that traces back to Roman times, and eventual Arab influences added warm spices like cinnamon and cloves to the filling. Here, you have the components of a cuccidati filling, but deconstructed and mixed into a buttery scone with a simple Marsala glaze—and a little chocolate added, for good measure.*

### FOR THE DOUGH

| | | |
|---|---|---|
| Dried figs, diced | 150 grams | 5 ounces |
| Marsala | 30 grams | 2 tablespoons |
| Toasted walnuts, coarsely chopped | 75 grams | ¾ cup |
| All-purpose flour | 425 grams | 3 cups |
| Baking powder | 20 grams | 1 tablespoon plus 1 teaspoon |
| Granulated sugar | 75 grams | 6 tablespoons |
| Fine sea salt | 6 grams | 1 teaspoon |
| Ground cinnamon | 3 grams | 1 teaspoon |
| Pinch of ground cloves | | |
| Unsalted butter, cubed and chilled | 125 grams | 9 tablespoons |
| Candied orange, chopped | 30 grams | 1 ounce |
| Mini chocolate chips | 90 grams | ½ cup |
| Heavy cream, cold, plus more as needed | 385 grams | 1⅔ cups |
| Pure vanilla extract | 5 grams | 1 teaspoon |

### FOR THE GLAZE

| | | |
|---|---|---|
| Powdered sugar, plus more as needed | 120 grams | 1 cup |
| Wildflower honey | 20 grams | 1 tablespoon |
| Grated orange zest | 2 grams | 1 teaspoon |

**Make the dough** ▶ Place the diced figs in a medium bowl with 1 tablespoon of the Marsala and enough hot tap water to barely cover, approximately 75 grams (⅓ cup). Let soak for 30 minutes. Reserving the liquid to make the glaze, drain the figs and set aside.

Preheat the oven to 375°F (190°C) and set a rack in the center. Line a baking sheet with parchment paper.

In the bowl of a stand mixer fitted with the paddle, mix the flour, baking powder, granulated sugar, salt, cinnamon, and cloves. Add the cold, cubed butter and mix on low speed until the butter pieces are pea-sized and the overall mixture resembles a coarse meal.

Add the toasted nuts, soaked figs, candied orange, and chocolate chips. Remove the bowl from the mixer, make a well in the middle of the dry ingredients, and slowly pour in half the heavy cream and vanilla. Using a rubber spatula, mix to incorporate and then add the second half of the cream. Mix again until just combined, but do not overwork the dough. Use your hands to bring the dough together. The mixture should be on the dry side but hold its shape. If the dough is crumbly and falling apart, add more heavy cream, 1 tablespoon at a time, as needed.

Transfer the dough to a lightly floured surface and fold it in half over itself. Roll the dough into a roughly 8-inch (20 cm) round about 1½ inches (4 cm) thick. Transfer the round to the lined baking sheet and place in the refrigerator to chill for at least 30 minutes (or overnight) before cutting. This will give you cleaner edges.

Once chilled, cut the dough into 8 wedges. Return them to the prepared baking sheet, evenly spaced. Place on the center rack and bake until golden brown, 30 to 40 minutes, rotating the pan halfway through. Transfer the scones to a wire rack placed over a baking sheet to cool.

**Make the glaze** ▶ In a small bowl, whisk together the powdered sugar, honey, orange zest, and 30 grams (2 tablespoons) of the reserved soaking liquid until smooth and pourable. If the mixture is too thick, add some more soaking liquid. If too loose, add some more sugar. Drizzle the glaze over the cooled scones and let the glaze set for a few minutes before serving.

Scones can be stored in an airtight container at room temperature and are best enjoyed day of. That said, this dough freezes fantastically well. Freeze and bake on demand!

# TRICOLORE BOMBOLONI

**MAKES 16 BOMBOLONI**

*I've always been obsessed with donuts, but as much as I would like to slowly transform Ciao, Gloria's menu into a donut-only paradise, we have a tiny kitchen with an even tinier fryer. So, instead, I look forward to Saturday: bomboloni day. Bomboloni are Italy's filled donut—originally from the Tuscany region, but commonly found all over—replete with cream, chocolate, or jam. This recipe is the blueprint for the most soft and supple donuts; what goes inside is completely up to you . . . words to live by.*

| | | |
|---|---|---|
| Large egg | 1 | |
| Large egg yolks | 3 | |
| Whole milk | 225 grams | 1 cup |
| Active dry yeast | 9 grams | 1 tablespoon |
| Pure vanilla extract | 5 grams | 1 teaspoon |
| Bread flour, plus more | 500 grams | 3½ cups |
| Granulated sugar | 65 grams | 5 tablespoons |
| | plus 200 grams | plus 1 cup |
| Fine sea salt | 3 grams | ¾ teaspoon |
| Unsalted butter, cubed and chilled | 70 grams | 5 tablespoons |
| Canola or other neutral oil, for deep-frying | | |
| Pastry Cream (page 268), Pistachio Pastry Cream (page 268), jam, or Nutella, for filling | | 2 cups |

**NOTE**

You can use 2 cups of pastry cream or jam in any flavor to fill these donuts, but to create the full tricolore, fill some with standard pastry cream, some with pistachio pastry cream, and the remaining ones with strawberry jam.

In a stand mixer fitted with the whisk, beat the whole egg, egg yolks, milk, yeast, and vanilla on low speed to combine, about 1 minute. Let the mixture rest for about 5 minutes until the yeast is frothy and fragrant.

In a medium bowl, whisk together the bread flour, 65 grams (5 tablespoons) of the sugar, and the salt. Switch to the dough hook on the mixer and add the dry ingredients to the bowl in two parts. Mix on low speed until just incorporated, about 2 minutes. Increase the speed to medium and add the butter one piece at a time. Mix the dough until all the butter is absorbed and the dough strengthens, 6 to 8 minutes. The dough should feel smooth and sturdy, not sticky. Transfer the dough to a large bowl coated with cooking spray. Cover tightly with plastic wrap and refrigerate for at least 1 hour or overnight.

Line two baking sheets with parchment paper and coat with cooking spray. Turn the dough out onto a lightly floured surface. Using a rolling pin, roll the dough out to a 12 by 16-inch (30 by 40 cm) rectangle about ½ inch (1 cm) thick. Use a 3-inch (8 cm) round cutter to cut out donuts, making cuts close together to maximize the dough. (Any leftover scraps can be fried up, tossed in sugar, and enjoyed.) Arrange the cut rounds on the prepared baking sheets, evenly spaced, and cover loosely with plastic wrap. Let them proof at room temperature for 1 to 2 hours, until puffy and soft. ▶▶▶

When done proofing, add the remaining sugar to a medium bowl. Add 2 to 3 inches (5 to 8 cm) of the oil to a large, deep pot (I recommend a Dutch oven), with a deep-fry thermometer clipped to the side. Set over medium heat and heat the oil to 350°F (163°C). Keep an eye on the thermometer while frying, increasing, or decreasing the heat to maintain a steady oil temperature.

Set a wire rack in a baking sheet. Working in batches of 4 or 5 to not crowd the pot, fry the bomboloni until golden brown, 2 to 4 minutes, using a spider strainer or large slotted spoon to flip them halfway through. Transfer to the wire rack to drain. Use tongs to toss each one in the sugar while they're still hot, before returning to the rack. Let cool for 30 minutes before filling.

When ready to use the pastry cream (or the filling of your choice), give it a vigorous whisk until smooth and fluid. Transfer to a piping bag fitted with a large round tip. Insert a paring knife into the side of the bomboloni, about halfway in, and rotate to make a small hole, then pipe to fill. If you have a Bismark piping tip, use that instead, and you can skip using the paring knife and simply insert and fill. Repeat with the remaining bomboloni. As the urge to overfill is natural for a generous baker like yourself, be careful not to, as your bomboloni will effectively become "boom-boloni" and explode. Once all are successfully filled, serve immediately.

The bomboloni are best enjoyed on the day they are fried.

Erice, Sicily, Italy

Brioche con Tuppo and
Granita Four Ways (page 236)

# BRIOCHE CON TUPPO

MAKES 12 BRIOCHE

*This style of brioche, a free-form bun with a tiny ball nestled on top, is specific to Sicily—tuppo was the same word Sicilians used to describe the common women's hairstyle of the time. A little bun on the top of the head. Brioche are usually eaten for breakfast or a late-afternoon snack, with icy granita (as seen opposite) or a few scoops of gelato. If you want to lean Italian American savory, add a sprinkle of everything bagel seasoning on top after the egg wash and then fill with scrambled egg, pesto, provolone, and prosciutto while they're still warm from the oven.*

| Master Brioche (page 279) | | |
|---|---|---|
| Large egg | 1 | |
| Whole milk | 15 grams | 1 tablespoon |

**Make the brioche dough as directed.** Let the chilled dough rest at room temperature for 30 to 60 minutes.

Line two baking sheets with parchment paper and coat with cooking spray. Divide the dough into 12 equal portions (roughly 100 grams each), then cut off 10 grams from each portion. Form each large piece into a tight ball by cupping your hand over it and using your thumb and pinky to shape while rolling, then press your thumb into the center to create an indent. Roll each small piece of dough into a ball and nestle it into the dent of a large piece. Arrange on the prepared baking sheets, evenly spaced, and cover loosely with plastic wrap. Let the dough proof at room temperature until it is puffy and springs back halfway after a light finger touch, 2 to 3 hours.

Before the buns finish proofing, preheat the oven to 375°F (190°C) and set racks in the upper and lower thirds.

When the buns are proofed, whisk the egg and milk in a small bowl. Brush the surface of each brioche with the egg wash.

Bake until risen and dark golden brown (the internal temperature should reach 190°F/88°C), about 20 minutes, rotating the pan halfway through. Let the brioche cool for 5 minutes on the baking sheets, then transfer to a wire rack to cool enough to handle and enjoy.

The brioche can be stored in an airtight container at room temperature for up to 3 days or wrapped and frozen up to one month.

# AMERICAN CINNAMON ROLLS

**MAKES 12 ROLLS**

*Some kids go to college and develop a drinking problem. I went to college and got hooked on Cinnabon. As often as I could, I would drive the thirty minutes from my college campus in Saratoga Springs to the Crossgates Mall in Albany to spend a few minutes of bliss in the food court. These are the memories that last a lifetime. After decades of testing and tasting, I think I've finally landed on perfection. This recipe is my homage to the oversized, overglazed, overly gooey roll of classic Americana, but the rolls can have a slight Italian accent with the addition of orange blossom water, an ingredient popular in many sweets in Italy and throughout the Mediterranean.*

### FOR THE DOUGH

Master Brioche (page 279)

### FOR THE FILLING

| | | |
|---|---|---|
| Unsalted butter, at room temperature | 85 grams | 6 tablespoons |
| Dark brown sugar | 150 grams | ¾ cup packed |
| Ground cinnamon | 18 grams | 2 tablespoons |
| Fine sea salt | 1 gram | ¼ teaspoon |

### FOR THE FROSTING

| | | |
|---|---|---|
| Cream cheese, at room temperature | 340 grams | 12 ounces |
| Powdered sugar | 120 grams | 1 cup |
| Wildflower honey | 60 grams | 3 tablespoons |
| Heavy cream, plus more as needed | 30 grams | 2 tablespoons |
| Pure vanilla extract | 10 grams | 2 teaspoons |
| Orange blossom water (optional) | 3 grams | ½ teaspoon |
| Pinch of fine sea salt | | |

**Make the brioche dough as directed.** Let the chilled dough rest at room temperature for 30 to 60 minutes.

**Make the filling** ▶ In a stand mixer fitted with the paddle, combine the butter, brown sugar, cinnamon, and salt and mix at medium speed to form a paste, about 4 minutes.

  Coat a 9 by 13-inch (23 by 33 cm) baking pan with cooking spray and line with parchment paper, creating a sling with a 2-inch (5 cm) overhang lengthwise. Turn the chilled dough out onto a lightly floured surface. Roll into a 9 by 16-inch (23 by 40 cm) rectangle and spread the filling in an even layer, leaving a ½-inch (1 cm) border on all sides. Starting with a long edge, roll the dough into a tight cylinder. Moisten the final lip with water and pinch to seal the roll. Place the roll in the freezer for about 15 to 20 minutes to facilitate a clean cut. Remove from the freezer and use a serrated knife to trim ½ inch (1 cm) off each end of the cylinder, then cut crosswise into twelve 1¼-inch-wide (3 cm) rolls. Arrange the rolls in the prepared baking dish, cut side down, evenly spaced in  ▶ ▶ ▶

American Cinnamon Rolls and
Sicilian Sticky Buns (page 23)

4 rows of 3. Cover loosely with plastic wrap and proof at room temperature until doubled, about 2 hours. The dough should feel soft and light, have some small air bubbles in it, and bounce back when lightly pressed.

**Meanwhile, make the frosting** ▶ In a stand mixer fitted with the paddle, beat the cream cheese on medium-high speed until smooth. Add the powdered sugar and beat on low speed until smooth, about 2 minutes. Add the honey, 2 tablespoons of heavy cream, the vanilla, orange blossom water (if using), and salt and beat on medium speed until smooth and pliable. Add heavy cream 1 tablespoon at a time as needed to achieve a smooth, spreadable consistency. Cover the bowl with plastic wrap and refrigerate until ready to use.

Before the buns finish proofing, preheat the oven to 350°F (180°C) and set a rack in the center.

Remove the plastic and bake the rolls until golden brown (the internal temperature should reach 190°F/88°C), 25 to 35 minutes.

Let the rolls cool in the baking pan for about 15 minutes, then remove from the pan using the parchment sling and transfer to a serving platter. Use an offset spatula to spread the rolls with the cream cheese frosting while still on the warmer side, so that the sweet deliciousness seeps into all the crevices, and serve immediately, because there is truly nothing as good as a warm cinnamon bun.

Cinnamon rolls are best enjoyed on the day they are baked.

# SICILIAN STICKY BUNS

**MAKES 12 BUNS**

*I'll admit, I didn't understand sticky buns until later in life. Probably because they were always overshadowed by my undying love for cinnamon rolls (see previous recipe). That is, until Ciao, Gloria's first pastry chef, Ginger Fisher Baldwin, insisted on putting them on the holiday menu a couple of months after we opened. And now I can only wax poetic about this pastry: It's a gorgeous swirl of breakfast heaven, with sweet caramel ribbons that pull as you tear away the soft and buttery brioche. This version takes a cue from the heavy Middle Eastern influences you find across Sicily and Southern Italy. Warm notes of cinnamon mingle with cardamom and sumac, pairing with the tangy sweetness of the pomegranate and orange caramel, finished with a crunchy topping of chopped pistachio.*

### FOR THE DOUGH

| | | |
|---|---|---|
| Master Brioche (page 279) | | |

### FOR THE CARAMEL

| | | |
|---|---|---|
| Orange juice (from 2 oranges) | 120 grams | ½ cup |
| Heavy cream | 230 grams | 1 cup |
| Unsalted butter | 55 grams | 4 tablespoons |
| Pomegranate molasses | 95 grams | 4 tablespoons |
| Pure vanilla extract | 5 grams | 1 teaspoon |
| Fine sea salt | 2 grams | ½ teaspoon |
| Granulated sugar | 400 grams | 2 cups |
| Pistachios, toasted and roughly chopped | 180 grams | 1½ cups |

### FOR THE FILLING

| | | |
|---|---|---|
| Unsalted butter, at room temperature | 85 grams | 6 tablespoons |
| Dark brown sugar | 200 grams | 1 cup packed |
| Grated orange zest (from 1 orange) | 6 grams | 1 tablespoon |
| Ground cinnamon | 3 grams | 1 teaspoon |
| Sumac (optional) | 4 grams | 1 teaspoon |
| Fine sea salt | 1 gram | ¼ teaspoon |
| Pinch of ground cardamom | | |

**Make the brioche dough as directed.** Let the chilled dough rest at room temperature for 30 to 60 minutes.

**Make the caramel** ▶ In a medium saucepan, cook the orange juice over medium heat until reduced by half (roughly ¼ cup), about 10 minutes. Add the cream, butter, pomegranate molasses, vanilla, and salt and stir occasionally until the mixture comes to a simmer. Remove from the heat.

In a large pot, combine the sugar and 115 grams (½ cup) water. Whisk until you have the consistency of wet sand, then set over medium-high heat and bring to a boil without stirring. Continue to boil until the syrup is thick and straw colored, then reduce the heat to medium, insert a candy thermometer, and continue to heat until the temperature reaches 350°F (177°C) ▶ ▶ ▶

and the syrup is dark, golden brown. Remove from the heat, carefully pour about one-quarter of the cream mixture into the sugar pot and let it bubble. Once the steam has subsided, whisk in the rest of the cream mixture and stir until the sauce is smooth. Bring the mixture back to a simmer over low heat, then remove from the heat and let the caramel cool to room temperature in the pot, about 1 hour.

**Meanwhile, make the filling** ▶ In a stand mixer fitted with the paddle, combine the butter, brown sugar, orange zest, cinnamon, sumac (if using), salt, and cardamom and mix at medium speed to form a smooth paste, about 2 minutes. Cover the bowl with plastic wrap and set aside at room temperature.

When the caramel is cooled, coat a 9 by 13-inch (23 by 33 cm) baking dish with cooking spray, line with parchment, and spray again. Pour the caramel into the bottom of the dish and sprinkle the pistachios evenly over the caramel.

Turn the chilled dough out onto a lightly floured surface. Roll into a 9 by 16-inch (23 by 40 cm) rectangle and use an offset spatula to spread the filling in an even layer, leaving a ½-inch (1 cm) border on all sides. Starting with a long edge, roll the dough into a long, tight cylinder. Moisten the final lip with water and pinch to seal the roll. Place the roll in the freezer for about 15 to 20 minutes to facilitate a clean cut. Remove from freezer and use a serrated knife to trim ½ inch (1 cm) off each end of the cylinder, then cut crosswise into twelve 1¼-inch-wide (3 cm) rolls. Arrange the rolls in the prepared baking dish, cut side up, on top of the caramel and pistachios, evenly spaced in 4 rows of 3. Cover loosely with plastic wrap and proof at room temperature until doubled, about 2 hours. The dough should feel soft and light, have some small air bubbles in it, and bounce back when lightly pressed.

Before the buns finish proofing, preheat the oven to 350°F (180°C) and set a rack in the center.

Remove the plastic and bake the buns until golden brown (the internal temperature should reach 190°F/88°C), 30 to 35 minutes, rotating the pan halfway through. Let them cool in the pan for about 5 minutes, then carefully invert onto a serving platter. Spoon any leftover caramel and pistachios over the top of the buns.

Sticky buns are best enjoyed on the day they are baked.

# PUMPKIN NUTELLA BREAD

**MAKES 1 LOAF**

*When you work in a café, you get to know the unique mania bubbling under the surface as summer comes to an end and pumpkin spice season rears its gigantic, orange head. Just like Christmas, it comes earlier every year. It's not uncommon seeing it show up on menus on a balmy, humid August day. This take on a classic pumpkin loaf—with a moist, dense crumb, and all those warm autumnal spices certain people go absolutely hysterical over—gets ribbons of Nutella (something I go absolutely hysterical over) swirled throughout, for a pleasantly unexpected Italian touch.*

| | | |
|---|---|---|
| All-purpose flour | 215 grams | 1½ cups |
| Baking powder | 7 grams | 1½ teaspoons |
| Baking soda | 5 grams | ¾ teaspoon |
| Fine sea salt | 4 grams | 1 teaspoon |
| Ground cinnamon | 5 grams | 1½ teaspoons |
| Ground ginger | 3 grams | 1 teaspoon |
| Ground nutmeg | 1 gram | ¼ teaspoon |
| Pinch of ground cloves | | |
| Unsweetened pumpkin puree | 300 grams | 2½ cups |
| Granulated sugar | 265 grams | 1⅓ cups |
| Canola oil | 100 grams | ½ cup |
| Large eggs, at room temperature | 3 | |
| Nutella | 150 grams | ½ cup |

Preheat the oven to 350°F (180°C) and set a rack in the center. Coat a 9 by 5-inch (23 by 13 cm) loaf pan with cooking spray.

In a medium bowl, sift together the flour, baking powder, baking soda, salt, cinnamon, ginger, nutmeg, and cloves.

In a stand mixer fitted with the paddle, beat the pumpkin, sugar, and oil on low speed until combined, about 2 minutes. With the mixer still running on low, add the eggs, one at time, beating to fully incorporate each one. Stop and scrape down the sides as needed. Add the dry ingredients and beat again on low until just incorporated, being careful not to overmix.

Transfer half of the batter to the prepared loaf pan. Spoon half of the Nutella over top and use a table knife or wooden skewer to swirl into the batter. Add the remaining batter to the pan and top with the remaining Nutella, swirling it into the batter one last time.

Bake until a cake tester comes out clean (the Nutella will stick to the tester regardless, so look to make sure there is no pumpkin batter on it), 60 to 70 minutes. If the top of the bread begins to get too dark, tent with aluminum foil. Once done, set on a wire rack and let cool completely, or for at least 1 hour, before removing from the pan, slicing, and serving.

The loaf can be wrapped in plastic and stored at room temperature for up to 4 days or wrapped in foil and frozen up to three months.

# MARITOZZI

**MAKES 12 LARGE MARITOZZI**

*Maritozzi have been a Roman specialty since the Middle Ages, a surprisingly deca-dent allowance during the fasting period of Lent. A fluffy brioche roll is stuffed to the heavens with freshly whipped cream, and because the components are both so airy, it's a surprisingly light treat, indulgent but not overly rich. While maritozzi are technically an all-day snack, I recommend leaning into the most luxurious breakfast ever and making them with jam and espresso fillings. The cream to bun ratio is not as extreme as the Roman version, but it is still generous and would go oh so well with your morning coffee or tea.*

| | | |
|---|---|---|
| Master Brioche (page 279) | | |
| Large egg | 1 | |
| Whole milk | 15 grams | 1 tablespoon |
| Basic Whipped Cream (page 271), any flavor, for filling | | |

**Make the brioche dough as directed.** Let the chilled dough rest at room temperature for 30 to 60 minutes.

Line two baking sheets with parchment paper and coat with cooking spray. Divide the dough into 12 equal portions of roughly 100 grams each. Form each piece into a tight ball by cupping your hand over it and using your thumb and pinky to shape while rolling. Arrange on the prepared baking sheets, evenly spaced, and cover with plastic wrap. Let proof at room temperature until puffy and the dough springs back halfway after a light finger touch, 2 to 3 hours.

Before the buns finish proofing, preheat the oven to 375°F (190°C) and set racks in the upper and lower thirds.

When the buns are proofed, in a small bowl, whisk together the egg and milk. Brush the surface of the brioche with the egg wash. Bake until risen and golden brown, 15 to 18 minutes, switching racks and rotating the pans halfway through.

Cool for 5 minutes on the pan, then transfer to a wire rack to cool completely, about 1 hour.

Use a serrated knife to make a vertical cut three-quarters of the way down, through the tops of the buns, without cutting through the base. Gently pry each roll open and spoon 3 to 4 tablespoons of the whipped cream into the center, making a strip about 1½ inches (4 cm) wide. Run the edge of an offset spatula or a table knife along the surface to make a smooth, even layer of cream flush with the bun. Use a wet paper towel to wipe the surface of the bun clean of any excess cream and then dust lightly with powdered sugar before serving.

Maritozzi are best enjoyed on the day they are baked.

# TRECCINE

MAKES 20 BISCUITS

*A package of Stella D'oro Roman Egg Biscuits were a year-round staple in my parents' house. They were the perfect treat to present with coffee when friends or neighbors dropped by, and I would always sneak a couple extra from the table to snack on later. I knew I wanted to include a homemade version in this book, but anything resembling my memory of Roman Egg Biscuits seemed to only exist in a Stella D'oro wrapper. Until, that is, I discovered a braided Sicilian biscuit called treccine that has shockingly similar characteristics. This recipe sits somewhere between Sicilian tradition and my personal American nostalgia, paying homage to both the egg biscuit and its Sicilian cousin. It embodies everything I love about the cookies of my childhood: the sturdy bite that lends itself to limitless dunkable options, the gentle notes of citrus and vanilla, the braided dough. These biscuits may be slightly updated for my adult palate, but they still hit the sweet spot when gathering around the table.*

| | | |
|---|---|---|
| All-purpose flour, plus more for shaping cookies | 450 grams | 3¼ cups |
| Baking powder | 6 grams | 1¼ teaspoons |
| Fine sea salt | 2 grams | ½ teaspoon |
| Unsalted butter, at room temperature | 125 grams | 9 tablespoons |
| Granulated sugar | 150 grams | ¾ cup |
| Grated orange zest (from 1 orange) | 6 grams | 1 tablespoon |
| Whole milk, warmed to room temperature | 50 grams | ¼ cup |
| Large egg, at room temperature | 1 | |
| Pure vanilla extract | 15 grams | 1 tablespoon |
| Orange blossom water (optional) | 3 grams | ½ teaspoon |
| Heavy cream, for brushing | 15 grams | 1 tablespoon |

In a medium bowl, whisk together the flour, baking powder, and salt.

In a stand mixer fitted with the paddle, cream the butter and sugar together at medium-high speed until light and fluffy, 3 to 5 minutes. Add the orange zest, milk, egg, vanilla, and orange blossom water (if using) and mix until incorporated, stopping to scrape the sides as needed. Reduce the speed to low. Add the flour mixture in two parts, mixing on low to incorporate and scraping down the sides as needed, until the dough forms, about 3 minutes. Transfer the dough to a lightly floured surface and knead until uniform. Tightly wrap in a sheet of plastic wrap and refrigerate for 1 hour or overnight.

Preheat the oven to 350°F (180°C) and set racks in the upper and lower thirds. Line two baking sheets with parchment paper.

Lightly flour a work surface. Taking pieces of dough, roll each piece into a 1-inch (2½ cm) thick rope, about 8 inches (20 cm) long. Loop the rope into a U-shape, bring the two ends together, and twist the bottom of the U twice to create a braided look. Place the braided cookies on one of the prepared baking sheets about 2 inches (5 cm) apart. Repeat until both baking sheets are full.

Brush each biscuit with cream and bake until the cookies are golden brown, 15 to 18 minutes, switching racks and rotating the baking sheets halfway through. Transfer the cookies to a wire rack to cool.

The cookies can be stored in an airtight container at room temperature for up to a week, if they last that long.

# MORNING GLORIA

**MAKES 18 COOKIES**

This is the Ciao, Gloria riff on the Morning Glory muffin, famously created by Pam McKinstry, owner of the Morning Glory Cafe on Nantucket Island. There are countless takes on the original—cookies, cakes, bars—but they all hold true to the healthy blend of oats, carrots, apples, raisins, coconut, walnuts, and spices. This version doesn't stray far from its predecessors and is one of the most sought-after breakfast items in the café—a healthy-ish, hand-held treat that goes perfectly with a cappuccino. Although there's nothing uniquely Italian about this recipe, it's so beloved at Ciao, Gloria that my regulars would kill me if I didn't include it!

### FOR THE CANDIED CARROT TOPPING

| | | |
|---|---|---|
| Sugar | 115 grams | ½ cup |
| Medium carrot, shredded | 1 | 2.6 ounces, ½ cup |

### FOR THE DOUGH

| | | |
|---|---|---|
| All-purpose flour | 215 grams | 1½ cups |
| Whole wheat flour | 85 grams | ¾ cup |
| Baking powder | 6 grams | ½ teaspoon |
| Baking soda | 3 grams | ½ teaspoon |
| Fine sea salt | 4 grams | 1 teaspoon |
| Ground cinnamon | 6 grams | 2 teaspoons |
| Ground ginger | 2 grams | ¾ teaspoon |
| Rolled oats | 165 grams | 1½ cups |
| Walnuts, toasted and roughly chopped | 75 grams | ¾ cup |
| Sweetened coconut flakes | 60 grams | ½ cup |
| Golden raisins | 80 grams | ½ cup |
| Dark brown sugar | 150 grams | ¾ cup packed |
| Granulated sugar | 100 grams | ½ cup |
| Unsalted butter, at room temperature | 85 grams | 6 tablespoons |
| Canola oil | 150 grams | ¾ cup |
| Large eggs | 2 | |
| Pure maple syrup | 20 grams | 1 tablespoon |
| Pure vanilla extract | 10 grams | 2 teaspoons |
| Shredded peeled Honeycrisp apple (about 1 medium apple) | 150 grams | 1 cup |
| Peeled, grated carrots (about 4 medium carrots) | 265 grams | 3 cups |

**Make the candied carrot topping** ▶ In a small saucepan over medium heat, combine the sugar with ½ cup of water. Whisk until the sugar is mostly dissolved. Add the carrots and bring to a boil, about 3 to 5 minutes. Remove from the heat, strain the carrots, and transfer to a small bowl, discarding the syrup. Let the carrots cool to room temperature. Store in an airtight container and refrigerate until ready to use.  ▶ ▶ ▶

**Make the dough** ▶ In a medium bowl, whisk together both flours, the baking powder, baking soda, salt, cinnamon, and ginger. Stir in the oats, walnuts, coconut, and raisins.

In a large bowl, whisk the brown sugar, granulated sugar, butter, and canola oil until smooth and creamy. Add the eggs, maple syrup, and vanilla and mix until incorporated. Add the flour and oat mixture in two parts and fold until incorporated. Stir in the shredded apple and grated carrot. Cover the bowl tightly with plastic wrap. Refrigerate the dough for at least 1 hour or overnight.

Preheat the oven to 350°F (180°C) and set racks in the upper and lower thirds. Line two baking sheets with parchment paper.

Use an ice cream scoop or measuring cup to portion about 85 grams (⅓ cup) of the dough onto the lined baking sheets spaced 3 inches (8 cm) apart. Dollop a ½ teaspoon of sugared carrot topping in the center of each cookie, pressing down gently to adhere.

Bake until the cookies are puffy and golden brown, 20 to 25 minutes, switching racks and rotating the baking sheets halfway through. Transfer to a wire rack to cool completely, about 1 hour.

The cookies can be stored in an airtight container at room temperature for up to 2 days.

# ODE TO IRIS

**MAKES 20 BUNS**

*When I told my mom that I was writing this book, she asked if the iris was going to make it into one of the chapters. A ricotta-filled, bread-crumb-crusted, and deep-fried Sicilian pastry, the iris never made it over to the U.S. in the way cannoli or sfogliatelle did. But it's extremely popular in Sicily and she often talks about it fondly, being a favorite treat from her childhood. Instead of inflicting another deep-fried pastry on you (we've achieved maximum capacity in this book), I decided to create an homage to the iris: tender baked brioche buns filled with a rich dark chocolate filling infused with orange and tossed in sugar to give the exterior just a little crunch. It's a little lighter than the original, more akin to a cream bun, but just as delicious—even my mom agrees.*

### FOR THE FILLING

|  |  |  |
|---|---|---|
| Cornstarch | 35 grams | ¼ cup |
| Granulated sugar | 100 grams | ½ cup |
| Large egg yolks | 4 | |
| Whole milk | 680 grams | 3 cups |
| Unsalted butter, cut into pieces | 55 grams | 4 tablespoons |
| Pure vanilla extract | 10 grams | 2 teaspoons |
| Fine sea salt | 1 gram | ¼ teaspoon |
| Dark chocolate, preferably Valrhona Caraïbe, chopped | 170 grams | 6 ounces |
| Grated orange zest (from 1 orange) | 6 grams | 1 tablespoon |

### FOR THE BUNS

|  |  |  |
|---|---|---|
| Master Brioche (page 279) | | |
| Large egg | 1 | |
| Whole milk | 15 grams | 1 tablespoon |
| Granulated sugar | 400 grams | 2 cups |
| Grated zest of 1 orange | | |
| Unsalted butter, melted | 225 grams | 16 tablespoons |
| Cocoa powder, for garnish | | |
| Candied orange peel (optional), for garnish | | |

**NOTE**

I am aware this is a generous yield of iris. If you aren't feeding a party, the buns freeze fantastically well. So go ahead and wrap up the unused baked brioche in foil and freeze them until ready to use. As for the extra chocolate pastry cream, well, I won't say anything if you eat the leftovers right out of the bowl.

**Make the filling** ▶ In a small bowl, whisk together the cornstarch and 50 grams (¼ cup) of the sugar, breaking up any lumps. Whisk in the egg yolks and 115 grams (½ cup) of the milk.

In a medium saucepan, stir together the remaining milk and sugar. Bring to a simmer over medium heat, stirring to dissolve the sugar. Whisk a ladleful of the hot milk mixture into the egg mixture to temper, then pour the warmed egg yolk mixture into the simmering milk mixture. Bring to a boil, stirring constantly with a whisk, until the mixture thickens and you see boiling bubbles reach the center of the saucepan. Continue to whisk for 1 minute while boiling.

Remove from the heat and strain through a fine-mesh sieve into a medium bowl. Whisk in the butter, vanilla, and salt. Whisk in the chocolate and ▶▶▶

orange zest until the chocolate is melted and the filling is smooth and shiny. Press plastic wrap directly on the surface of the pastry cream and refrigerate until chilled, at least 2 hours or up to 24 hours.

**Make the buns** ▶ Make the brioche dough as directed. Let the chilled dough rest at room temperature for 30 to 60 minutes.

Line four baking sheets with parchment paper. Turn the dough out onto a lightly floured work surface. Pat the dough down to get rid of any bubbles. Use a bench knife to divide the dough into 60-gram pieces, 20 balls total. Form each piece into a ball by cupping your hand over it and using your thumb and pinky to shape while rolling. Place 5 balls on each lined baking sheet, arranging them 3 inches (8 cm) apart to allow for the buns to expand in the oven. Cover the buns loosely with plastic wrap and let proof at room temperature for 3 to 4 hours. The buns should appear puffy and spring back slowly when pressed.

Before the buns finish proofing, preheat the oven to 375°F (190°C) and set racks in the upper and lower thirds.

When the buns are ready to bake, in a small bowl, whisk together the egg and milk to make an egg wash. Working in batches of 2 sheets at a time, lightly brush egg wash over the tops and sides of the buns on two of the baking sheets.

Bake until golden brown all over (the internal temperature should reach 190°F/88°C), about 20 minutes, switching racks and rotating the baking sheets halfway through.

While the buns are baking, in a shallow medium bowl, combine the granulated sugar and orange zest. Massage the zest into the sugar using a pinching motion, evenly incorporating and releasing the oils. Place the melted butter in a small bowl.

Once the buns are out of the oven, brush the exterior of each bun with the melted butter. Using tongs, quickly roll the buns in the orange sugar to coat. Set on a wire rack to cool completely.

Repeat with the remaining two sheets of buns.

When all the buns are cooled, transfer the filling to a piping bag fitted with a small round tip. Use a large open star piping tip to cut a hole in the top center of a bun, going almost all the way down but not cutting through the other side. (Alternatively, do this with a paring knife.) Pipe the filling into the hole, letting it overflow a little, then lightly press the tip down to create a little button top.

Before serving, add a spoonful of cocoa powder to a small fine-mesh sieve or sifter. Give the top of each bun one tap of cocoa powder. Garnish the top of the button with candied orange peel (if using).

The iris can be refrigerated in an airtight container for up to 2 days, but are best enjoyed on the day they are baked.

Cinque Terre, Liguria, Italy

# 2

# COOKIES, BARS + BISCOTTI

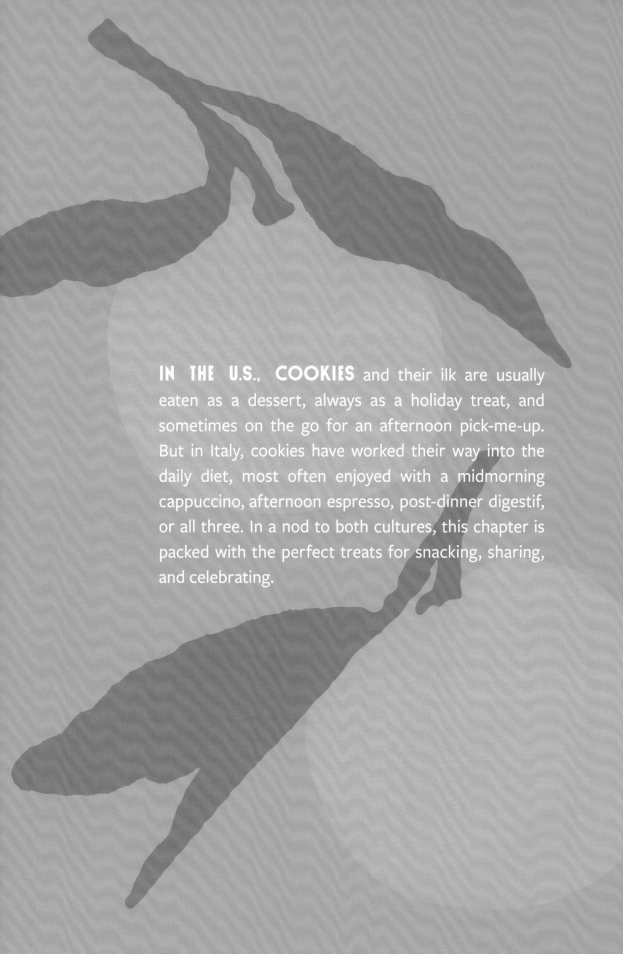

**IN THE U.S., COOKIES** and their ilk are usually eaten as a dessert, always as a holiday treat, and sometimes on the go for an afternoon pick-me-up. But in Italy, cookies have worked their way into the daily diet, most often enjoyed with a midmorning cappuccino, afternoon espresso, post-dinner digestif, or all three. In a nod to both cultures, this chapter is packed with the perfect treats for snacking, sharing, and celebrating.

Triple-Chocolate Biscotti and Cantucci (page 43)

# TRIPLE-CHOCOLATE BISCOTTI

**MAKES 32 COOKIES**

*My philosophy has always been: Why have one chocolate when you can have three? Biscotti—the Italian blanket term for cookies, but whose literal translation is "twice-baked"—is the perfect vehicle for a chocolate explosion. I've carried this biscotti recipe with me for years and I consider it the Big Mac of biscotti, super-sized for American cravings. These are extra large and extra chocolatey, thanks to cocoa powder and chocolate chips, plus a final dip in melted chocolate. As with all chocolate-based recipes, it's smart to invest in high-quality cocoa powder (Valrhona makes a fantastic one). You'll notice a distinct difference in taste and color right away. This recipe makes an abundant number of biscotti, but like most twice-baked cookies, they keep well for a long time, for a superior snack at any time of day.*

| | | |
|---|---|---|
| All-purpose flour | 355 grams | 2½ cups |
| Cocoa powder | 70 grams | ¾ cup |
| Baking soda | 6 grams | 1 teaspoon |
| Fine sea salt | 2 grams | ½ teaspoon |
| Granulated sugar | 250 grams | 1¼ cups |
| Unsalted butter, at room temperature | 115 grams | 8 tablespoons |
| Large eggs, at room temperature | 3 | |
| Pure vanilla extract | 5 grams | 1 teaspoon |
| Semisweet chocolate chips | 225 grams | 1⅓ cups |
| Dark chocolate, chopped | 455 grams | 16 ounces |

Preheat the oven to 350°F (180°C) and set a rack in the center. Line a baking sheet with parchment paper.

In a medium bowl, whisk together the flour, cocoa powder, baking soda, and salt until combined.

In a stand mixer fitted with the paddle, combine the sugar and butter. Beat on medium-high speed until light and fluffy, 3 to 5 minutes. Reduce the speed to low and add the eggs one at a time, scraping down the sides as needed. Add the vanilla and mix to combine. Add the flour mixture in two parts and mix on low until combined, stopping to scrape the sides as needed. Add the chocolate chips and mix until just combined. The dough will be tacky and a little sticky.

On a lightly floured surface, with floured hands, divide the dough in half and shape into 2 even logs almost the length of the baking sheet, about 16 inches (40 cm) long. Arrange on the lined baking sheet and pat down evenly until each log is about 2½ inches (6 cm) in width. Bake until the logs are firm to the touch, 35 to 45 minutes. Remove from the oven but leave the oven on and reduce the temperature to 275°F (135°C).

Let the logs cool on the baking sheet for about 30 minutes, or until cool enough to handle. Transfer the logs to a cutting board and discard the parchment. Set a wire rack in the baking sheet. Use a serrated knife to slice each log on the bias into 16 cookies, about ¾ inch (2 cm) wide, trimming off the ends of the logs and reserving for a bakers' snack. Place the cookies ▶▶▶

cut-side up on the wire rack, spacing evenly. Bake until the biscotti give just slightly when pressed, 10 to 15 minutes. Let cool for about 30 minutes.

Remove the wire rack and reline the baking sheet with parchment. Fill a medium saucepan with 1 inch (2.5 cm) of water and bring to a simmer over medium heat. Set a heatproof medium bowl over the saucepan, making sure the bowl doesn't touch the water. Add the chopped dark chocolate to the bowl and use a silicone spatula to stir occasionally as the chocolate melts. Remove the bowl from the saucepan. Dip one end of each biscotti into the chocolate at a 45-degree angle and arrange, bottom side down, on the lined baking sheet to set, about 30 minutes at room temperature or 10 minutes in the refrigerator.

The biscotti can be stored in an airtight container at room temperature for up to 2 weeks.

# CANTUCCI

**MAKES 40 COOKIES**

*As a kid, I couldn't stand the licorice flavor of anise. But it is hard to escape in an Italian household. As I grew older and developed a more nuanced palate, anise became a favorite, especially in cantucci form. Cantucci, originating in Tuscany, are the smaller, more rustic cousin to what we know as the classic biscotti. These cookies are not for the anise-shy, but when balanced with almond and orange, they have a perfectly rounded, classically Italian flavor profile. They're glorious cookies that come together easily.*

| | | |
|---|---|---|
| All-purpose flour | 500 grams | 3½ cups |
| Anise seeds | 8 grams | 1 tablespoon |
| Baking powder | 10 grams | 2 teaspoons |
| Fine sea salt | 3 grams | ¾ teaspoon |
| Unsalted butter, at room temperature | 170 grams | 12 tablespoons |
| Granulated sugar | 300 grams | 1½ cups |
| Grated orange zest (from 1 orange) | 6 grams | 1 tablespoon |
| Large eggs, at room temperature | 3 | |
| Pure vanilla extract | 5 grams | 1 teaspoon |
| Almond extract | 3 grams | ½ teaspoon |
| Sliced almonds, toasted | 215 grams | 2¼ cups |

**NOTE**

If you're truly anise averse, you can totally omit it from this recipe and customize with another seed, spice, or even dried fruit. This is a great base recipe to make your own.

Preheat the oven to 350°F (180°C) and set a rack in the center. Line a baking sheet with parchment paper.

In a medium bowl, whisk together the flour, anise seeds, baking powder, and salt. In a stand mixer fitted with the paddle, combine the butter, sugar, and orange zest and beat on medium-high speed until light and fluffy, 3 to 5 minutes. Reduce the speed to low and add the eggs one at a time, followed by the vanilla and almond extracts, stopping to scrape the sides as needed. Add the flour mixture in two parts and mix on low until combined. Scrape down the sides. Add the almonds and mix until just combined.

On a lightly floured surface, with floured hands, divide the dough in half and shape into 2 even logs almost the length of the baking sheet, about 16 inches (40 cm) long. Arrange on the lined baking sheet and pat down evenly until each log is about 2 inches (5 cm) in width. Bake until the logs are lightly golden brown and firm to the touch, 35 to 40 minutes. Leave the oven on but reduce the oven temperature to 275°F (135°C).

Let the logs cool on the baking sheet for about 30 minutes, or until cool enough to handle. Transfer the logs to a cutting board and discard the parchment. Set a wire rack in the baking sheet. Use a serrated knife to slice each log into 20 cookies about ¾ inch (2 cm) wide, trimming off the ends of the log. Place the cookies cut-side up on the wire rack, spacing evenly. Bake until the cantucci give just slightly when pressed, 10 to 12 minutes. Remove from the oven and let cool completely.

The cantucci can be stored in an airtight container at room temperature for up to 2 weeks.

# BACIONI

## MAKES 20 COOKIES

*In the mid '80s, my older sister would commute to Manhattan where she worked for an Italian bank. She would often bring me little gifts and treats from the city, and my favorite were Baci chocolates from the Perugina shop near her office. These Italian truffle-like chocolates are filled with creamy gianduja (a mixture of chocolate and hazelnut cream) and crunchy hazelnuts, wrapped in foil with a romantic bon mot tucked inside. It's an impossibly delicious flavor memory that I have carried with me into adulthood, and these cookies—chocolatey and studded with hazelnut—are my homage to the glorious flavors of my favorite truffle.*

| | | |
|---|---|---|
| Dark chocolate, chopped | 340 grams | 12 ounces |
| All-purpose flour | 285 grams | 2 cups |
| Cocoa powder | 70 grams | ¾ cup |
| Baking soda | 12 grams | 2 teaspoons |
| Fine sea salt | 2 grams | ½ teaspoon |
| Unsalted butter, at room temperature | 225 grams | 16 tablespoons |
| Granulated sugar | 150 grams | ¾ cup |
| Dark brown sugar | 130 grams | ⅔ cup packed |
| Large eggs, at room temperature | 4 | |
| Pure vanilla extract | 10 grams | 2 teaspoons |
| Milk chocolate, chopped | 140 grams | 5 ounces |
| Blanched hazelnuts, toasted and chopped | 140 grams | 1 cup |
| Flaky sea salt, for garnish | | |

Fill a medium saucepan with 1 inch (2.5 cm) of water and bring to a simmer over medium heat. Set a heatproof medium bowl over the saucepan, making sure the bowl doesn't touch the water. Add the chopped dark chocolate to the bowl and use a silicone spatula to stir occasionally as the chocolate melts. Remove the bowl from the saucepan and let cool.

In a medium bowl, sift together the flour, cocoa powder, baking soda, and salt.

In a stand mixer fitted with the paddle, combine the butter, granulated sugar, and brown sugar and beat on high speed until light and fluffy, about 3 to 5 minutes. Reduce the speed to low and add the eggs one at a time, scraping down the sides after each addition. Add the vanilla and mix until combined. With the mixer on low speed, stream in the melted chocolate and mix until incorporated. Add the dry ingredients in two parts, scraping down as needed, and mix on low speed to combine. Add the chopped milk chocolate and hazelnuts. Mix on low until combined.

Line two baking sheets with parchment paper.

Using a 4-tablespoon cookie scoop (¼ cup or 2 ounces), scoop the dough into balls and place them in a lidded container. Refrigerate the dough for at least 12 hours to set. Chilling the dough makes for a more flavorful cookie with a tighter structure.

Preheat the oven to 325°F (160°C) and set racks in the upper and lower thirds.

Divide the dough between the prepared baking sheets and sprinkle the tops of each dough ball with a pinch of flaky sea salt. Bake, rotating halfway through, for about 18 to 20 minutes or until the cookies are firm on the edges but still soft in the center. Cool for 10 minutes on the baking sheets, then transfer to a wire rack to cool completely.

The bacioni can be stored in an airtight container at room temperature for up to 3 days.

# AMARETTO CARAMEL BROWNIES

**MAKES 24 BROWNIES**

*Brownies and I go way back. The reputation of my first bakery, Baked, was built on a classically American approach to desserts that put us on the map. In building the menu for Ciao, Gloria, I wanted to breathe new life into my well-trodden dessert. By leading with a good-quality cocoa powder (which you always should!), you'll get a brownie so complex and rich, it actually tastes more chocolatey than the traditional brownie I made with melted chocolate. To give this bar a little Italian twist, I added swirls of amaretto-infused caramel throughout. If you are a traditionalist, these are fantastic on their own, studded with mini chocolate chips. But why not go the extra mile and swirl in some caramel for good measure?*

| | | |
|---|---|---|
| Granulated sugar | 400 grams | 2 cups |
| Cocoa powder | 95 grams | 1 cup |
| Fine sea salt | 2 grams | ½ teaspoon |
| Unsalted butter | 225 grams | 16 tablespoons |
| Large eggs | 3 | |
| Pure vanilla extract | 5 grams | 1 teaspoon |
| All-purpose flour | 105 grams | ¾ cup |
| Semisweet mini chocolate chips | 170 grams | 1 cup |
| Amaretto Caramel (recipe follows) | 105 grams | ⅓ cup |

Preheat the oven to 325°F (160°C) and set a rack in the center. Coat a 9 by 13-inch (23 by 33 cm) baking dish with cooking spray. Line with parchment paper, leaving a 2-inch (5 cm) overhang on the two short sides of the baking dish for easy removal.

In a large bowl, whisk together the sugar, cocoa powder, and salt. In a small saucepan over low heat, melt the butter until very hot and starting to bubble. Pour the hot butter over the cocoa mixture and whisk well until gritty. Let cool for about 5 minutes, then whisk in the eggs, one at a time, followed by the vanilla. Sift the flour over the bowl and use a rubber spatula to fold it in until a few streaks remain. Add the chocolate chips and mix until just combined.

Transfer the batter into the prepared baking dish and spread evenly. Transfer the amaretto caramel to a piping bag fitted with a small round tip. With a long side of the baking dish facing you, pipe vertical parallel lines of caramel across the top of the batter. Rotate the baking dish a quarter-turn so that a short side is facing you and use a toothpick to pull swirls through the lines of caramel lengthwise in alternating directions, back and forth, creating a feathered effect.

Bake the brownies until a cake tester comes out with just a few crumbs, 30 to 40 minutes. The edges should look firm and the center should look moist but not gooey. Let the brownies cool completely in the baking dish, about 1 hour.

Use the parchment to lift the brownies to a cutting board. (For an extra-clean cut, chill the cooled brownies in the refrigerator until set, about 1 hour.) Cut your brownies into 2-inch (5 cm) squares, making sure to wipe the knife clean after each cut.

The brownies can be stored in an airtight container at room temperature for up to 5 days. ▶▶▶

Amaretto Caramel Brownies and
Albi Crunch Bars (page 50)

Circo's, Bushwick, Brooklyn

# AMARETTO CARAMEL

**MAKES 320 GRAMS (1 CUP)**

*A rich caramel with just a hint of booziness, this is equally great drizzled over gelato or stirred into a latte.*

| | | |
|---|---|---|
| Granulated sugar | 200 grams | 1 cup |
| Heavy cream, at room temperature | 115 grams | ½ cup |
| Unsalted butter, at room temperature | 30 grams | 2 tablespoons |
| Fine sea salt | 1 gram | ¼ teaspoon |
| Amaretto | 30 grams | 2 tablespoons |

In a medium saucepan, combine the sugar and 115 grams (½ cup) water. Set over medium-high heat and simmer, without stirring, until the sugar has turned a deep shade of amber, 10 to 15 minutes, or a few degrees under 350°F (177°C) on a candy thermometer. Remove from the heat and slowly pour in half of the heavy cream. The mixture will bubble and steam, so be careful! Once the steam subsides, add the remaining heavy cream plus the butter and salt and whisk well.

Return to low heat, whisking constantly, until the mixture comes to a boil. Boil until thickened, 1 to 2 minutes. Remove from the heat and whisk in the amaretto. Pour the caramel into an airtight container and refrigerate for 2 hours or overnight.

The caramel can be stored in an airtight container in the refrigerator for up to 2 weeks.

# ALBI CRUNCH BARS

**MAKES 24 BLONDIES**

*"How do we make an Italian blondie?" That's the question I posed to my bakers one spring morning. After lots of testing and tasting, we reached our answer. It's a simple browned butter bar, with chopped hazelnuts, and a river of apricot jam flowing throughout. Albi is short for albicocca, "apricot," which is seemingly Italy's favorite flavor of jam. The crunch is thanks to the hazelnuts, another unmistakable Italian favorite. Cut into small pieces, they're perfect two-bite treats for a midday sweet.*

| | | |
|---|---|---|
| Unsalted butter | 250 grams | 18 tablespoons |
| All-purpose flour | 215 grams | 1½ cups |
| Fine sea salt | 8 grams | 2 teaspoons |
| Baking powder | 5 grams | 1 teaspoon |
| Apricot preserves | 115 grams | ⅓ cup |
| Fresh lemon juice | 5 grams | 1 teaspoon |
| Dark brown sugar | 300 grams | 1½ cups packed |
| Large eggs | 2 | |
| Large egg yolk | 1 | |
| Blanched hazelnuts, toasted and chopped | 120 grams | 1 cup |

**NOTE**

You can easily customize this recipe to your liking. Add any nut (or chocolate chip) or preferred jam for a bar you can call your own.

Preheat the oven to 325°F (160°C) and set a rack in the center. Coat a 9 by 13-inch (23 by 33 cm) baking dish with cooking spray, then line with parchment paper, leaving a 2-inch (5 cm) overhang on two sides.

In a small saucepan, melt the butter over high heat. Reduce the heat to medium and cook, watching closely, until the butter is dark golden and smells nutty, about 10 minutes. There should be small brown flecks of toasted milk solids visible and the foam should be gone. Pour into a small bowl to cool slightly.

In a medium bowl, sift the flour, salt, and baking powder. In a small bowl, combine the apricot preserves and lemon juice and whisk until incorporated.

In a stand mixer fitted with the whisk, combine the brown sugar, whole eggs, and egg yolk and whisk on medium speed until the mixture falls from the whisk in pale, foamy ribbons that are thick enough to draw a figure-eight, about 5 minutes. With the mixer running on low speed, stream in the brown butter. Stop and scrape the sides as needed. Remove the bowl from the mixer and fold in the flour mixture. Add the hazelnuts and fold until combined.

Spread the batter evenly in the prepared baking dish. Use a spoon to dollop the pureed preserves evenly on top and use a table knife or skewer to swirl it into the batter.

Bake until the edges are golden brown and the center is puffed up but firm to the touch, 30 to 35 minutes, rotating halfway through.

Cool completely in the dish, then use the parchment overhang to transfer to a cutting board. (For an extra-clean cut, chill the cooled blondies in the refrigerator until set, about 1 hour.) Cut into 2-inch (5 cm) squares before serving.

The albi bars can be stored in an airtight container at room temperature for up to 5 days.

# MOSTACCIOLI

MAKES 16 COOKIES

*Like most things in Italy, there are endless names and variations for the same foods. Take mostaccioli: with multiple names, varied ingredients and techniques. Every region in Italy thinks theirs is the original and absolute best version. At their core, they are a classic holiday cookie, soft, spiced, and warming. I've settled on this recipe, which is really just an amalgam of all of the best elements I uncovered, including a decadent chocolate dip to finish. The warm spices and hit of orange almost scream Christmas, which makes this a popular cookie among Italians and Italian Americans alike. (Once in a while, we can all agree on something!)*

| | | |
|---|---|---|
| Blanched almonds, toasted | 30 grams | 3 tablespoons |
| Blanched hazelnuts, toasted | 30 grams | 3 tablespoons |
| All-purpose flour | 200 grams | 1½ cups |
| Granulated sugar | 50 grams | ¼ cup |
| Cocoa powder | 12 grams | 2 tablespoons |
| Ground cinnamon | 3 grams | 1 teaspoon |
| Ground nutmeg | 1 gram | ¼ teaspoon |
| Pinch of ground cloves | | |
| Baking powder | 3 grams | ½ teaspoon |
| Fine sea salt | 1 gram | ¼ teaspoon |
| Large egg | 1 | |
| Boiling water | 30 grams | 2 tablespoons |
| Instant espresso powder | 3 grams | 2 teaspoons |
| Pure vanilla extract | 5 grams | 1 teaspoon |
| Wildflower honey | 80 grams | ¼ cup |
| Canola oil | 25 grams | 2 tablespoons |
| Grated zest of ½ orange | | |
| Dark chocolate, chopped | 225 grams | 8 ounces |

In a food processor, process the almonds and hazelnuts until ground into a coarse meal, about 1 minute.

In a large bowl, whisk the ground nuts, flour, sugar, cocoa powder, cinnamon, nutmeg, cloves, baking powder, and salt. Whisk the egg in a small bowl.

In a separate small bowl, combine the boiling water, espresso powder, and vanilla. In a small saucepan, warm the honey, canola oil, and orange zest over low heat until runny, then whisk in the espresso mixture.

Pour the liquid ingredients into the bowl with the dry ingredients, add the whisked egg, and fold to combine. The dough will come together and feel a little tacky, but not wet.

Place the dough between two pieces of parchment paper and use a rolling pin to roll into a 10-inch (25 cm) round between ¼ and ⅜ inch (6 mm to 9.5 mm) thick. Remove the top parchment and use a knife or pastry wheel cutter to cut the dough into 1½-inch-wide (4 cm) strips. Use the bottom parchment to rotate the dough round 45 degrees and cut again in 1½-inch-wide (4 cm) strips, to make diamonds. Line a baking sheet with parchment and ▶▶▶

carefully arrange the diamond cookies on the baking sheet, leaving about 1 inch (2.5 cm) between them. Reroll any scrap to yield more cookies. Chill the dough for about 1 hour, until firm.

Preheat the oven to 350°F (180°C).

Bake until slightly firm to the touch, about 12 to 15 minutes, rotating the baking sheet halfway through. Transfer the cookies to a wire rack to cool.

Fill a medium saucepan with 1 inch (2.5 cm) of water and bring to a simmer over medium heat. Set a heatproof medium bowl over the saucepan, making sure the bowl doesn't touch the water. Add the chopped dark chocolate to the bowl and use a silicone spatula to stir occasionally as the chocolate melts. Once smooth, remove the bowl from the saucepan.

Use two forks to dip each cookie in the chocolate, turning to coat and letting the excess drip off, before returning to the wire rack. Let the chocolate fully set, about 30 minutes.

Reheat the remaining chocolate in the bowl. Dip the tines of a fork into the chocolate and drizzle over each cookie, making a zig-zag pattern, to re-create the design seen on page 53. Let the zig-zag set for an additional 15 minutes before removing the cookies from the wire rack.

The mostaccioli can be stored in an airtight container at room temperature for up to 7 days.

*Clockwise from far left:*
**Gingerbread Amaretti (page 66),**
**Zaletti (page 68),**
**Butter Cookies (page 57),**
**Espresso Almond Icebox Cookies (page 60),**
**Occhi di Bue (page 69), and**
**Mostaccioli (page 51)**

# MOCHA ORANGE WHOOPIE PIES

**MAKES 14 WHOOPIE PIES**

*For decades, the whoopie pie seemed to be either the exclusive property of Pennsylvania Dutch country or the state of Maine (both lay claim to its creation, and I am not getting involved in that drama). But a few years back, they came roaring onto the bakery scene and now you can find them everywhere, in all sorts of flavors. At Ciao, Gloria, we will occasionally make whoopie pies for special occasions: pumpkin in the fall, red velvet for Valentine's Day. But none of them are particularly Italian. So I thought it would be fun to create one for this book that captures some of my favorite Italian flavors. This mocha-inspired whoopie pie has coffee in its chocolate cake, which sandwiches an orange-infused Italian buttercream and a surprise orange marmalade center. It hits all the pleasure points of Italian dessert in a uniquely American vessel.*

### FOR THE WHOOPIE PIES

| | | |
|---|---|---|
| Hot coffee | 225 grams | 1 cup |
| Cocoa powder | 95 grams | 1 cup |
| All-purpose flour | 535 grams | 3¾ cups |
| Fine sea salt | 4 grams | 1 teaspoon |
| Baking powder | 5 grams | 1 teaspoon |
| Baking soda | 6 grams | 1 teaspoon |
| Dark brown sugar | 345 grams | 1¾ cups packed |
| Canola oil | 150 grams | ¾ cup |
| Large egg | 1 | |
| Pure vanilla extract | 5 grams | 1 teaspoon |
| Buttermilk | 115 grams | ½ cup |

### FOR ASSEMBLY

| | | |
|---|---|---|
| Italian Buttercream (page 267) | | |
| Orange Marmalade, store-bought or homemade (recipe follows) | 85 grams plus 210 grams | ¼ cup plus heaping ½ cup |

Preheat the oven to 350°F (180°C) and set racks in the upper and lower thirds. Line two baking sheets with parchment paper.

**Make the whoopie pies** ▶ In a medium bowl, whisk the hot coffee and cocoa powder. In a separate medium bowl, sift the flour, salt, baking powder, and baking soda. In a large bowl, whisk the brown sugar and oil until combined. Whisk in the coffee mixture, followed by the egg and vanilla. Scoop about half of the dry ingredients into the wet ingredients and fold to combine. Fold in the buttermilk, then the remaining dry ingredients until incorporated with no streaks. Cover the bowl tightly with plastic wrap and let sit for 30 minutes at room temperature.

Use a 3-tablespoon cookie scoop (1.5 ounces) to portion the batter onto the prepared baking sheets, leaving 2 inches (5 cm) between each scoop to allow for spread while baking.

Bake until the whoopies are puffed and dry to the touch, about ▶▶▶

15 minutes, switching racks and rotating halfway through. Cool completely on the baking sheets before filling.

**To assemble the whoopie pies** ▶ In a stand mixer fitted with the whisk, whip together the buttercream and 85 grams (¼ cup) of the marmalade. Place the orange buttercream in a piping bag fitted with a large star tip.

Flip the cooled whoopies over so that the flat sides are facing up. Onto half of the whoopies, pipe a ring of buttercream on the outer edge, leaving a small empty space in the middle. Fill the middle of each with 15 grams (2 teaspoons) marmalade. Top with the unfilled halves, creating a sandwich, and gently press down to seal in the marmalade. Enjoy right away.

The whoopie pies can be stored in an airtight container at room temperature for up to 2 days or in the refrigerator for up to 3 days, bringing to room temperature before enjoying.

# ORANGE MARMALADE

### MAKES 465 GRAMS (1½ CUPS)

*This recipe makes a little more than you need for the Mocha Orange Whoopie Pies (page 55), but rest assured, you will want to spread it on your toast the next morning . . . and the morning after that, too!*

| | | |
|---|---|---|
| Navel oranges (1 to 2 medium) | 360 grams | 13 ounces |
| Granulated sugar | 200 grams | 1 cup |
| Fresh lemon juice | 5 grams | 1 teaspoon |
| Wildflower honey | 10 grams | 1½ teaspoons |

Wash the oranges thoroughly and slice off the stem tops. Roughly chop the entire orange, discarding any seeds. In a large pot, combine the chopped oranges with 225 grams (1 cup) water. Bring to a boil over medium heat, then remove from the heat. Transfer to a medium bowl to cool for 30 minutes. Cover tightly with plastic wrap and refrigerate for at least 2 hours or overnight.

Transfer the oranges to a food processor and process until finely chopped, about 1 minute. Transfer the mixture to a large saucepan. Set over medium heat and simmer for about 30 minutes, stirring occasionally, until the liquid has evaporated.

Add the sugar and stir until dissolved. Simmer for another 30 minutes, stirring frequently to prevent burning. The marmalade should be thick and gel-like.

Remove from the heat and whisk in the lemon juice and honey. Return the marmalade to the medium bowl and let cool for 30 minutes. Cover tightly with plastic wrap and refrigerate overnight before enjoying.

The marmalade can be stored in an airtight container in the refrigerator for up to 2 weeks.

# BUTTER COOKIES

**MAKES 30 SANDWICH COOKIES**

*Where would an Italian cookie tray be without these? After the ubiquitous tricolor cookie, these might be the most iconic fixture of Italian American bakeries, found in an array of guises: rounds with a candied cherry in the middle, or dyed pink or green and in the shape of a leaf. This straightforward version has always been my favorite. Two buttery cookies sandwich a raspberry jam filling, then the tip of the cookie gets dipped in chocolate and covered in rainbow sprinkles. (This qualifies as "straightforward" in Italian American baking.) Once you get this cookie base down pat, feel free to play with shapes, colors, fillings, and toppings to load up your own personal cookie tray.*

| | | |
|---|---|---|
| All-purpose flour | 355 grams | 2½ cups |
| Fine sea salt | 2 grams | ½ teaspoon |
| Baking powder | 3 grams | ½ teaspoon |
| Unsalted butter, at room temperature | 225 grams | 16 tablespoons |
| Granulated sugar | 150 grams | ¾ cup |
| Large eggs, at room temperature | 2 | |
| Pure vanilla extract | 5 grams | 1 teaspoon |
| Raspberry preserves | 170 grams | ½ cup |
| Dark chocolate, chopped | 225 grams | 8 ounces |
| Rainbow sprinkles | 25 grams | 2 tablespoons |

Preheat the oven to 350°F (180°C) and set racks in the upper and lower thirds. Line two baking sheets with parchment paper.

In a medium bowl, whisk the flour, salt, and baking powder.

In a stand mixer fitted with the paddle, combine the butter and sugar. Beat on high until light and fluffy, about 3 minutes. Add the eggs one at a time, followed by the vanilla, and mix until incorporated, stopping to scrape the sides as needed. Reduce the speed to medium and continue mixing until well combined and fluffy. Add the flour mixture in two parts and mix, stopping to scrape the sides as needed. Increase the speed to high for 30 seconds for a final mix.

Transfer the dough into a pastry bag fitted with a large star tip. Pipe the dough onto the prepared baking sheets in strips 2½ inches (6 cm) long with 2 inches (5 cm) between the cookies. Refrigerate for 20 minutes to chill before baking.

Bake until the edges are golden brown, 15 to 20 minutes, switching racks and rotating the sheets halfway through. Let the cookies cool on the baking sheets for 5 minutes, then transfer to a wire rack to cool completely. Reserve the lined baking sheets.

Flip half of the cookies so that the flat sides are facing up. Transfer the raspberry preserves to a small piping bag fitted with a small round tip. Pipe a thin line down the center of the flat-side up cookies, about ½ teaspoon per cookie. Top with the remaining cookies to sandwich, pressing gently so the jam doesn't spill out. ▶▶▶

Fill a medium saucepan with 1 inch (2.5 cm) of water and bring to a simmer over medium heat. Set a medium bowl over the saucepan, making sure the bowl doesn't touch the water. Add the chopped dark chocolate to the bowl and use a silicone spatula to stir occasionally as the chocolate melts. Remove the bowl from the saucepan. Dip one end of the cookies in the chocolate at a 45-degree angle. Immediately sprinkle the chocolate with rainbow sprinkles, then arrange on the lined baking sheets to set, about 30 minutes at room temperature or 10 minutes in the refrigerator.

The butter cookies can be stored in an airtight container at room temperature for up to 5 days.

**Court Pastry Shop,
Cobble Hill, Brooklyn**

**Ciao, Gloria,
Prospect Heights, Brooklyn**

**Ciao, Gloria,
Prospect Heights, Brooklyn**

**Circo's,
Bushwick, Brooklyn**

# ESPRESSO ALMOND ICEBOX COOKIES

MAKES 36 COOKIES

*If it isn't yet obvious, chocolate has always been my go-to dessert. I'll take it any way you give it to me, from cake to candy bar, high quality to questionable, I'm there for it. I'm not above eating an Entenmann's devil's food cake with full conviction. When developing this recipe, my main goal was to build a cookie with cocoa and espresso content so dark and rich, it would border on savory. The flecks of sliced almonds give this cookie a pleasing crunch and texture, plus a gorgeous speckle when sliced. They're great straight out of the oven, but the flavor continues to deepen and develop as the cookies sit, which makes them ideal for making ahead, as they're even more delicious a few days later.*

| | | |
|---|---|---|
| Instant espresso powder | 12 grams | 3 tablespoons |
| Boiling water | 30 grams | 2 tablespoons |
| All-purpose flour | 250 grams | 1¾ cups |
| Cocoa powder | 95 grams | 1 cup |
| Fine sea salt | 2 grams | ½ teaspoon |
| Unsalted butter, at room temperature | 170 grams | 12 tablespoons |
| Granulated sugar | 200 grams | 1 cup |
| Large egg, at room temperature | 1 | |
| Whole milk | 30 grams | 2 tablespoons |
| Sliced almonds, toasted | 85 grams | ¾ cup |
| Semisweet chocolate chips | 45 grams | ¼ cup |

**NOTE**

For the Espresso Almond Icebox Towers (page 61), slice the cookies ¼-inch thick, but baking instructions remain the same. The thinner and crispier cookies will better absorb the whipped cream.

In a small bowl, whisk together the espresso powder and hot water until dissolved. In a medium bowl, sift the flour, cocoa powder, and salt.

In a stand mixer fitted with the paddle, cream the butter and sugar at medium-high speed until light and fluffy, about 3 minutes. Reduce the speed to low and add the egg, milk, and espresso mixture and mix until incorporated. With the mixer still on low, add the flour mixture in two parts, until combined, stopping to scrape the sides as needed. Remove the bowl from the mixer and use a rubber spatula to fold in the almonds and chocolate chips. The dough should have a fudgy texture and come together easily when pinched.

Turn out the dough onto a lightly floured surface and press and roll into a log that is about 12 inches (30 cm) long and 2 inches (5 cm) in diameter. Wrap in parchment paper or plastic wrap and freeze for at least 2 hours or overnight.

When you are ready to bake, preheat the oven to 350°F (180°C) and set racks in the upper and lower thirds. Line two baking sheets with parchment paper.

Unwrap the log and set on a cutting board. Use the parchment to hold the log in place and slice into rounds ⅓ inch (8 mm) thick. Arrange on the lined baking sheets about 1 inch (2.5 cm) apart.

Bake until the cookies have a matte finish, about 12 minutes, switching racks and rotating halfway through. Let them rest on the baking sheets for 5 minutes before transferring them to a wire rack to cool.

The icebox cookies can be stored in an airtight container at room temperature for up to 5 days.

# ESPRESSO ALMOND ICEBOX TOWERS

**MAKES 6 MINI ICEBOX TOWERS**

*Using the thinner espresso cookies, paired with a double batch of whipped cream, you can create individual icebox cakes that are an easy dessert to assemble, and an impressive finish to any dinner.*

| | | |
|---|---|---|
| Double batch Basic Whipped Cream (page 271) | | |
| Instant espresso powder | 4 grams | 1 tablespoon |
| Powdered sugar | 15 grams | 2 tablespoons |
| Espresso Almond Icebox Cookies | 24 | |
| Sliced almonds toasted, for garnish | 10 grams | 2 tablespoons |
| Cocoa powder, for dusting | | |

In a small bowl, combine the espresso powder with 1 tablespoon hot water. Stir until dissolved and cool completely. Transfer half of the whipped cream to a piping bag fitted with a large tip. In a large bowl, whisk together the remaining whipped cream, espresso mixture, and powdered sugar until incorporated. Transfer to another piping bag with a large tip.

Arrange four 3-inch (8 cm) ramekins on a work surface. Place a cookie in the bottom of each ramekin. Pipe about 10 grams (2½ tablespoons) of the espresso whipped cream onto each cookie. Top with another cookie and pipe 10 grams (2½ tablespoons) of the plain whipped cream on top. Repeat the process, alternating whipped creams, until each stack is 4 cookies tall, finishing with 12 grams (3 tablespoons) of the plain whipped cream. Refrigerate for 6 hours or overnight.

Before serving, top each tower with a few sliced almonds and a dusting of cocoa powder.

The towers can be refrigerated in an airtight container for up to 2 days.

# HONEY-RICOTTA BLACK AND WHITES

**MAKES 15 LARGE COOKIES**

*The black and white cookie must be the official cookie of NYC. It's as much a part of the fabric of the city as cheap pizza slices, halal carts, and coffee on the go. You can reliably find the mass-produced, fondant-covered, plastic-wrapped versions at delis and bodegas, but biting into a freshly baked version makes it nearly impossible to ever go back to store-bought. This recipe infuses the zingy lemon cookie base with ricotta and honey for extra sweetness and moisture. And, let's admit it, black and whites have always been more cake than cookie, so it only makes sense to swap the pourable glaze or sticky fondant for a rich, spreadable frosting.*

### FOR THE COOKIES

| | | |
|---|---|---|
| All-purpose flour | 425 grams | 3 cups |
| Baking powder | 10 grams | 2 teaspoons |
| Fine sea salt | 4 grams | 1 teaspoon |
| Unsalted butter, at room temperature | 115 grams | 8 tablespoons |
| Granulated sugar | 400 grams | 2 cups |
| Grated lemon zest (from 1 lemon) | 4 grams | 2 teaspoons |
| Large eggs, at room temperature | 2 | |
| Ricotta cheese | 425 grams | 1¾ cups |
| Wildflower honey | 20 grams | 1 tablespoon |
| Fresh lemon juice (from 1 to 2 lemons) | 45 grams | 3 tablespoons |

### FOR THE FROSTING

| | | |
|---|---|---|
| Light corn syrup, plus more if needed | 80 grams | ¼ cup |
| Heavy cream | 155 grams | ⅔ cup |
| | plus 30 grams | plus 2 tablespoons |
| Pure vanilla extract | 5 grams | 1 teaspoon |
| Powdered sugar, sifted | 660 grams | 5½ cups |
| Cocoa powder, sifted | 25 grams | ¼ cup |

**Make the cookies** ▶ Preheat the oven to 325°F (160°C) and set racks in the upper and lower thirds. Line two baking sheets with parchment paper.

In a medium bowl, whisk the flour, baking powder, and salt.

In a stand mixer fitted with the paddle, combine the butter, sugar, and lemon zest. Beat on medium-high speed until the butter is smooth and the mixture resembles wet sand, about 5 minutes. Add the eggs, one at a time, scraping down the sides as needed. Continue beating on medium-high for 1 minute until the batter is light and fluffy. Add the ricotta, honey, and lemon juice. Beat on low until combined, scraping down the sides as needed. The mixture will look curdled, but don't worry!

Add the flour mixture in two parts and mix on low until combined, scraping down the sides after each addition. Increase the speed to medium-high and beat for 30 seconds to make sure the batter is mixed.

Use a 6-tablespoon cookie scoop (⅓ cup or 2.7 ounces) to portion ▶▶▶

generous scoops of batter onto the lined baking sheets 3 inches (8 cm) apart (these cookies will spread, so give them space).

Bake until the cookies are firm to the touch in the center and slightly golden on the edges, 20 to 25 minutes, switching racks and rotating halfway through. Transfer to a wire rack to cool completely before frosting.

**Make the frosting** ▶ In a large bowl, combine the corn syrup, 155 grams (⅔ cup) of the heavy cream, and the vanilla. Add the powdered sugar and whisk until the frosting is smooth and very thick.

Divide the frosting between two bowls. To one bowl, add the cocoa powder and the remaining heavy cream. Use a rubber spatula to mix until smooth and thick. Add more corn syrup to each bowl, a teaspoon at a time, for a glossy and spreadable consistency, if needed.

Flip each cookie, flat side up. Starting with the vanilla frosting, use an offset spatula to generously frost half of each cookie, making a distinct line down the center. Clean the offset spatula, then generously frost the other half of each cookie with chocolate, maintaining a clear center line. Return to the wire rack and let set for 1 hour before serving. The frosting will become shinier as it sets.

The black and white cookies can be refrigerated in an airtight container for up to 3 days.

Siena, Tuscany, Italy

# GINGERBREAD AMARETTI

**MAKES 30 SMALL COOKIES**

*Italians have a soft spot for most nuts, but I believe their love for almonds surpasses all the rest combined. So when it comes to almond cookies, it's no surprise that every mamma, nonna, and pasticceria offer a dozen different types. And with each region having its own specific varieties, and with twenty regions, well . . . you do the math. Almonds, in one form or another, are infused into almost every sweet in Italy. Even pistachio-based sweets often use almond extract to—get this!—enhance the flavor of the pistachio. Amaretti are almond cookies in their truest, most almond-y sense, and an easy base recipe that adapts well to a variety of flavors, like cocoa, matcha, or pulverized freeze-dried fruit. This gingerbread version has a slightly crunchy exterior and a soft, chewy interior. Infused with warm winter spices, it's an easy and delicious addition to your seasonal baking repertoire.*

| | | |
|---|---|---|
| **FOR THE COATING** | | |
| Powdered sugar | 120 grams | 1 cup |
| Gingerbread Spice Mix (recipe follows) | 6 grams | 1 tablespoon |
| **FOR THE AMARETTI** | | |
| Granulated sugar | 400 grams | 2 cups |
| Blanched almond flour | 375 grams | 3¾ cups |
| Gingerbread Spice Mix | 12 grams | 2 tablespoons |
| Fine sea salt | 3 grams | ½ teaspoon |
| Large egg whites | 4 | |
| Cream of tartar | 2 grams | ½ teaspoon |
| Almond extract | 5 grams | 1 teaspoon |

**NOTE**

For classic amaretti, simply omit the spice mix from the recipe. For any flavor variations, use ground spices in an amount equivalent to the gingerbread spice mix.

Preheat the oven to 325°F (160°C) and set a rack in the center. Line a baking sheet with parchment paper.

**Make the coating** ▸ In a small bowl, sift together the powdered sugar and spice mix.

**Make the amaretti** ▸ In a large bowl, whisk the sugar, almond flour, spice mix, and salt.

In a stand mixer fitted with the whisk, whip the egg whites on medium speed until foamy. Add the cream of tartar and continue whisking until soft peaks form. Add the almond extract and whisk to medium peaks.

Add the egg whites to the almond flour mixture in two parts, using a rubber spatula to fold until no streaks remain. Don't worry about deflating the egg whites in this step, you want to make sure that the dough is well combined. It will resemble wet sand and come together easily when squeezed.

Using a 2-tablespoon cookie scoop (1 ounce), scoop the dough one scoop at a time into the coating. Use your hands to toss until covered and roll into a ball. Arrange the balls of dough on the lined baking sheet about 2 inches (5 cm) apart.

Bake until the cookies are golden brown at the edges, but still soft in the center, 25 to 30 minutes, rotating the baking sheet halfway through. Transfer to a wire rack and cool completely.

The amaretti can be stored in an airtight container at room temperature for up to 5 days.

# GINGERBREAD SPICE MIX

**MAKES 44 GRAMS (SCANT 6 TABLESPOONS)**

*This recipe makes more than you need for Gingerbread Amaretti (page 66), but you're definitely going to want to make these cookies again, so why not save yourself a step? Or, if there is a winter chill in the air, use a pinch of this spice in your morning coffee.*

| | | |
|---|---|---|
| Ground ginger | 20 grams | 3 tablespoons |
| Ground cinnamon | 18 grams | 2 tablespoons |
| Ground cloves | 5 grams | 1½ teaspoons |
| Freshly grated nutmeg | 1 gram | ½ teaspoon |

In a small bowl, whisk the ginger, cinnamon, cloves, and nutmeg. Transfer to a spice jar or small airtight container. The mix will remain fresh for about 3 months.

# ZALETTI

**MAKES 34 COOKIES**

*Zaletti, a cornmeal and sultana cookie, have been around in Italy since the six-teenth century. Originating in Venice (zálo means "yellow" in Venetian dialect) and popular with the upper classes of the time, it eventually spread throughout the country, traveled to America with Italian immigrants, and now resides mostly in nonna's recipe box. Its crunchy yet soft texture makes for an interesting bite, and a simple swap of dried cranberries for the sultanas in this recipe lends a slight tartness, which I think goes perfectly with the sweet corn notes.*

| | | |
|---|---|---|
| All-purpose flour | 570 grams | 4 cups |
| Cornmeal | 215 grams | 1¼ cups |
| Baking powder | 10 grams | 2 teaspoons |
| Baking soda | 6 grams | 1 teaspoon |
| Fine sea salt | 6 grams | 1½ teaspoons |
| Granulated sugar | 400 grams | 2 cups |
| Unsalted butter, at room temperature | 225 grams | 16 tablespoons |
| Grated lemon zest (from 2 lemons) | 12 grams | 2 tablespoons |
| Large eggs, at room temperature | 4 | |
| Large egg yolks, at room temperature | 2 | |
| Olive oil | 50 grams | ¼ cup |
| Fresh lemon juice (from 1 to 2 lemons) | 60 grams | ¼ cup |
| Pure vanilla extract | 5 grams | 1 teaspoon |
| Dried cranberries | 135 grams | 1 cup |
| Raw sugar, for rolling | 180 grams | 1 cup |

Preheat the oven to 350°F (160°C) and set racks in the upper and lower thirds. Line two baking sheets with parchment paper.

In a medium bowl, whisk the flour, cornmeal, baking powder, baking soda, and salt.

In a stand mixer fitted with the paddle, combine the sugar, butter, and lemon zest. Beat on medium-high speed until light and fluffy, 3 to 5 minutes. Reduce the speed to low and add the whole eggs and yolks one at a time, scraping down the sides as needed. Add the olive oil, lemon juice, and vanilla and mix until combined. Add the flour mixture in two parts and mix until just combined. Scrape down the sides, then mix in the cranberries.

Pour the raw sugar into a medium shallow bowl. Use a 3-tablespoon cookie scoop (1.5 ounces) to portion the dough, rolling each piece in the sugar, then arranging on the baking sheets, leaving 3 inches (8 cm) between the balls.

Bake until the edges are golden brown and the middle is puffed and slightly firm to the touch, 15 to 18 minutes, switching racks and rotating halfway through. Transfer to a wire rack to cool completely.

The zaletti can be stored in an airtight container at room temperature for up to 5 days.

# OCCHI DI BUE

**MAKES 24 SANDWICH COOKIES**

*These cookies originated in the Lombardy region, along Italy's northern border. It's no coincidence, then, that they strongly resemble linzer cookies, popular in neighboring Switzerland, Austria, and a little further north in Germany. Occhi di bue, literally "ox eyes," are a simple cut-out sandwich cookie that can be made with a filling of your choosing, chocolate or jam being the most common.*

Pasta Frolla (page 283)

Fruit jam, any flavor          255 grams          ¾ cup

Powdered sugar, for dusting

**NOTE**

As an alternative, use the Chocolate Pasta Frolla (page 283) and fill with your favorite chocolate ganache or chocolate spread.

**Make the pasta frolla and refrigerate as directed.**

When ready to bake, preheat the oven to 350°F (180°C) and set racks in the upper and lower thirds. Line two baking sheets with parchment paper.

Divide the chilled pasta frolla in half. Wrap and refrigerate one half while working with the other half and let it temper for about 5 minutes. Set the dough between two pieces of parchment paper and use a rolling pin to roll into an 8 by 10-inch (25 cm) rectangle about ¼ inch (6 mm) thick, flipping and releasing the dough from the parchment, or lightly flouring as needed if the dough starts to stick. Once rolled out to ¼-inch (6 mm) thickness, chill in the refrigerator for 15 minutes to firm up before cutting. Using a small (about 2¼ inches or 6 cm) round cookie cutter, cut out 24 cookies. Transfer 12 cookies to each lined baking sheet. Chill in the refrigerator for an additional 15 minutes to firm up before baking. In the meantime, collect the scrap to combine, wrap in plastic wrap and refrigerate.

Bake until the cookies have just started to brown on the edges, about 15 minutes, switching racks and rotating halfway through. Transfer the cookies to a wire rack. Let the lined baking sheets cool for the next batch of cookies.

While the first batch of cookies bakes, set the other half of the frolla between two pieces of parchment, rolling about ¼ inch (6 mm) thick. Chill in the refrigerator for 15 minutes to firm up before cutting. Using the same cookie cutter (about 2¼ inches or 6 cm), cut out 24 cookies. Then use a smaller (about 1¼-inch or 3 cm) round cookie cutter to cut out the centers.

When the baking sheets are cooled, transfer 12 cookies to each one. Chill in the refrigerator for an additional 15 minutes to firm up before baking. Bake as for the first batch. Transfer the cookies to a wire rack. Repeat this process with all the scrap pieces, reroll as stated above, chill, cut, chill, bake.

Let all cookies cool completely before filling, about 1 hour.

Separate the whole cookies and the cut-out cookies. Spread 10 grams (1.5 teaspoons) of fruit jam over each of the whole cookies, then place the cut-out cookies over the cookies with jam to make sandwiches. Dust all the sandwich cookies with powdered sugar.

The occhi di bue can be stored in an airtight container at room temperature for up to 5 days. They soften up a bit the day after assembly, which is my favorite way to enjoy them.

Volterra, Tuscany, Italy

# ITALIAN KRISPIE TREATS

**MAKES 16 BARS**

*Honestly, I can't think of many things more uniquely American than a Rice Krispies Treat. It's an impossibly easy recipe that has found its way into bake sales and school lunch boxes the country over. Similarly, I can't think of many things more uniquely Italian than tiramisù. A mainstay on trattoria menus worldwide, tiramisù translates to "pick me up," a reference to the effects of all that coffee, liquor, and sugar. So as an adult who is still very in touch with his inner child, both American and Italian, addicted to sugar, who drinks espresso several times a day, I can't think of many things more uniquely me than a tiramisù-inspired Rice Krispies Treat. Mascarpone, espresso powder, and a splash of rum join the marshmallow mixture, wrapping the Rice Krispies in a flavor combo that is troppo delizioso.*

| | | |
|---|---|---|
| Mascarpone | 60 grams | ¼ cup |
| Unsalted butter | 55 grams | 4 tablespoons |
| Instant espresso powder | 4 grams | 1 tablespoon |
| Cocoa powder | 6 grams | 1 tablespoon |
| Mini marshmallows, from 2 (10-ounce/283-gram) bags | 565 grams | 20 ounces |
| Rum | 40 grams | 3 tablespoons |
| Rice Krispies or other crisped rice cereal | 340 grams | 13½ cups |
| Cocoa powder, for garnish | | |

Coat a 9 by 13-inch (23 by 33 cm) baking dish with cooking spray. Line with parchment paper, leaving 2 inches (5 cm) of overhang on all sides for easy removal later, and coat again with cooking spray.

In a large Dutch oven, combine the mascarpone, butter, espresso powder, and cocoa. Cook, stirring constantly, over medium heat, until the butter and mascarpone melt together. Add the marshmallows and rum and stir until the marshmallows are melted and the espresso is evenly incorporated. Remove the pot from the heat and stir in the Rice Krispies.

Transfer the mixture into the prepared baking dish, then spray your hands with cooking spray (to prevent the mixture from sticking to them) and press the mixture into an even layer.

Let sit at room temperature or refrigerate for 1 hour to set. Use the parchment to lift the bars out of the baking dish and onto a cutting board. Spoon some cocoa powder into a fine-mesh sieve and tap over the bars to coat. Cut into 16 bars and serve.

The bars can be refrigerated in an airtight container for up to 3 days.

Palermo, Sicily, Italy

# 3

# PIES, TARTS + CROSTATAS

**PIES AND CROSTATAS** have a similar history in Italy and the U.S., namely as vessels for a wide variety of sweet fillings. Whereas pies in the U.S. are mostly saved for Thanksgiving or summer produce, Italian crostatas are a natural part of daily life. They're a perfect snack throughout the day alongside an espresso or as a finale to a full meal served with sparkling dessert wine. (Both countries agree that they make an ideal breakfast.) Pulling from traditional flavors of both countries, here are a few of my favorite sweet slices to end (or begin) the day.

*From top:* **Crostata Classica, Crostata della Nonna (page 78), and Torta del Nonno (page 79)**

# CROSTATA CLASSICA

**MAKES ONE 9-INCH (23 CM) CROSTATA**

*Sicily, 2018. It was already 140°F at 10 a.m. I was about to take a walking tour of an archaeological museum in Siracusa. Previous trips to Sicily had been strictly spent in or around my parents' village, so exploring more of the island felt new and exciting. After a couple of hours of swooning over different column styles (was it the columns or dehydration?), I decided to head to the museum's café. There, possibly with a mild heat stroke, I ordered a very ordinary looking slice of crostata—and I was never the same again.*

*The frolla was so tender, the apricot filling was just right. Maybe an odd place to find the perfect crostata, but this recipe exists in the DNA of most every Italian and excellent versions exist in coffee bars across the country. When I began developing my own crostata, my number one goal was to get it as close as I could to the one I tasted on that impossibly hot day. I like to think that this recipe does it justice, its soft and tender crust wrapping around a thin layer of apricot jam.*

| | | |
|---|---|---|
| Pasta Frolla (page 283) | | |
| All-purpose flour, for dusting | | |
| Good quality apricot jam | 170 grams | ½ cup |
| Powdered sugar, for dusting | | |

**Make the pasta frolla and refrigerate as directed.**

When ready to bake, preheat the oven to 350°F (180°C) and set a rack in the center. Coat a 9-inch (23 cm) tart pan with a removable bottom with cooking spray.

Remove the dough from the refrigerator and let rest for about 5 minutes before rolling. Divide into 3 equal portions. Dust a work surface with flour and combine 2 of the pieces of dough into a ball. Use a rolling pin to roll it into an 11-inch (28 cm) round about ¼ inch (6 mm) thick. Roll the dough up onto the pin and transfer to the prepared pan, pressing to line the bottom and sides. Roll the remaining dough between two sheets of parchment paper into an 11-inch (28 cm) rectangle about ⅛ inch (3 mm) thick. Slide the parchment-covered sheet of dough onto a baking sheet and freeze for about 10 minutes to firm up the dough.

Spread the apricot jam on the bottom of the crostata shell, smoothing with an offset spatula into an even layer.

Remove the sheet of dough from the freezer and remove the top parchment. Cut into 10 strips at least 1 inch (2.5 cm) wide. Place 5 of the strips over the crostata, spaced evenly apart. Place the remaining 5 strips across them at a diagonal, to create a lattice, in the style of your choosing. Cut off any excess dough and press all the strips to adhere to the crust edge.

Bake until golden brown, 35 to 45 minutes, rotating the pan halfway through. Cool completely in the pan. Remove the tart pan and dust with powdered sugar just before serving.

The crostata can be wrapped in plastic and stored at room temperature for up to 5 days. The flavor improves as it sits, so make it a day ahead!

# CROSTATA DELLA NONNA

**MAKES ONE 9-INCH (23 CM) CROSTATA**

*Neither of my grandmothers ever made me a torta della nonna. Partly because they lived in Sicily and I lived in New York, but mostly because neither of them quite fit the stereotype of the flour-dusted nonna of golden daydreams. Sure, they could whip up a meal to feed twenty-six people without breaking a sweat, but sweets were relegated to other cherubic, doting grandmothers. I hadn't even tried a torta della nonna until I had a slice at Babbo in NYC many years ago, and I fell for it instantly. Here, a pasta frolla crust serves as the base to a bright and creamy vanilla-forward filling. But in a nod to the baking nonnas I never had, I finish with a beautiful lattice crust, in the spirit of the nostalgic American pie cooling on the windowsill. Topped with a sprinkling of pine nuts and a dusting of sugar, this is an easy dessert to make for those you love. Release your inner nonna!*

Pasta Frolla (page 283)
Pastry Cream (page 268)
All-purpose flour, for dusting
Pine nuts, toasted     15 grams     2 tablespoons
Powdered sugar, for garnish

**Make the pasta frolla and pastry cream and refrigerate as directed.**

When ready to bake, preheat the oven to 350°F (180°C). Coat a 9-inch (23 cm) tart pan with a removable bottom with cooking spray and dust with flour, knocking out any excess.

Remove the dough from the refrigerator and divide into 3 equal pieces. Dust a work surface with flour and combine 2 of the pieces of dough into a ball. Use a rolling pin to roll it into an 11-inch (28 cm) round about ¼ inch (6 mm) thick. Roll the dough up onto the pin and transfer to the prepared pan, pressing to line the bottom and up the sides. Dock the bottom of the crust with a fork. Roll the remaining dough between two sheets of parchment paper into an 11-inch (28 cm) round about ⅛ inch (3 mm) thick. Slide the parchment-covered sheet of dough onto a baking sheet and freeze for about 10 minutes to firm up the dough.

Transfer the pastry cream into the crostata shell and smooth into an even layer.

Remove the sheet of dough from the freezer and remove the top parchment. Cut into 10 strips, at least 1 inch (2.5 cm) wide. Place 5 of the strips over the crostata, spaced evenly apart. Place the remaining 5 strips across them at a diagonal, to create a lattice in the style of your choosing. Cut off any excess dough and press all the strips to adhere to the crust edge.

Bake until golden brown, 40 to 50 minutes, rotating the pan halfway through. If the tart is getting too dark, tent with foil until baked through. Cool completely in the pan.

Remove the crostata from the tart pan, top with pine nuts, and dust with powdered sugar before serving.

The crostata can be wrapped in plastic and stored in the refrigerator for up to 3 days.

# TORTA DEL NONNO

**MAKES ONE 9-INCH (23 CM) TORTA**

*If you skipped my intro, first of all, shame on you! But secondly, you would have learned that my parents came to Brooklyn from Sicily in the late 1950s. By the time I arrived on the scene—much, much later, thank you very much—they were comfortably situated homeowners and business owners, living a relatively quiet life. And although we were surrounded by Sicilians, our family was an ocean away. My grandfather on my mom's side came to visit only once, right when I was born. I have no real memory of him, but always carry this mental picture of him holding me as an infant. It could have been from a photograph I saw, or an actual memory, who knows. But I always envied people with grandparents. I only saw mine a few times in my life, and wondered what my relationship with them would have been like had we lived near each other. So I decided to add a torta del nonno to this book, for my grandfathers. I love the idea of a nonno version of the Crostata della Nonna (page 78), both of them wonderful on their own and a perfect pair together. This torta is a true chocolate lovers' dessert. With a hit of espresso and a sneaky nip of bourbon, it's guaranteed nonno-approved.*

| | | |
|---|---|---|
| Chocolate Pasta Frolla (page 283) | | |
| Granulated sugar | 65 grams | ⅓ cup |
| Cornstarch | 9 grams | 1 tablespoon |
| Cocoa powder, plus more for dusting | 6 grams | 1 tablespoon |
| Instant espresso powder | 4 grams | 1 tablespoon |
| Pinch of fine sea salt | | |
| Heavy cream | 120 grams | ½ cup |
| Large egg yolks | 2 | |
| Pure vanilla extract | 5 grams | 1 teaspoon |
| Whole milk | 285 grams | 1¼ cups |
| Dark chocolate, chopped | 115 grams | 4 ounces |
| Unsalted butter | 15 grams | 1 tablespoon |
| Bourbon (optional, but highly recommended) | 15 grams | 1 tablespoon |
| All-purpose flour, for dusting | | |
| Powdered sugar, for dusting | | |

**Make the chocolate pasta frolla and refrigerate as directed.**

In a medium saucepan, whisk the sugar, cornstarch, cocoa powder, espresso powder, and salt. Add 60 grams (¼ cup) of the heavy cream and whisk until smooth. Whisk in the egg yolks and vanilla until incorporated. Set over low heat and slowly whisk in the milk and remaining heavy cream. Bring to a simmer, whisking constantly, until the mixture thickens, about 1 minute.

Remove the pan from the heat and add the chopped chocolate, butter, and bourbon (if using). Whisk until smooth. Set a fine-mesh sieve over a medium bowl and pour the pastry cream through, using a rubber spatula to help it pass through. Press plastic wrap directly on the surface of the cream. Let cool for 30 minutes then refrigerate for 1 hour, until completely cooled.  ▶▶▶

When ready to bake, preheat the oven to 350°F (180°C) and set a rack in the center. Coat a 9-inch (23 cm) tart pan with a removable bottom with cooking spray and dust with cocoa powder, knocking out any excess.

Remove the dough from the refrigerator and divide into 2 portions: one potion should weigh roughly 330 grams and the other 490 grams. Dust a work surface lightly with flour, then roll the 330-gram portion into a 9½-inch (24 cm) round about ¼ inch (6 mm) thick. Use the tart pan as a cutting guide, to cut out a round of dough and trim off the excess. Roll the dough up onto the pin and transfer to a parchment-lined baking sheet. Use a 1-inch (2.5 cm) cookie cutter to cut a round out of the center of the dough. Transfer to the freezer to chill.

Roll the remaining dough into an 11-inch (28 cm) round about ¼ inch (6 mm) thick. Roll the dough up onto the pin and transfer to the prepared pan, pressing to line the bottom and sides. Trim any dough overhang. Transfer the pastry cream onto the crust and smooth into an even layer.

Remove the round of dough from the freezer. Center it over the torta. Cut off any excess and press to adhere to the crust edge.

Bake for 45 to 55 minutes, rotating the pan halfway through. Cool completely in the pan. Remove from the tart pan and dust with powdered sugar around the edges just before serving.

The torta can be stored, covered, in the refrigerator for up to 3 days.

Capri, Campania, Italy

# PEAR AND ALMOND SBRICIOLATA

**MAKES ONE 9-INCH (23 CM) TART**

*Sbriciolata is a most unfussy tart. From one dough, you get both a shell base and a crumble topping. You can fill the space in between with whatever you wish: jam, sweetened ricotta, chocolate, pastry cream . . . It's an anything-goes situation! To make this recipe a bit more special than the formulaic crust, filling, crumb, I decided to add a frangipane base layer, in addition to a sweet pear filling. Because a food processor does most of the work for you, it's a perfect last-minute dessert for a dinner party or picnic.*

### FOR THE DOUGH

| | | |
|---|---|---|
| All-purpose flour | 215 grams | 1½ cups |
| Almond flour | 50 grams | ½ cup |
| Baking powder | 15 grams | 1 tablespoon |
| Fine sea salt | 1 gram | ¼ teaspoon |
| Unsalted butter, cubed and chilled | 115 grams | 8 tablespoons |
| Granulated sugar | 100 grams | ½ cup |
| Large egg yolks | 2 | |

### FOR THE PEAR FILLING

| | | |
|---|---|---|
| Ripe pears (about 3), such as Bosc, Bartlett, or Anjou, peeled, cored, and cut into ½-inch (1 cm) pieces | 390 grams | 14 ounces |
| Dark brown sugar | 50 grams | ¼ cup packed |
| Unsalted butter | 15 grams | 1 tablespoon |
| Ground cinnamon | 1 gram | ½ teaspoon |
| Fresh lemon juice | 15 grams | 1 tablespoon |
| Pure vanilla extract | 10 grams | 2 teaspoons |

### FOR THE FRANGIPANE

| | | |
|---|---|---|
| Unsalted butter, at room temperature | 55 grams | 4 tablespoons |
| Granulated sugar | 50 grams | ¼ cup |
| Almond flour | 50 grams | ½ cup |
| Large egg | 1 | |
| Pure vanilla extract | 10 grams | 2 teaspoons |
| Almond extract | 5 grams | 1 teaspoon |
| All-purpose flour | 20 grams | 2 tablespoons |

### FOR ASSEMBLY

| | | |
|---|---|---|
| Sliced almonds | 20 grams | ¼ cup |
| Powdered sugar, for dusting | | |

**Make the dough ▶** In a medium bowl, whisk the all-purpose flour, almond flour, baking powder, and salt. Set aside. In a food processor, combine the butter and granulated sugar and pulse about 6 to 8 times to combine. Add the flour mixture and pulse 15 to 20 times until you achieve a crumbly texture. Add the egg yolks and process until the dough begins to clump together, about

2 minutes. Transfer the dough to a medium bowl, cover with plastic wrap, and refrigerate. Wipe down the bowl and blade of the processor.

**Meanwhile, make the pear filling** ▶ In a large skillet over medium heat, combine the pears, brown sugar, butter, cinnamon, and lemon juice. Cook, stirring occasionally, until the pears have softened and are just fork-tender, 6 to 8 minutes. Remove from the heat, stir in the vanilla. Cool completely in the skillet, about 30 minutes.

**Make the frangipane** ▶ Combine the butter, granulated sugar, and almond flour in a food processor. Process until the mixture is fluffy and pale in color, 30 to 45 seconds. Add the egg, vanilla, and almond extract and pulse to combine. Add the flour and pulse again to combine, scraping down the bowl as needed. Transfer to a small bowl.

Preheat the oven to 350°F (180°C) and set a rack in the center. Coat a 9-inch (23 cm) tart pan with a removable bottom with cooking spray.

**To assemble** ▶ Crumble one third (roughly 160 grams) of the dough into a medium bowl and toss with the sliced almonds. Crumble the remaining dough into the bottom of the prepared tart pan. Use the bottom of a measuring cup to press the dough into an even layer along the bottom of the pan.

Spoon the frangipane into the center of the tart shell. Use a small offset spatula to spread the frangipane within ½ inch (1 cm) from the edge of the tart in an even layer. Dollop the pear filling into the center of the frangipane and again, spread within ½ inch (1 cm) from the edge in an even layer. Sprinkle the reserved almond and dough crumbles over the pears, covering as much of the filling as possible and breaking into smaller crumbs if necessary.

Bake until deep golden brown, 35 to 40 minutes, rotating the pan halfway through. Cool completely in the pan before removing from the sides and bottom. Dust with powdered sugar before serving.

The sbriciolata can be wrapped in plastic and stored at room temperature for up to 5 days. This tart ages well, so make sure to save some for the day after!

# LIMONCELLO PISTACHIO TART

MAKES ONE 9-INCH (23 CM) TART

*As any Italian will tell you, the best lemons are from the Amalfi Coast. These gargantuan, mutant-scaled citrus fruits are known for their floral bouquet, thick pith, and bright, tart flavor. They make their way into most desserts you find in the region, as well as the neon-yellow liqueur, limoncello, which practically flows from the kitchen faucets in Positano. Sadly, Amalfi lemons are a bit difficult to come by in Brooklyn, but limoncello is not, so we make do with what we have. This lemon-forward dessert is bursting with Mediterranean flavor, with the pistachios adding a contrasting savory note to the tart base. Cooking the curd (a tip I learned from friend and fellow Italian baker Tina Zaccardi) ensures a bright yellow filling, free of bubbles or pale yellow film.*

### FOR THE DOUGH

| | | |
|---|---|---|
| Unsalted butter, at room temperature | 195 grams | 14 tablespoons |
| Powdered sugar | 60 grams | ½ cup |
| All-purpose flour | 250 grams | 1¾ cups |
| Unsalted pistachios, toasted and finely ground | 65 grams | ½ cup |

### FOR THE CURD FILLING

| | | |
|---|---|---|
| All-purpose flour | 40 grams | 4½ tablespoons |
| Granulated sugar | 350 grams | 1¾ cups |
| Grated lemon zest | 4 grams | 2 teaspoons |
| Fresh lemon juice, from 4 to 5 large lemons | 240 grams | 1 cup |
| Large eggs | 5 | |
| Large egg yolks | 4 | |
| Limoncello | 30 grams | 2 tablespoons |
| Fine sea salt | 1 gram | ¼ teaspoon |
| Unsalted pistachios, toasted and finely chopped, for garnish | 25 grams | ¼ cup |

Preheat the oven to 350°F (175°C). Coat a 9-inch (23 cm) tart pan with a removable bottom with cooking spray.

**Make the dough** ▶ In a stand mixer fitted with the paddle, beat the butter and powdered sugar on low speed until combined. Add the flour and pistachios and mix until large clumps form, but don't let the dough fully come together. Sprinkle clumps of the dough in the prepared tart pan. Use floured hands to press the dough into an even layer along the bottom and sides of the pan.

Line the dough with parchment paper, extending past the sides of the pan. Fill the base with pie weights, dried beans, or uncooked rice. Bake until the bottom is set, about 30 minutes. Remove the parchment and weights, then return to the oven and bake for another 10 minutes, or until the crust is lightly browned. Remove from the oven but leave the oven on. Reduce the oven temperature to 275°F (135°C). ▶▶▶

Meanwhile, make the curd filling ▶ Sift the flour into a heatproof medium bowl. Add the sugar, lemon zest, and lemon juice and whisk until the sugar is dissolved. In a separate medium bowl, whisk the whole eggs, yolks, limoncello, and salt. Pour into the flour mixture, then whisk well until combined and homogeneous.

Fill a medium saucepan with 1 inch (2.5 cm) of water and bring to a simmer over medium heat. Set the bowl over the saucepan, making sure it doesn't touch the water. Whisk the curd as it heats up, until it's thick and turns bright yellow, about 5 minutes.

Pour the lemon curd into the tart shell and bake until the center of the custard is no longer wobbly, about 20 to 25 minutes.

Cool completely in the pan, and refrigerate for at least 4 hours or overnight. Remove from the pan sides and bottom. Sprinkle the tart with the chopped pistachios around the rim before serving.

The tart can be stored, loosely covered, in the refrigerator for up to 3 days.

# MONTE BIANCO

**MAKES EIGHT 4-INCH (10 CM) TARTS**

*When I was a kid, a bowl of roasted chestnuts and walnuts (along with the requisite nutcracker) was always presented after wintertime dinners and I have happy memories, on the streets of Rome and NYC alike, of roasted chestnuts heralding the holiday season. The Monte Bianco, named after the highest mountain in the Alps, is a traditional chestnut tart and an elegant way to impress family and friends. Here, I chose to use a chocolate frolla dough plus chocolate meringues to pair with the slightly savory chestnut filling and sweet whipped cream. Although reading the recipe might seem like you're scaling Monte Bianco itself, this multistep endeavor is easily attainable.*

**Chocolate Pasta Frolla (page 283)**

**FOR THE COCOA MERINGUES**

| | | |
|---|---|---|
| **Large egg whites** | 4 | |
| **Pinch of fine sea salt** | | |
| **Powdered sugar** | 240 grams | 2 cups |
| **Good-quality cocoa powder** | 25 grams | ¼ cup |

**FOR THE CHESTNUT PUREE**

| | | |
|---|---|---|
| **Peeled chestnuts** | 215 grams | 7½ ounces |
| **Whole milk** | 170 grams | ¾ cup |
| **Powdered sugar** | 40 grams | ⅓ cup |
| **Cocoa powder** | 6 grams | 1 tablespoon |
| **Pure vanilla extract** | 10 grams | 2 teaspoons |
| **Rum** | 15 grams | 1 tablespoon |
| **Pinch of fine sea salt** | | |

**FOR ASSEMBLY**

| | | |
|---|---|---|
| **Cold heavy cream** | 575 grams | 2½ cups |
| **Powdered sugar, for garnish** | | |
| **Cocoa powder, for garnish** | | |
| **Shaved chocolate, for garnish (optional)** | | |

**SPECIAL EQUIPMENT**

**Eight 4-inch (10 cm) tart pans**

**NOTE**

If you want to speed up the process, you can buy premade chocolate meringues as well as chestnut puree. Skip ahead to blending the puree with the sugar and other ingredients, add ¼ cup of whole milk and proceed as directed from there.

Make the Chocolate Pasta Frolla and refrigerate as directed.

**Make the cocoa meringues ▶** Preheat the oven to 250°F (120°C) and set a rack in the center. Line a baking sheet with parchment paper.

In a stand mixer fitted with the whisk, combine the egg whites and salt and beat on low speed until frothy, about 2 minutes. Increase the speed to medium and slowly add the powdered sugar a little at a time, until stiff peaks form, about 6 minutes. Add the cocoa powder and mix on low until just combined.

Transfer the mixture to a piping bag fitted with a large round tip. ▶▶▶

Pipe eight 4-inch (10 cm) spiral disks onto the parchment paper about 2 inches (5 cm) apart.

Bake until the exterior shell of the meringues has hardened, about 1 hour. Remove from the oven and transfer to a wire rack to cool completely.

**Meanwhile, make the chestnut puree ▶** In a medium saucepan, combine the chestnuts and milk and simmer over medium heat, stirring often, until the chestnuts are soft, about 12 minutes. Use a potato masher to mash them. Once most of the milk has been absorbed by the mashed chestnuts, remove from the heat.

In a blender, combine the chestnut puree, powdered sugar, cocoa powder, vanilla, rum, and salt. Process until very smooth, 2 to 3 minutes. Transfer to a bowl, cover with plastic wrap, and refrigerate until ready to use.

When ready to bake, preheat the oven to 350°F (180°C) and set a rack in the center. Grease eight 4-inch (10 cm) tart pans with cooking spray and line a baking sheet with parchment.

Remove the chocolate pasta frolla from the fridge and divide it into 8 equal portions (about 105 grams each). Dust a work surface with flour and roll each portion into a 6-inch (15 cm) round about ⅛ inch (3 mm) thick. Press each round into a tart pan to fill the bottom and sides of the pan. Trim off any excess dough and use a fork to poke holes along the bottom of the dough.

Line the dough in each pan with a parchment paper round that extends past the sides of the pan. Fill with pie weights, dried beans, or uncooked rice. Place each pan on the parchment-lined baking sheet and bake until the bottoms are set, 20 to 25 minutes, rotating halfway through. Remove the weights and parchment. Let the tart shells cool completely in the pans, about 1 hour.

**When the tarts are cool, begin the assembly ▶** In a stand mixer fitted with the whisk, beat the heavy cream on medium speed to stiff peaks, about 4 minutes. Remove 370 grams (3 cups) of the whipped cream to a medium bowl. Add the chestnut puree to the whipped cream remaining in the stand mixer and beat again on medium until smooth, about 2 minutes. Transfer the chestnut puree to a piping bag fitted with a small round tip (or a Mont Blanc tip, if you have one in your possession). Chop the meringues into ½-inch (1 cm) pieces and fold into the medium bowl of reserved whipped cream.

Scoop about 120 grams (about ½ cup) of the meringue and whipped cream mixture into each tart shell, forming a dome shape and smoothing any edges with an offset spatula. Pipe the chestnut cream around the base of the filling, filling in the gap between the meringue mixture and the tart shell. Pipe in a spiral, moving up the dome until you reach the top center. Repeat with the remaining tarts.

Before serving, dust the tarts with powdered sugar and a tap of cocoa powder. If desired, also decorate with shaved chocolate.

The tarts can be stored, uncovered, in the refrigerator for up to 24 hours.

# PASTIERA

MAKES ONE 9-INCH (23 CM) TART

*Our parents never made us go to church on Sundays or pray before meals or bedtime while we were growing up. They weren't overly religious, but my dad really enjoyed celebrating Easter. Because of that, he loved pastiera, a traditional Neapolitan dessert that is synonymous with the holiday. An early version of this pastry originated during the Roman Empire, as an offering to Ceres, the goddess of agriculture, and the rustic ingredient list points to its ancient heritage. It is made from a combination of wheat berries, ricotta cheese, and candied orange peel, flavored with cinnamon, vanilla, and orange blossom water. Pastiera is typically made a few days ahead of time, to allow the flavors to meld together.*

| Pasta Frolla (page 283) | | |
|---|---|---|
| FOR THE GRANO COTTO | | |
| Grano cotto (cooked wheat berries) | 275 grams | 9¾ ounces |
| Whole milk | 115 grams | ½ cup |
| Strip of orange zest | | |
| Pinch of ground cinnamon | | |
| Pure vanilla extract | 3 grams | ½ teaspoon |
| FOR THE FILLING | | |
| Fresh Ricotta (page 272) or good-quality ricotta cheese, drained overnight | 500 grams | 17 ounces/2 cups |
| Granulated sugar | 170 grams | ¾ cup |
| Fine sea salt | 1 gram | ¼ teaspoon |
| Large eggs | 2 | |
| Large egg yolk | 1 | |
| Diced candied orange peel | 80 grams | ½ cup |
| Wildflower honey | 20 grams | 1 tablespoon |
| Orange blossom water (optional) | 15 grams | 1 tablespoon |
| Pure vanilla extract | 5 grams | 1 teaspoon |
| Powdered sugar, for garnish | | |

**Make the pasta frolla and refrigerate as directed.**

**Make the grano cotto** ▶ In a small saucepan, combine the grano cotto, milk, orange zest, and cinnamon. Simmer over low heat, stirring constantly, until thickened, about 15 minutes. Stir in the vanilla. Discard the strip of zest and transfer the wheat to a medium bowl. Let cool for 30 minutes, then cover with plastic wrap and refrigerate until chilled, about an hour.

**When the grano cotto is cooled, make the ricotta filling** ▶ In a stand mixer fitted with the whisk, combine the ricotta, granulated sugar, and salt. Beat on low speed until combined. Add the whole eggs and yolk one at a time, stopping to scrape down the sides as needed. Mix in the candied orange, honey, orange blossom water (if using), and vanilla. Add the cooled grano cotto ▶▶▶

We are using a shortcut here by purchasing a jar of grano cotto, already cooked wheat berries, easily found in Italian markets or ordered online, especially in the weeks leading up to Easter. However, you can purchase dried wheat berries and cook them yourself in a large pot of boiling water for 2 hours until tender, then drain and cool completely.

If you are having trouble finding either dried or cooked wheat berries, you can swap them out for Arborio rice for an equally delicious pastiera. The process for cooking the rice is similar to making rice pudding. In a medium saucepan over low heat, cook 150 grams (¾ cup) rice in 455 grams (2 cups) whole milk, a strip of orange zest, and a pinch of cinnamon. Stir frequently, until the milk has been absorbed and rice is tender and creamy, about 15 minutes. Add 3 grams (½ teaspoon) of vanilla extract and remove the strip of zest. Transfer to a bowl, let cool for 30 minutes, then cover with plastic wrap and chill in the refrigerator until ready to use.

### ANOTHER NOTE

Goat milk ricotta is the traditional filling, if you can find it, but cow's milk is welcome here, too!

and mix again to combine. Remove the bowl from the mixer and scrape the sides and bottom to fully combine.

Preheat the oven to 375°F (190°C) and set a rack in the lowest position. Coat a 9-inch (23 cm) springform pan with cooking spray, line with a round of parchment paper, and spray again.

Remove the dough from the refrigerator and divide into 3 equal portions. Dust a work surface with flour and combine two of the portions of dough into a ball. Use a rolling pin to roll it into an 11-inch (28 cm) round about ¼ inch (6 mm) thick. Roll the dough up onto the pin and transfer to the prepared pan, pressing to line the bottom and sides. Roll the remaining dough between two sheets of parchment paper into a 9½ by 10-inch (24 by 25 cm) rectangle about ¼ inch (6 mm) thick. Remove the top parchment and cut the dough into 10 strips about 1 inch (2.5 cm) wide. Replace the top parchment and slide onto a baking sheet and freeze for about 10 minutes to firm up the dough.

Transfer the ricotta filling into the torta shell and smooth into an even layer.

Remove the sheet of dough from the freezer and remove the top parchment. Place 5 of the strips over the torta, spaced evenly apart. Place the remaining 5 strips across them at a diagonal, to create a lattice. Cut off any excess dough and press all the strips to adhere to the crust edge.

Bake the torta until the top is dark golden brown, about 1 hour, rotating the pan halfway through. Cool completely in the pan, about 2 hours.

Remove the torta from the springform, cover in plastic wrap, and refrigerate overnight to set and let the flavors meld.

Before serving, bring to room temperature and dust the edges of the tart with powdered sugar.

The torta can be wrapped in plastic and stored in the refrigerator for up to 1 week.

# CHOCOLATE AMARO PECAN PIE

**MAKES ONE 9-INCH (23 CM) DEEP-DISH PIE**

*My brother insists that a pecan pie is not a pecan pie if it has chocolate in it. I beg to differ, and this is my cookbook so I have the final word. My stance is if it doesn't have chocolate (and booze, for that matter), why bother? Just eat a handful of nuts and call it a day. But I digress. The milk chocolate here adds a creamy sweetness that pairs perfectly with the buttery pecans. And like bourbon in American pecan pies, Italian amaro adds a depth of flavor and a sharp boozy finish. This pie is my idea of pecan perfection.*

### FOR THE PIE DOUGH

| | | |
|---|---|---|
| All-purpose flour | 285 grams | 2 cups |
| Fine sea salt | 2 grams | ¼ teaspoon |
| Unsalted butter, cubed and chilled | 195 grams | 14 tablespoons |
| Ice-cold water, plus more as needed | 55 grams | ¼ cup |

### FOR THE FILLING

| | | |
|---|---|---|
| Large eggs, at room temperature | 3 | |
| Corn syrup | 230 grams | ½ cup plus 2 tablespoons |
| Unsalted butter, melted | 40 grams | 3 tablespoons |
| Dark brown sugar | 65 grams | ⅓ cup packed |
| Amaro, such as Faccia Brutto or Amaro Nonino | 30 grams | 2 tablespoons |
| Pure vanilla extract | 5 grams | 1 teaspoon |
| Fine sea salt | 2 grams | ¼ teaspoon |
| Milk chocolate chips | 115 grams | ⅔ cup |
| Pecans, toasted and chopped | 340 grams | 3 cups |

**NOTE**

If you have trouble sourcing amaro, good old-fashioned bourbon will do the trick!

**Make the pie dough** ▶ In a stand mixer fitted with the paddle, combine the flour, salt, and butter. Mix on low speed until the butter pieces are pea-sized. Slowly stream in the ice water, using only what you need until the ingredients hold together evenly in a smooth dough. If there are noticeable cracks, add a small amount more water. If it's wet or tacky, add a small amount more flour.

Form the dough into a disk and pat down until 1 inch (2.5 cm) thick. Wrap tightly in plastic wrap and refrigerate for at least 1 hour or overnight. Bring the dough to room temperature for 10 minutes before using.

Dust a work surface with flour. Roll the dough into a 12-inch (30 cm) round about ¼ inch (6 mm) thick. Roll the dough up onto the pin and transfer to a 9-inch (23 cm) deep-dish pie plate, pressing to line the bottom and sides. Dock the bottom with the tines of a fork. Trim any excess and crimp the edges. Refrigerate for 1 hour to firm up.

Preheat the oven to 375°F (190°C).

Line the dough with a parchment round that extends past the sides of the pie plate. Fill the base with pie weights, dried beans, or uncooked rice. Bake until the bottom is set, 25 to 30 minutes. Remove the weights and parchment, ▶▶▶

and place back in the oven to bake for an additional 10 to 20 minutes, or until firm to the touch. Remove and let cool slightly. Leave the oven on and reduce the temperature to 350°F (180°C).

**Meanwhile, make the filling** ▶ In a medium bowl, whisk together the eggs and corn syrup. Add the melted butter, brown sugar, amaro, vanilla, and salt and whisk until the mixture is smooth.

Scatter the chocolate chips and pecans into the pie shell and give it a quick toss to combine. Pour in the filling up to the rim of the pie crust.

Bake until the filling is set and puffed up, 40 to 50 minutes. Let cool completely, about 2 hours. The pie can be rewarmed in a 300°F (150°C) oven for 15 minutes before serving.

The pecan pie can be refrigerated for up to 3 days.

4

BREADS, SAVORIES + STREET SNACKS

Naples, Campania, Italy

**STREET FOOD IS A** vibrant part of the culture in both Italy and New York. In Italy, where something good to eat is always within arm's reach and snacking is a full-time job, making multiple stops at the bar isn't just common, it's expected. In the busier rush of New York, walking while eating something grabbed from a food truck is the norm. But in both places, the food sold on the street is, in my opinion, the truest way to stitch your way into the culinary fabric of the culture.

# SOURDOUGH FOCACCIA THREE WAYS

**MAKES 1 BAKING SHEET OF FOCACCIA**

*The focaccia at Ciao, Gloria is a godsend, if I do say so myself. Our recipe uses a sourdough starter, which is worth the effort for giving the bread that indelible tanginess that only comes from lengthy fermentation, which carb aficionados like myself deeply appreciate. If you don't have a starter going, there's a handy guide to making your own on page 275; it just requires a little time, patience, and Sicilian witchcraft (or science). This recipe includes a trio of my favorite toppings, from simple to loaded, but feel free to experiment with the flavors you love. There's no shame in going heavy on the shredded cheese, pepperoni cups, and sliced mushrooms.*

| | | |
|---|---|---|
| Sourdough Starter (page 275) | 225 grams | 1 cup |
| All-purpose flour | 640 grams | 4½ cups |
| Instant dry yeast | 3 grams | 1 teaspoon |
| Good-quality olive oil, plus more for the dough | 65 grams | ⅓ cup |
| Fine sea salt | 12 grams | 1 tablespoon |

**NOTE**

If you don't want to go through the process of making your own starter, ask your local bakery if they have some to give. Most bakeries will be happy to share some with you free of charge.

In a stand mixer fitted with the dough hook, combine the sourdough starter, flour, yeast, olive oil, and 425 grams (1¾ cups plus 2 tablespoons) warm water. Mix on low speed until combined, about 3 minutes. Add the salt, increase the speed to medium, and mix for an additional 3 minutes to continue to develop the dough. It will be very loose and sticky, do not fret.

Generously rub a baking sheet with olive oil. Transfer the dough to the baking sheet and pat into a rough square shape. Fold the dough over itself by lifting the edge farthest from you and pulling it toward you to fold in half. Turn the baking sheet 90 degrees and repeat this process until all four sides have been folded on top of each other. Cover the baking sheet with a kitchen towel and let the dough rest at room temperature for 30 minutes.

Repeat the folding and resting process two more times. After the final rest, stretch out the dough to reach all four corners of the baking sheet. If you are experiencing any snap back, cover the dough and let it rest for 10 to 15 minutes until pliable. Brush the top of the dough with olive oil and cover the entire baking sheet loosely with plastic wrap. Refrigerate overnight to rest.

The following day, remove the dough from the fridge and let proof for about 2 hours until bubbly and doubled in size.

About 30 minutes before the dough is done proofing, preheat the oven to 425°F (220°C) and set racks in the center and lower third. Place a baking dish filled with 1 cup of water on the lower rack while the oven preheats. The steam will help create a nice crispy crust and chewy interior on the focaccia.

Discard the plastic wrap and dimple the focaccia with your fingers for the classic, undulating surface. Pop any large bubbles as those may blister and char, unless that's the look you're going for.

You can bake the focaccia as is ▶ Top with flaky sea salt and a drizzle of olive oil and bake until dark golden brown, about 25 to 30 minutes, rotating the baking sheet halfway through. The plain version is especially great for sandwich bread. To take it to the next level, try one of these variations.

## D'OLIVA

Arrange marinated olives, homemade (see page 103) or store-bought, in the dimples of the dough, using as many as you'd like. Sprinkle some rosemary tips across the surface and top with flaky sea salt and freshly ground black pepper. Add another drizzle of olive oil and bake until dark golden brown, about 25 to 30 minutes, rotating the baking sheet halfway through. Let cool on the baking sheet for 10 minutes before slicing and serving.

## MORTAZZA

Top the focaccia with flaky sea salt and a drizzle of olive oil. Bake until dark golden brown, about 25 to 30 minutes, rotating the baking sheet halfway through. Let cool on the baking sheet for 10 minutes.

Meanwhile, in a small bowl, mix 250 grams (1 cup) ricotta (homemade, page 272, or store-bought), 5 grams (1 tablespoon) grated Pecorino Romano cheese, and a big pinch of salt and black pepper.

When the focaccia has cooled for 10 minutes, spread the cheese mixture in a thin, even layer over the focaccia, leaving a 1-inch (2.5 cm) border around the edges. Drape about 115 grams (¼ pound) thinly sliced mortadella over the ricotta, folding the slices to give some height. Top with about 80 grams (4 cups) baby arugula, a drizzle of olive oil, a handful of chopped pistachios, and another pinch of salt and pepper. Slice and serve immediately.

## QUATTRO STAGIONI

NOTE

If you aren't one for tradition, go ahead and mix all the seasons together to top your focaccia. It will still look beautiful and taste delicious.

Bake the focaccia until the dough begins to brown on top, 10 to 12 minutes, rotating the baking sheet halfway through.

Meanwhile, in a medium skillet, heat 15 grams (1 tablespoon) butter over medium heat. Add 50 grams (½ cup) thinly sliced cremini mushrooms. Season with a pinch of salt and freshly ground black pepper. Cook, stirring occasionally, until browned, about 5 minutes. Remove from the heat.

Remove the focaccia from the oven and spread 225 grams (2 cups) tomato sauce in an even layer, leaving a 1-inch (2.5 cm) border on all sides. Top with 230 grams (2 cups) shredded mozzarella cheese, 115 grams (1 cup) shredded smoked mozzarella, and a sprinkle of dried oregano. Top one quadrant of the focaccia with the sautéed mushrooms, top another with 115 grams (¼ pound) folded prosciutto cotto, another with 85 grams (½ cup) diced cured artichoke hearts, and the last corner with 70 grams (½ cup) diced marinated olives (homemade, below, or store-bought) to create the "quattro stagioni," or four seasons, of the focaccia. Bake for another 10 to 12 minutes, rotating halfway through, until the cheese is melted and bubbling.

Let cool on the baking sheet for 10 minutes before drizzling with a little olive oil. Cut each quadrant into 4 slices, for a total of 16 slices. The focaccia is best served immediately. There will be no leftovers.

# MARINATED OLIVES

## MAKES 1 LITER (1 QUART)

*As a child, I was obsessed with Moroccan black olives, which were readily available by the barrel at our local Italian market. I could eat an entire pint container in one sitting. As I got older, like most teenagers, I began to experiment . . . with different kinds of olives. Kalamata, Cerignola, Manzanilla, I've tried all of them. My obsession ultimately moved toward the meaty, green Sicilian Castelvetrano olive, where my heart has been ever since. I suggest using a mixed assortment for this recipe, as all varieties benefit from resting in this fragrant oil bath.*

| | | |
|---|---|---|
| Extra-virgin olive oil | 400 grams | 2 cups |
| Garlic cloves, crushed | 6 | |
| Sprigs fresh thyme | 4 | |
| Bay leaves | 2 | |
| Strips of zest from 1 orange | | |
| Pitted mixed olives, any variety | 910 grams | 2 pounds |

NOTE

This recipe can be easily doubled, if you would like to make a large batch and always have delicious olives at the ready for your next aperitivo or focaccia topping.

In a medium saucepan, combine the olive oil and garlic. Bring to a simmer over medium heat. Remove from the heat and let the oil cool for 30 minutes. Add the thyme, bay leaves, and orange zest. Let the oil continue to cool for 1 hour.

Meanwhile, line a baking sheet with paper towels. Drain and rinse the olives under cold water, then transfer to the lined baking sheet and pat dry with more paper towels. Set aside to air-dry while the oil cools.

Add the olives to a 2-quart mason jar. Pour the oil and seasonings over the olives, adding more oil if needed to ensure that the olives are submerged. Seal the jar and refrigerate until ready to use. The olives will continue to develop in flavor the longer they sit. Let the jar sit at room temperature for at least 30 minutes before enjoying.

The olives can be stored in an airtight container in the refrigerator for up to 3 months.

# IMPANATA

## MAKES ONE 10-INCH IMPANATA

Impanata was on constant rotation during my childhood. Think of it as an inside-out pizza, typically filled with broccoli, anchovy, olives, and pecorino primosale. And as much as I am one for tradition, I would always ask my mom to vary the fillings. She serves the impanata in hearty slices and, as most Italian mothers do, expects you to go back for seconds (and thirds). It's something I often crave and make for myself as an adult. In my home, fillings are truly chef's choice, but I am sharing my favorite combination here: broccoli rabe, sausage, mozzarella, and pecorino.

| | | |
|---|---|---|
| Pizza Dough (page 276) | | |
| 4 links of Italian sausage (2 sweet and 2 hot, or any combo) | | |
| Extra-virgin olive oil, plus more for brushing | 25 grams | 2 tablespoons |
| Broccoli rabe, cleaned, trimmed, and chopped | 430 grams | 1 bunch |
| Garlic cloves, peeled | 2 | |
| Pinch of crushed red pepper (optional) | | |
| Fine sea salt, to taste | | |
| Low-moisture mozzarella cheese, shredded | 170 grams | 2 cups |
| Grated Pecorino Romano | 30 grams | ¼ cup |
| Freshly ground black pepper, to finish | | |

**A day ahead** ▶ Make the pizza dough and refrigerate as directed.

Remove the dough from the refrigerator and let sit at room temperature for 30 to 45 minutes before using.

Remove the sausage from its casings. In a 10-inch (25 cm) cast-iron skillet, heat 1 tablespoon of the oil over medium-high heat. When the oil shimmers, add the sausage and cook until browned and cooked through, 8 to 9 minutes, breaking up the larger pieces of sausage with a spoon. Transfer the sausage to a paper towel–lined plate and reserve the oil in the skillet. (Do not wipe out.)

Meanwhile, in a large pot of salted boiling water over medium heat, cook the broccoli rabe and garlic cloves until the broccoli rabe is tender, but still vibrant green, about 4 minutes.

While the broccoli is cooking, fill a large bowl with ice water and place a colander in it. Set aside.

Remove the garlic cloves from the pot. Strain the broccoli and place in the colander. (This will shock the rabe and keep its coloring.) Let sit for about a minute and then squeeze out the excess liquid and place in a medium bowl. Thinly slice the garlic cloves.

In the same skillet over medium heat, add 1 tablespoon of olive oil, the garlic, and the crushed red pepper (if using) and sauté until fragrant, about 2 minutes. Add the broccoli rabe and sausage back to the skillet, then cook for another 2 to 3 minutes. Add salt to taste, remove from heat, and transfer to a plate to cool. Let the skillet cool slightly, then wipe out the oil.

Preheat the oven to 400°F (200°C) and set a rack in the center. Lightly brush the skillet with oil.

Divide the pizza dough in 2 pieces: one piece weighing roughly 330 grams and the other 190 grams. On a generously floured surface, use a floured rolling pin to roll the larger half into a 12-inch (30 cm) round. Transfer the dough to the skillet draping it over the bottom and up the sides. Sprinkle half of the mozzarella over the dough. Place the broccoli rabe and sausage filling in the center of the mozzarella, smoothing into an even layer and leaving about a 1-inch (2.5 cm) border around the edge. Sprinkle the grated pecorino and the remaining mozzarella over the filling. Roll the remaining half of dough into a 10-inch (25 cm) round and drape, centered, over the filling. Roll the overhang of the bottom dough over the top dough and pinch tightly to secure. Using a knife or fork, dock the top crust with a few slits or holes to allow the steam to release. Brush the top and edges with olive oil and sprinkle with a little salt and a few grinds of pepper.

Bake until the dough is golden brown, 40 to 45 minutes. Let cool for 30 minutes before slicing and serving.

The impanata can be wrapped in plastic and stored in the refrigerator for up to 3 days.

# 'NDUJA PIZZETTE

## MAKES 12 PIZZETTE

*Pizzette are the ultimate Italian quick bite. Mountains of small dough rounds, baked with a variety of regional and seasonal toppings, are featured in display cases across the country. But unlike our typical American walk-and-eat culture, Italians pause, even if only for a few minutes, standing at the bar or seated at a sidewalk table, accompanying food with an espresso, acqua minerale, or an aperitivo cocktail, depending on time of day. The classic pizzette you will find almost anywhere is made with fresh tomato sauce, topped with mozzarella, a sprinkling of dried oregano, and a finish of olive oil. A schmear of 'nduja livens things up here, but mix and match as you see fit.*

| | | |
|---|---|---|
| Pizza Dough (page 276) | | |
| Semolina flour, for dusting | | |
| 'Nduja | 170 grams | 6 ounces |
| Grape tomatoes, halved | 340 grams | 1 pint |
| Fresh mozzarella or scamorza cheese, shredded | 240 grams | 8 ounces |
| Extra-virgin olive oil, for brushing and garnish | | |
| Dried oregano, for garnish | | |

**A day ahead ▸** Make the pizza dough and refrigerate as directed.

Dust a baking sheet with flour. Divide the dough into 12 equal portions (45 to 50 grams each). On a generously floured surface, roll each portion into a little ball and then place on the prepared baking sheet, a few inches apart from one another. Let the dough rest for about 30 minutes.

Line two baking sheets with parchment paper and dust with some semolina flour.

On the same lightly floured surface, shape the dough balls into little pizzette. Using your fingers, flatten out the balls by turning and pressing outward until you have a 4-inch (10 cm) round. Use a spatula to transfer the pizzette to the lined baking sheets, 6 on each one, evenly spaced.

On each round, spread 15 grams (2 rounded teaspoons) of 'nduja. Top with tomato halves and 20 grams (2 rounded tablespoons) of shredded mozzarella. Make sure to leave a ½-inch (1 cm) border around each pizzette. Brush the edges of each pizzette with olive oil and let rest for an additional 10 to 15 minutes.

Preheat the oven to 400°F (245°C) and set two racks in the center.

Bake until the crust is golden brown and the cheese is melted, 15 to 20 minutes, switching racks and rotating the pans halfway through. Immediately garnish each pizzette with a pinch of dried oregano and a drizzle of olive oil. Transfer to a wire rack to cool slightly.

The pizzette are best enjoyed on the day they're baked.

# CAPONATA BOMBAS

**MAKES 10 BOMBAS**

*We serve a full menu of sandwiches, salads, and grain bowls at Ciao, Gloria, but the one thing customers are always asking for is savory pastries. Bombas, an Italian-sounding snack we invented at the café, were created to fill exactly that need. Literally meaning "bombs," these filled dough balls puff up while baking, housing a wide variety of fillings. I'm partial to these vegetarian caponata-filled ones. They make a delicious snack or great appetizer.*

| | | |
|---|---|---|
| Pizza Dough (page 276) | | |
| Caponata (recipe follows) | | |
| Extra-virgin olive oil, plus more for brushing | 25 grams | 2 tablespoons |
| Minced fresh parsley | 5 grams | 1 tablespoon |
| Garlic clove, grated | 1 | |
| Flaky sea salt, for garnish | | |

**A day ahead** ▶ Make the pizza dough and caponata and refrigerate as directed.

When ready to bake, let the dough sit at room temperature for 30 to 45 minutes before using.

Preheat the oven to 400°F (200°C) and set a rack in the center. Brush 10 cups of a muffin tin with olive oil.

On a generously floured surface, cut the dough into 10 equal portions (50 grams each). Working with one piece at a time, roll into a 4-inch (10 cm) round. Scoop 50 grams (2 tablespoons) of caponata in the center of the round. Brush the rim of the round with olive oil. Lift the edges of the dough up and to the center of the filling, pinching together to join like a satchel. Once completely sealed, set in the muffin tin, seam-side down. Repeat with the remaining dough and caponata.

Brush the tops with a little olive oil and bake until golden brown, 25 to 35 minutes, rotating the muffin tin halfway through.

While the bombas bake, in a small bowl, whisk the olive oil, parsley, and garlic. Set a wire rack over a baking sheet.

Remove the bombas from the oven and, while still hot, use an offset spatula to transfer to the wire rack. Brush the oil and parsley mixture over the bombas and top with a sprinkle of flaky salt. Let cool for 15 minutes before serving.

The bombas can be stored in an airtight container in the refrigerator for up to 3 days.  ▶ ▶ ▶

# CAPONATA

MAKES 1,200 GRAMS (6 CUPS)

*Caponata is most popular in its place of origin, Sicily. A flavor punch of roasted eggplant, briny capers and olives, sweet raisins, and a little vinegar makes for a very balanced, very addictive mix.*

| | | |
|---|---|---|
| Eggplant, cut into 1-inch (2.5 cm) cubes | 900 grams | 2 pounds |
| Fine sea salt, divided | 15 grams | 4 teaspoons |
| Extra-virgin olive oil, divided | 75 grams | ⅓ cup |
| Diced yellow onion (from 1 large onion) | 140 grams | 1 cup |
| Diced celery (from 2 stalks) | 140 grams | 1 cup |
| Diced red bell pepper (from 2 peppers) | 290 grams | 2 cups |
| Cloves garlic, sliced | 3 | |
| Pinch crushed red pepper flakes | | |
| Tomato paste | 60 grams | 4 tablespoons |
| Drained capers | 40 grams | ¼ cup |
| Golden raisins | 40 grams | ¼ cup |
| Pitted Castelvetrano olives, halved | 140 grams | 1 cup |
| Cherry tomatoes, quartered | 110 grams | 4 ounces |
| Granulated sugar | 35 grams | 3 tablespoons |
| Red wine vinegar | 55 grams | ¼ cup |
| Chopped fresh basil | 30 grams | 1 cup |

**NOTE**

If you would like to make enough caponata to use for the bombas only, just halve this recipe. However, I don't recommend limiting your caponata intake. The flavors improve with time, so make this at least a day in advance.

Preheat the oven to 400°F (200°C) and set a rack in the center. Brush a baking sheet with a generous amount of olive oil.

Arrange the eggplant on the prepared baking sheet and toss with 8 grams (2 teaspoons) of the salt and 50 grams (¼ cup) of the olive oil. Roast until nicely browned, 30 to 40 minutes, tossing halfway through. Remove from the oven.

In a large skillet, heat the remaining olive oil over medium heat. When the oil shimmers, add the onion, celery, bell peppers, and garlic. Season with the remaining salt and the pepper flakes. Cook, stirring often, until softened, 8 to 10 minutes.

Push the veggies to one side and add the tomato paste in the empty area. Warm for 30 seconds, then stir into the veggies. Stir in the capers, raisins, olives, cherry tomatoes, sugar, and vinegar. Simmer, stirring occasionally, until the liquid is almost reduced, 2 to 3 minutes.

Stir in the eggplant. Continue to cook until the caponata has thickened slightly and there is little residual liquid left, 5 to 10 minutes. Taste for seasoning. Remove from the heat and stir in the basil. Let the mixture cool for 1 hour in the skillet, then transfer to an airtight container and refrigerate for up to 1 week.

San Gimignano,
Tuscany, Italy

Rome, Lazio, Italy

FAZOllO
BOROLdi
€ 2.50
AL-KG

€2·50
AL-KG

Lentticci
montania
€2.50
AL-KG

FAZZOLI
OCCHIO
€2.50

Palermo, Sicily, Italy

Catania, Sicily, Italy

# PANELLE FRIES

SERVES 6 TO 8

*It might seem excessive to eat fried chickpea flour between two pieces of bread—carbs on carbs—but Sicilians, especially in Palermo, don't seem to mind one bit. Panelle street stands are pretty ubiquitous in the city (think New York City's hot dog and pretzel carts). Panelle are made by cooking chickpea flour and water into a thick paste, cut into squares, and quickly fried for a crispy exterior. The great thing about the panelle base is how endlessly adaptable it is, so we're skipping the bread here and instead making panelle sticks, all the better to be dipped in a flavorful red pepper spread. The panelle are an ideal canvas for other flavors and ingredients, so top yours with whatever you like. And se vuoi fare come un Palermítano, go ahead and sandwich it on a good, crusty semolina roll, I won't judge.*

| | | |
|---|---|---|
| Chickpea flour | 480 grams | 4 cups |
| Fine sea salt | 4 grams | 1 teaspoon |
| Extra-virgin olive oil, plus more for shallow-frying | 100 grams | ½ cup |
| Freshly grated Pecorino Romano cheese | 200 grams | 2 cups |
| Minced fresh parsley | 65 grams | 1 cup |
| Lemon, cut into wedges, for squeezing | 1 | |
| Red Pepper Dip (recipe follows), for serving | | |

Line a 9 by 13-inch (23 by 33 cm) baking dish with parchment paper, leaving a 1-inch (2.5 cm) overhang on all sides.

In a heatproof medium bowl, whisk the chickpea flour and salt.

In a large saucepan, combine the olive oil and 6 cups water. Bring to a rolling boil over high heat. Slowly pour in the chickpea mixture, whisking constantly. Switch to an immersion blender to pulse the mixture until it is completely smooth. (This step is optional but makes for a great final texture.) Return to low heat, whisking constantly, until the mixture releases a few thick bubbles, 1 to 2 minutes. Remove from the heat and whisk in the pecorino and parsley until combined. Transfer the batter into the prepared baking dish and smooth into an even layer. Cool for 30 minutes, then cover loosely with plastic wrap and refrigerate for 1 hour.

Use the parchment sling to lift the panelle to a cutting board. Cut in half lengthwise to form 2 rectangles Cut each rectangle crosswise into 16 equal strips for 32 pieces total.

Line a baking sheet with paper towels. In a medium skillet, heat ¼ inch (6 mm) olive oil over medium heat. When the oil shimmers, work in batches to fry the panelle for about 2 minutes on each side, flipping with tongs, until lightly golden brown. Transfer to the paper towels to drain while frying the rest.

Serve the panelle warm with a squeeze of lemon juice and red pepper dip.

Panelle are best served immediately. There will be no leftovers.

# RED PEPPER DIP

**MAKES 500 GRAMS (1½ CUPS)**

*We're using this as a dip here, but it can also work as a spread for sandwiches or tossed with pasta and vegetables for a cold pasta salad.*

| | | |
|---|---|---|
| Garlic clove, grated | 1 | |
| Fresh lemon juice | 15 grams | 1 tablespoon |
| Fine sea salt | 1 gram | ¼ teaspoon |
| Marinated Roasted Peppers, homemade (page 117) or store-bought | 455 grams | 1½ cups |
| Minced fresh parsley | 5 grams | 1 tablespoon |
| Olive oil | 50 grams | 2 tablespoons |

In a small bowl, stir the grated garlic, lemon juice, and salt. Let sit for 5 minutes. Remove the peppers from the marinade. In a food processor, combine the garlic mixture, peppers, salt, parsley, and olive oil. Process until mostly smooth with some texture, stopping to scrape the sides as needed, about 2 minutes. Transfer to an airtight container and refrigerate until ready to use.

The red pepper dip can be stored in an airtight container in the refrigerator for up to 5 days.

D. Coluccio & Sons,
Borough Park, Brooklyn

# PIADINA

MAKES SIX 9-INCH (23 CM) PIADINAS

*Piadina is a flatbread from the Emilia-Romagna region that looks a lot like a large tortilla. A centuries-old recipe, it has become a popular snack food across Italy. Instead of rolling up the tortilla, like a burrito, a piadina is simply folded in half and stuffed with all sorts of fillings. The most traditional version is a mix of prosciutto, stracchino cheese, and plenty of peppery arugula. But like most of the recipes in this chapter, amounts and ingredients are mostly suggestions. That's the beauty with savory dishes, you can easily experiment and make them your own.*

| | | |
|---|---|---|
| All-purpose flour | 355 grams | 2½ cups |
| Fine sea salt | 4 grams | 1 teaspoon |
| Baking powder | 5 grams | 1 teaspoon |
| Whole milk, at room temperature | 170 grams | ¾ cup |
| Unsalted butter, melted | 55 grams | 4 tablespoons |
| Warm tap water | 55 grams | ¼ cup |
| Vegetable oil, for brushing | | |

OPTIONAL FILLINGS

Fresh Ricotta (page 272)
Marinated Roasted Peppers (page 117)
Red Pepper Dip (page 113)
'Nduja
Prosciutto
Mortadella
Soppressata
Mozzarella
Provolone
Arugula

In a medium bowl, sift the flour, salt, and baking powder.

In a stand mixer fitted with the dough hook, combine the milk, melted butter, and warm tap water. With the mixer running on low speed, slowly add the flour mixture. Mix until the dough comes together, then increase the speed to medium-high and knead for 5 minutes, until soft and pliable.

Wrap the dough tightly in plastic and let rest at room temperature for 30 minutes.

Divide the dough into 6 equal portions (about 100 grams each). On a lightly floured work surface, use a rolling pin to roll each portion into a 9-inch (23 cm) round. (It's okay if the round is a little rustic in shape.)

Heat a 10-inch (25 cm) cast-iron skillet over medium heat for 10 minutes, until very hot. Brush the surface of the skillet with a little vegetable oil. Working one at a time, lay a piadina in the skillet. Cook until the top bubbles and the bottom is golden with brown spots, about 1 minute. Flip and cook the other side for 1 minute more. Transfer to a kitchen towel to keep warm while making the rest. Brush the skillet with a little oil as needed to prevent sticking.

Spread your choice of fillings over the surface of the piadina, using a light touch. Fold the piadina in half and enjoy.

The piadinas without fillings can be wrapped in plastic and stored at room temperature for up to 2 days. Warm briefly in a skillet before using.

# CROSTINI

MAKES 36 CROSTINI

*It's wild to think that something as ubiquitous and simple as crostini are actually an Italian creation dating back to the Middle Ages, when peasants would use bread in place of plates. When the bread was a little stale, the liquid from the toppings helped bring everything back to life. What would they think of us now, enjoying crostini artfully arranged on the plates they lacked, served for aperitivo alongside a cocktail? This version leans very rustic with homemade ricotta and marinated roasted peppers, an ingredient brought over from the New World during the late Middle Ages, in a nod to the dish's DIY origins.*

| | | |
|---|---|---|
| Large baguette (about 26 inches or 66 cm), ends trimmed and cut into ½-inch-thick (1 cm) slices | 1 | |
| Extra-virgin olive oil, for brushing and drizzling | | |
| Garlic clove, halved | 1 | |
| Fresh Ricotta (page 272) | 570 grams | 2¼ cups |
| Flaky sea salt | | |
| Freshly ground black pepper | | |
| Marinated Roasted Peppers (recipe follows) | | |

Preheat the oven to 400°F (200°C) and set two racks in the center.

Arrange the baguette slices on two baking sheets, brush the tops with olive oil, and bake until toasted, 5 to 10 minutes. Immediately rub the warm bread with the cut sides of the garlic clove.

While the bread is still warm, spread about 1 tablespoon ricotta on each crostini. Drizzle with a little olive oil and add a pinch of flaky salt and a few grinds of pepper over the ricotta. Lay a tablespoon of marinated peppers over the top, cutting larger ones to fit.

Crostini are best served immediately. There will be no leftovers.

# MARINATED ROASTED PEPPERS (PEPERONATA)

MAKES 455 GRAMS (1½ CUPS)

*Are you even Italian if you don't have a jar of marinated peppers in the fridge? They're best known as an antipasto staple, but also handy for slicing to dress up pizza, pulsing into dips (see Red Pepper Dip, page 113), chopping up to toss into a salad, and draping over crostini, as we're doing here. I strongly recommend keeping a batch on hand at all times.*

| | | |
|---|---|---|
| Bell peppers (red, yellow, orange or a combination of all three) | 4 | |
| Extra-virgin olive oil | 150 grams | 6 tablespoons |
| Garlic cloves, thinly sliced | 2 | |
| Capers, drained | | 2 tablespoons |
| Minced fresh parsley | 5 grams | 1 tablespoon |
| Fine sea salt | | |

Preheat the oven to 500°F (260°C) and set a rack in the center. Line a baking sheet with foil.

In a large bowl, toss the peppers with 50 grams (2 tablespoons) of the olive oil. Arrange on the lined baking sheet. Roast until charred, turning over as needed to char evenly on all sides. About 30 minutes.

Return to the same bowl and cover tightly with plastic wrap. Let the peppers steam for 30 minutes, until the skins are very loose and they are cool enough to handle.

Peel off the skins and discard, don't worry about leaving some charred bits behind. Transfer the peppers to a cutting board. Slice in half lengthwise and discard the stems and seeds. Slice each piece in half lengthwise again to create long wide strips.

In a pint jar, combine the pepper strips, remaining olive oil, garlic, capers, and parsley. Add a generous pinch of salt, then twist the lid on the jar and gently shake to mix. Make sure the peppers are submerged in the marinade, then refrigerate until ready to use. The longer they sit, the better the flavor, so make well in advance.

Red peppers can be stored in an airtight container in the refrigerator for up to 2 weeks.

# MOZZARELLA IN CARROZZA

**MAKES 4 SANDWICHES**

Mozzarella in carrozza—literally mozzarella "in a carriage"—is what would happen if grilled cheese and mozzarella sticks had a baby. The popular street food is pure comfort, a simple mix of sandwich bread cradling a gooey mozzarella interior. The whole thing gets coated in bread crumbs and fried until melty and crisp. Every region of Italy has its own variations, of course, but this version takes it to the umami max with prosciutto, mozzarella, sun-dried tomatoes, and a dash of smoked paprika.

| | | |
|---|---|---|
| Large eggs | 4 | |
| Panko bread crumbs | 75 grams | 1½ cups |
| Smoked paprika | 2 grams | ¼ teaspoon |
| Slices white sandwich bread, crusts trimmed off | 8 | |
| Fresh mozzarella cheese, sliced ¼ inch (6 mm) thick | 330 grams | 12 ounces |
| Oil-packed sun-dried tomatoes, drained and finely chopped | 40 grams | ¼ cup |
| Slices prosciutto | 8 | |
| Extra-virgin olive oil, for frying | 50 grams | ¼ cup |
| Canola oil, for frying | 50 grams | ¼ cup |
| Flaky sea salt | | |
| Minced fresh parsley, for garnish | | |

Preheat the oven to 200°F (95°C) and set a rack in the center. Set a wire rack in a baking sheet and slide it into the oven to preheat.

Set up a dredging station with two shallow medium bowls. In one bowl, whisk the eggs. In the second bowl, combine the panko and smoked paprika and mix together.

Line a baking sheet with parchment paper. Arrange 4 slices of the bread on the lined baking sheet. Evenly divide the mozzarella and sun-dried tomatoes among the slices, leaving ½-inch (1 cm) border around the edges of the bread. Arrange 2 slices of prosciutto over the mozzarella. Top each sandwich with another slice of bread and press around the edges to seal.

Working one at a time, dip a sandwich into the egg, coating on all sides. Let the excess drip off, then transfer to the panko, pressing to adhere on all sides. Return to the baking sheet and continue coating the remaining sandwiches.

In a large skillet, heat the olive oil and canola oil over medium heat. When the oil shimmers, lay 2 of the coated sandwiches in the skillet and fry for 2 minutes per side, until the sandwiches are golden brown. Immediately transfer to the preheated wire rack in the oven. Fry the remaining 2 sandwiches, then transfer to the oven for 5 minutes.

Remove the warmed sandwiches to a cutting board. Season with flaky salt and a sprinkling of parsley before slicing diagonally and serving.

Mozzarella in carrozza is best served immediately. There will be no leftovers.

*Clockwise from left:*
**Polenta Crackers (page 122),**
**Perfect Grissini, and**
**Cheddar Taralli (page 123)**

# PERFECT GRISSINI

**MAKES 24 GRISSINI**

*Grissini, thin and crispy breadsticks, are usually a disappointing affair on both sides of the ocean. Individually wrapped, stuffed in a glass, and forgotten until they're long past stale—I've been burned too many times. So while it might be a low bar, these are the best I've ever had. Not just okay, but actually good! Enriched with pecorino, fresh rosemary, and plenty of black pepper, these grissini are spicy, cheesy, and delicious on their own, but are next level when wrapped in slices of prosciutto.*

| | | |
|---|---|---|
| Envelope active dry yeast | 7 grams | 2¼ teaspoons |
| Granulated sugar | 8 grams | 2 teaspoons |
| Warm tap water | 170 grams | ¾ cup |
| Extra-virgin olive oil | 50 grams | ¼ cup |
| Freshly grated Pecorino Romano cheese | 25 grams | ¼ cup |
| Finely chopped fresh rosemary | 5 grams | 1 tablespoon |
| Freshly ground black pepper | 7 grams | 1 tablespoon |
| All-purpose flour | 215 grams | 1½ cups |
| Whole wheat flour | 55 grams | ½ cup |
| Fine sea salt | 4 grams | 1 teaspoon |

In a stand mixer fitted with the dough hook, combine the yeast, sugar, and warm water. Let the mixture sit about 5 minutes, until the yeast is foaming and fragrant.

Add the olive oil, pecorino, rosemary, and black pepper. Mix on low speed until combined, about 1 minute. Sift in the all-purpose flour, whole wheat flour, and salt. Continue to mix on low speed until combined, about 2 minutes. Increase the speed to medium-high and mix until the dough is soft and pliable, about 6 minutes.

Coat a medium bowl with cooking spray. Transfer the dough to the bowl and cover tightly with plastic wrap. Rest until the dough has doubled in size, about 1 hour.

Line two baking sheets with parchment paper. Punch the dough down and divide in half (about 275 grams each). Roll one half of the dough into a 6 by 9-inch (15 by 23 cm) rectangle. Cut the rectangle lengthwise into 12 strips 9 inches (23 cm) long and ½ inch (1 cm) wide. Place each strip on one of the prepared baking sheets, spacing them ½ inch (1 cm) apart. Twirl the ends of each strip in opposite directions to create a twist. Roll, cut, and twist the remaining dough, arranging on the second baking sheet. Cover the baking sheets loosely with plastic wrap and let them rest for 30 minutes, until puffy.

While the grissini are resting, preheat the oven to 425°F (220°C) and set two racks in the center.

Bake until golden brown and crisp, 10 to 15 minutes, switching racks and rotating the baking sheets halfway through. Cool for 5 minutes on the baking sheets, then transfer the grissini to a wire rack to cool completely before serving.

The grissini can be wrapped in plastic and stored at room temperature for up to 3 days.

# POLENTA CRACKERS

**MAKES 32 CRACKERS**

*There's a toothsome bite to these crackers, thanks to the little bits of polenta holding them together. Neither Italian nor American, they are inspired by flavors and ingredients common in both places. They're addictively snackable on their own but deserve pride of place on any charcuterie board or antipasti spread.*

| | | |
|---:|---|---|
| Polenta | 165 grams | 1 cup |
| All-purpose flour | 140 grams | 1 cup |
| Grated Parmesan cheese | 25 grams | ¼ cup |
| Unsalted butter, at room temperature | 70 grams | 5 tablespoons |
| Fine sea salt | 10 grams | 3 teaspoons |
| Freshly ground black pepper | 2 grams | 1 teaspoon |
| Fresh thyme | 2 grams | 1 teaspoon |
| Warm tap water | 65 grams | 5 tablespoons |

In a food processor, combine the polenta, flour, Parmesan, butter, salt, pepper, thyme, and warm water. Process for about 2 minutes until the mixture forms a ball. Remove from the processor and press into a disk. Wrap tightly in plastic and rest at room temperature for 30 minutes.

While the dough rests, preheat the oven to 400°F (200°C) and set racks in the center and lower third of the oven.

Divide the dough in half (about 275 grams each). Place one of the halves between two pieces of parchment and roll into a roughly 9 by 13-inch (23 by 33 cm) rectangle about ⅛ inch (3 mm) thick. Remove the top piece of parchment. Trim the rectangle to create perfectly straight edges and to end up with an 8 by 12-inch (20 by 30 cm) rectangle when finished, reserving the scrap. Cut the dough in 4 equal strips in one direction, then rotate the parchment and cut in 4 equal strips in the opposite direction creating 16 rectangles measuring 2 by 3 inches (5 by 8 cm). Transfer the parchment to a baking sheet and slightly separate the crackers. Dock each cracker with a fork.

Roll, trim, cut, and dock the second batch and place on the second baking sheet. Repeat with whatever scraps are left over.

Bake until golden and crisp, 15 to 20 minutes, switching racks and rotating the baking sheets halfway through. Cool completely on the baking sheet.

The cornmeal crackers can be stored in an airtight container at room temperature for up to 2 weeks.

# CHEDDAR TARALLI

MAKES ABOUT 60 TARALLI

*Taralli are one of the most popular crackers across Italy. It's a common sight to see a bowl of them during aperitivo, enjoyed with a spritz or Negroni, as a salty complement to your drink while you rev up your appetite for dinner. When I was thinking of similarly salty and snackable foods in the U.S., I became obsessed with the idea of introducing a taralli inspired by Cheez-Its, loaded with sharp cheddar. I'll admit, I let out a little squeal as I typed the idea up and I hope you get as much giddy excitement as I did. Because, at the end of the day, aren't we all just waiting for our next great snack?*

| | | |
|---|---|---|
| All-purpose flour | 500 grams | 3½ cups |
| Sharp yellow cheddar cheese, finely grated on a Microplane | 350 grams | 12 ounces |
| Fine sea salt, plus more for salting the cooking water | 8 grams | 2 teaspoons |
| Paprika | 3 grams | 1 teaspoon |
| Extra-virgin olive oil | 100 grams | ½ cup |
| Dry Italian white wine, like Sangiovese or Pinot Grigio, plus more as needed | 150 grams | ⅔ cup |
| Flaky sea salt, for garnish | | |

In a stand mixer fitted with the dough hook, combine the flour, cheddar, salt and paprika. Mix on low until combined.

In a small saucepan, heat the olive oil over medium heat. When the oil shimmers, return the mixer to low speed. Very slowly pour a small amount of hot oil into the flour mixture. It might sizzle a little as it is absorbed. Continue pouring a little at time until the oil is incorporated.

Stream in the wine, letting it fully mix into the dough, about 2 minutes. Stop to check the dough. If it's a little dry, mix in more wine, about 1 tablespoon at a time, until the dough is hydrated and firm. Increase the speed to medium and mix until the dough is smooth and pliable, about 5 minutes. Wrap the dough tightly in plastic and rest at room temperature for 30 minutes.

Meanwhile, preheat the oven to 375°F (190°C) and set racks in the upper and lower thirds. Line two baking sheets with parchment paper. Bring a large pot of salted water to a boil over high heat.

Unwrap the dough. Break off small walnut-sized pieces (about 15 grams each). On an unfloured surface, roll each piece into a rope about 4 inches (10 cm) long and ½ inch (1 cm) thick. Loop each rope into a ring shape and pinch the ends together. Repeat until all the dough has been rolled and formed into rings.

Line a baking sheet with paper towels. Line a second baking sheet with parchment paper. Give the taralli an extra pinch to make sure the ends hold together. Working in batches so as not to crowd the pot, lower a few taralli at a time into the boiling water—the rings will drop to the bottom at first, then float to the top. Use a spider strainer or large slotted spoon to give them a gentle nudge so they don't stick to the bottom. As soon as they float to the ▶ ▶ ▶

surface, about 2 minutes, lift them out of the water and transfer them to the paper towels to drain. Sprinkle the still-wet taralli with a little flaky salt. Then transfer to the parchment-lined baking sheet, setting the taralli spaced about ½ inch (1 cm) apart.

Once the baking sheet is full, transfer to the oven and bake until light golden brown and crisp, 30 to 40 minutes, rotating the baking sheet halfway through. Cool on the baking sheet for about 5 minutes, then transfer the taralli to a wire rack to cool completely.

Continue boiling and baking the remaining taralli in batches. Cool completely before serving.

The taralli can be stored in an airtight container at room temperature for up to 2 weeks.

Pienza, Tuscany, Italy

# FRITTATA

SERVES 6 TO 8

*My mom's frittata is essentially a Spanish tortilla, made with potatoes and onions, but a lot less olive oil. She tells me that during and after World War II, olive oil didn't flow as freely as it used to, so adjustments to the recipe were made. This all tracks, since Sicily has been invaded by almost everyone on earth, and each conquest left an indelible mark on the island's population and culture, from the language to the architecture to the religious beliefs, but especially the food. It's safe to say that this frittata has a direct link to Spain's long rule over the island, where Sicilian and Spanish culture are interwoven even today in my mother's recipes.*

| | | |
|---|---|---|
| Yukon Gold potatoes, peeled, halved, rinsed, and cut into ¼-inch-thick (6 mm) slices | 675 grams | 1½ pounds |
| Fine sea salt | 8 grams | 2 teaspoons |
| Extra-virgin olive oil | 50 grams | ¼ cup |
| Yellow onion, halved and thinly sliced | 200 grams | 7 ounces |
| Freshly ground black pepper | 1 gram | ½ teaspoon |
| Large eggs | 8 | |
| Bomba Calabrese mayonnaise, for serving (recipe follows) | | |

**NOTE**

I decided to stay true to the Spanish method with the traditional pan flip. With a little bit of confidence, you can do it too. That said, if you lack the upper body strength for an assured flip, you can always finish it off in the oven, like my mom now does. For this method, use an ovenproof skillet and turn on the broiler with a rack set in the upper middle position. Broil for about 5 minutes or until just set.

In a 10-inch (25 cm) nonstick skillet, combine the potato, 4 grams (1 teaspoon) of salt, and 455 grams (2 cups) of water. Set over high heat and simmer until fork tender, about 5 to 7 minutes. Drain the potatoes and transfer to a medium bowl.

Wipe the same skillet clean and add 25 grams (2 tablespoons) of olive oil over medium heat. When the oil shimmers, add the onion and 1 gram (½ teaspoon) of salt. Cook for 7 to 10 minutes, stirring occasionally, until translucent. Add the cooked potatoes. Stir and continue to cook until both potatoes and onions are tender, another 2 to 3 minutes. Transfer the potatoes and onions back to the medium bowl and cool slightly, about 10 minutes.

In a large bowl, whisk the eggs with the remaining salt and the pepper. Add the cooled potatoes and onions and mix thoroughly. Let the mixture rest for 10 minutes.

Add the remaining olive oil to the same skillet over medium heat. When the oil shimmers, pour the egg mixture into the skillet. Stir occasionally as the eggs begin to set, about 3 to 5 minutes. Pull any set edges to the center of the skillet, letting raw egg flood the sides, and drag a spatula along the sides and bottom of the skillet to prevent any sticking.

When the sides and bottom of the frittata are set and golden brown, place a 12-inch (30 cm) plate over the skillet. In a careful but quick motion, flip the skillet and plate upside down so the frittata is on the plate. Then carefully slide the frittata back into the skillet so that the bottom is now the top. Working your way around the skillet, gently push in the sides of the frittata using a silicone spatula. This will help create the nice, rounded edge typical of Spanish tortillas. Cook for an additional 5 to 7 minutes or until the tortilla is just set.

Transfer the frittata to a clean platter and let cool for 30 minutes before serving, or cool completely, about 2 hours. Serve warm or at room temperature, with Bomba Calabrese mayonnaise.

The frittata can be stored in an airtight container in the refrigerator for up to 3 days.

# BOMBA CALABRESE MAYONNAISE

*Serve this frittata dish alongside a mayonnaise infused with Bomba Calabrese (a spicy Italian chili paste easily found in most Italian markets and online) for a welcome kick.*

| | | |
|---|---|---|
| Mayonnaise | 155 grams | ⅔ cup |
| Bomba Calabrese, to taste | 15 grams | 1 tablespoon |
| Lemon juice | 2 grams | ½ teaspoon |
| Salt and pepper, to taste | | |

Combine the mayonnaise, bomba, and lemon juice in a small bowl and whisk until combined. Add salt and pepper to taste. Cover with plastic wrap and refrigerate until serving.

# CACIO E PEPE ARANCINI

**MAKES 6 LARGE OR 12 SMALL ARANCINI**

*Although a lot of the Italian food you can find in New York is as good as what you can get in Italy, when it comes to the Sicilian arancino (or arancina, depending on what side of the island you are on), I can say with total authority that nothing compares to the ones in Sicily. Some historians believe they were a culinary gift from the Arab conquest. Others say they didn't make an appearance until the late 1960s, as rice was rarely consumed in Southern Italy until that point. The version I am most familiar with is a saffron-infused, conical-shaped rice ball stuffed with a classic ragu and melty caciocavallo cheese. These days, flavors vary widely by bar or stall, with popular fillings ranging from pistachios to ham and even chocolate. For my version, I decided to lean into America's current obsession with cacio e pepe for a cheesy, peppery ball of fried goodness that's a true chef's kiss.*

| | | |
|---|---|---|
| Vegetable broth | 625 grams | 2¾ cups |
| Arborio rice | 300 grams | 1½ cups |
| Fine sea salt, plus more as needed | 4 grams | 1 teaspoon |
| Unsalted butter | 55 grams | 4 tablespoons |
| Freshly grated pecorino cheese | 130 grams | 1⅓ cup |
| Freshly ground black pepper | 5 grams | 2 teaspoons |
| Caciocavallo or low-moisture mozzarella cheese, shredded | 110 grams | 3½ ounces |
| All-purpose flour | 140 grams | 1 cup |
| Panko bread crumbs | 110 grams | 1½ cups |
| Canola oil, for frying | 2 liters | 2 quarts |

**NOTE**

You can form the arancini into perfect rounds or make them into cones with a pointed top, in the Sicilian style. To make cones, press part of the ball in the nook between your thumb and index finger, while turning and applying pressure with your other hand, until a sloping peak forms.

Line a baking sheet with parchment paper and chill in the freezer.

In a medium saucepan over high heat, bring the vegetable broth to a boil. Add the rice and salt and give a quick stir. Reduce the heat to low and cover. Simmer, undisturbed, for 15 minutes or until all the liquid has been fully absorbed and the rice is cooked through. Remove from the heat. Stir in the butter, pecorino, and pepper. Spread the cooked rice on the chilled baking sheet in a flat, even layer and let cool completely, 30 minutes to 1 hour.

Once cool, depending on the size of arancini you are making, cut the sheet of rice into 6 or 12 equal squares. This will help you portion your rice out easily for shaping. Line a second baking sheet with parchment.

Take one square of rice into your hand and flatten it out slightly, creating a small indentation in your palm. Depending on arancino size, place 10 grams (1 tablespoon) or 20 grams (2 tablespoons) of shredded caciocavallo cheese into the indentation. Press to wrap the rice around the cheese and form into a ball (see Note). Transfer the shaped arancini onto the lined baking sheet, then continue filling and shaping the rest.

Set up a dredging station with two medium, shallow bowls. In one bowl, whisk the flour with a generous pinch of salt plus 200 grams (¾ cup) of water. In the second bowl, combine the panko with another generous pinch of salt. ▶▶▶

Working with one at a time, roll each arancino in the flour mixture to coat on all sides. Let the excess drip off, then roll in the panko, pressing to adhere. Return to the same baking sheet. Once all the arancini are coated, store the baking sheet in the refrigerator to let them set while you heat the oil.

Line a large plate with paper towels. Pour 3 inches (8 cm) canola oil into a large pot or Dutch oven with a deep-fry thermometer attached. Heat the oil over medium heat until it reaches 350°F (180°C).

Remove the arancini from the refrigerator. Working in batches of 3, use a spider strainer or large slotted spoon to gently lower the arancini into the oil. Fry until golden brown, flipping halfway, about 3 to 4 minutes, depending on size. Transfer to the paper towels to drain while frying the rest. Let the arancini rest for about 2 minutes before serving.

The arancini can be stored in an airtight container in the refrigerator for up to 5 days. To reheat, preheat your oven to 250°F (120°C), place the arancini on a baking sheet with a wire rack and warm through, about 10 minutes.

# TAGLIOLINI SUPPLI

**MAKES 12 SUPPLI**

*In the early twenty-first century, Italians, who rarely welcome new culinary ideas into the fold, suddenly embraced a new form of suppli, made from pasta. It feels like a cousin to American state fair food, like deep-fried macaroni and cheese after a study abroad. Throughout Southern Italy, pizzerias have started putting them on the menu and Italians are nuts about them. I mean, what's not to love? It's pasta, it's cheese, it's deep-fried. This version pays tribute to the classic Roman dish pasta Amatriciana, with a smoky guanciale-flecked tomato sauce for dipping. Just think of it as a deconstructed plate of pasta.*

| | | |
|---|---|---|
| Dried pasta, such as tagliolini or spaghetti | 250 grams | ½ pound |
| Freshly grated Parmesan cheese | 70 grams | ¾ cup |
| Fine sea salt, plus more as needed | 8 grams | 2 teaspoons |
| Pinch of red pepper flakes | | |
| Unsalted butter | 30 grams | 2 tablespoons |
| Large eggs | 5 | |
| Shredded low-moisture mozzarella cheese | 120 grams | 1 cup |
| All-purpose flour | 140 grams | 1 cup |
| Bread crumbs | 120 grams | 1 cup |
| Freshly ground black pepper | 1 gram | ¼ teaspoon |
| Canola oil, for frying | 2 liters | 2 quarts |
| Amatriciana Sauce (recipe follows), for serving | | |

Bring a large pot of salted water to a boil over high heat. Stir in the pasta and cook to al dente, according to the package directions.

As the pasta is nearing the end of its cooking time, remove 55 grams (¼ cup) of the pasta water. In a large bowl, whisk the Parmesan, salt, red pepper flakes, butter, and pasta water until you have a creamy sauce. Once the pasta is al dente, drain well, and transfer to the bowl. Toss the pasta in the sauce and let cool completely, about 1 hour.

Beat 2 of the eggs and toss with the cooled pasta. Add the mozzarella and toss. Cover tightly with plastic wrap and refrigerate for at least 2 hours or overnight.

Line a baking sheet with parchment paper. Use wet hands to scoop up some of the pasta (about 70 grams) and press into a tight 2-inch (5 cm) ball. Repeat with the rest of the pasta to make 12 balls in total, arranging the formed suppli on the baking sheet. Transfer to the freezer to set for 1 hour.

Set up a dredging station with three medium shallow bowls: In one bowl, add the flour and a generous pinch of salt. In another, whisk the remaining 3 eggs with about 30 grams (2 tablespoons) of water. In the third bowl, stir together the bread crumbs with another generous pinch of salt and the black pepper.

Working with one at a time, roll the suppli in the eggs to coat on all sides. Let the excess drip off, then roll in the flour. Finally, roll in the bread crumbs, compacting and pressing to adhere on all sides, before returning them to the baking sheet. ▶▶▶

Line a large plate with paper towels. Pour 3 inches (8 cm) canola oil into a large Dutch oven with a deep-fry thermometer attached. Heat the oil over medium heat until it reaches 338°F (170°C).

Working in batches of 4, use a spider strainer or large slotted spoon to gently lower the suppli into the oil. Fry, turning halfway, until golden brown, 3 to 4 minutes. Transfer to the paper towels to drain while frying the remainder. Serve with the warm Amatriciana sauce for dipping.

The suppli can be stored in an airtight container in the refrigerator for up to 5 days. To reheat, preheat your oven to 250°F (120°C), place the suppli on a baking sheet with a wire rack and warm through, about 10 minutes.

# AMATRICIANA SAUCE

MAKES 430 GRAMS (1½ CUPS)

*One of the classic Roman sauces, Amatriciana is known for its potent fusion of guanciale, onion, and tomato, with a touch of heat from red pepper flakes. We're using it as a dip, but it's just as great tossed with hot pasta or as a base for pizza.*

| | | |
|---|---|---|
| Extra-virgin olive oil | 13 grams | 1 tablespoon |
| Thinly sliced guanciale (see Note), chopped | 57 grams | 2 ounces |
| Minced yellow onion | 36 grams | ¼ cup |
| Garlic cloves, minced | 2 | |
| Freshly ground black pepper | 1 gram | ½ teaspoon |
| Pinch of crushed red pepper flakes | | |
| Fine sea salt | 4 grams | 1 teaspoon |
| Can whole peeled tomatoes | 1 (411-gram) | (14.5-ounce) |

NOTE

If you can't find guanciale, pancetta or bacon in the same amount will work.

In a large Dutch oven or large heavy skillet, heat the oil over medium heat. When the oil shimmers, add the guanciale and onion and cook, stirring often, until the guanciale is browned and crisp, about 3 minutes. Add the garlic, black pepper, red pepper flakes, and salt and stir until fragrant, about 30 seconds. Pour in the liquid from the can of tomatoes, then crush the tomatoes by hand before adding to the sauce. Bring to a simmer, then reduce the heat to low. Cook, stirring occasionally, until the sauce thickens 10 to 15 minutes. Serve warm.

The Amatriciana sauce can be stored in an airtight container in the refrigerator for up to 3 days.

CIN CIN!

Sangue Sour (page 139),
Caffè Nocino Shakerato (page 138),
Amaro Root Beer Float (page 140),
and Americano Spritz (page 141)

Rome, Lazio, Italy

**JUST LIKE IN THE U.S.,** in Italy it's always 5 o'clock somewhere. (Or 17:00.) Aperitivo is the Italian version of Happy Hour, a moment to gather around drinks and enjoy a light snack after work and before dinner. These four cocktails play with drinks and flavors from both sides of the ocean in ways that feel both familiar and brand new.

# CAFFÈ NOCINO SHAKERATO

**MAKES 1 COCKTAIL**

*A friend visiting from Italy once gifted my husband and I a bottle of nocino (an Italian liqueur made from walnuts), which was in the shape of a walnut itself. I was impressed with the presentation, but completely unsure of what to do with it besides sip it straight, very slowly. It wasn't until some time later that we tested it in baked goods and cocktails, and this one, a mixture of espresso and orange bitters, is heavenly. As much as I am a fan of espresso martinis (and I have been a fan for an embarrassingly long time), I'll go out on a limb and say this is a welcome fresh take, adding a greater depth of flavor to accent the nutty, rich espresso.*

Ice

½ ounce Nocino liqueur

½ ounce simple syrup (see Note)

2 dashes orange bitters

2 ounces hot espresso

**NOTE**

To make simple syrup, boil an equal amount of granulated sugar and water in a small saucepan until the sugar is dissolved. Cool and store in an airtight container in the refrigerator for up to 1 month.

In an ice-filled cocktail shaker, combine the nocino, simple syrup, and bitters. Pour in the espresso and shake until the outside of the shaker is frosty, about 30 seconds. Strain into a coupe glass, allowing the foam to settle on top before serving.

# SANGUE SOUR

**MAKES 1 COCKTAIL**

*Italians are obsessed with the combo of sweet and sour, so much so that they named a sauce—agrodolce—after this exact contrast. I clocked plenty of hours in my twenties knocking back whiskey sours, but my adult palate craves something a little more complex and refreshing. In this very agrodolce drink, a lemon-infused gin is boosted with fresh lemon and blood orange juices, some sweetener to round it out, and an egg white foam for an elegant finish. Raise a glass to la (agro)dolce vita!*

**2 ounces lemon-flavored gin, such as Malfy Gin con Limone**

**1 ounce fresh lemon juice**

**½ ounce fresh blood orange juice**

**½ ounce rich syrup (see Note)**

**1 large egg white**

**Blood orange slice and Amarena cherry, for garnish**

**NOTE**

To make rich syrup, boil 2 parts granulated sugar and 1 part water in a small saucepan until the sugar is dissolved. Cool and store in an airtight container in the refrigerator for up to 3 months.

In a cocktail shaker, combine the gin, lemon juice, blood orange juice, syrup, and egg white. Shake for 20 seconds, without ice, until the egg white is frothy. Add ice and shake again until the outside of the shaker is frosty, about 10 more seconds. Strain into a rocks glass. Serve with a blood orange slice and a skewered cherry.

# AMARO ROOT BEER FLOAT

**MAKES 1 DRINK**

*No matter how old I get, I still feel like a kind of man-child. So, this is right up my alley. Root beer is a very traditional American flavor, but it's also innately spicy and herbaceous in a way that you don't often see anymore. When paired with Italian amaro, it almost feels like two long-lost relatives finally meeting. The finishing touch is a generous scoop of gelato, and the cream-forward flavor of fior di latte couldn't be a better choice.*

**2 ounces amaro, such as Faccia Brutto, Amaro Gorini, or Averna Amaro**

**1 scoop Fior di Latte Gelato (page 233), or a classic vanilla ice cream**

**Good-quality root beer, such as Boylan, for topping**

**NOTE**

You can turn this drink into a Boozy Brown Cow by swapping the fior di latte with cioccolato nero gelato.

Chill a milkshake or pint glass in the freezer for at least 1 hour.

Pour the amaro into the glass, add a big scoop of gelato, then top with root beer. Stir once with a bar spoon and serve with a straw.

# AMERICANO SPRITZ

**MAKES 1 COCKTAIL**

*The Americano was originally created in Milan in the 1860s by Gaspare Campari (sound familiar?). But the name likely came later as Americans fled to Europe in droves during Prohibition and found boozy refuge in the cocktail. The more famous spritz, Aperol, has bewitched Italian and American palates, but I also enjoy the bitter bite of Campari for a perfect aperitivo in the heat of lazy summer afternoons.*

**Ice**
**1½ ounces Campari**
**1½ ounces sweet vermouth, preferably Martini & Rossi**
**Sparkling water, for topping**
**Orange slice and pitted Castelvetrano olive, for garnish**

Fill a collins glass with ice. Add the Campari and vermouth, and top with sparkling water. Stir once with a bar spoon. Garnish with an orange slice and a skewered olive.

Florence, Tuscany, Italy

# 5
# SPECIALTIES

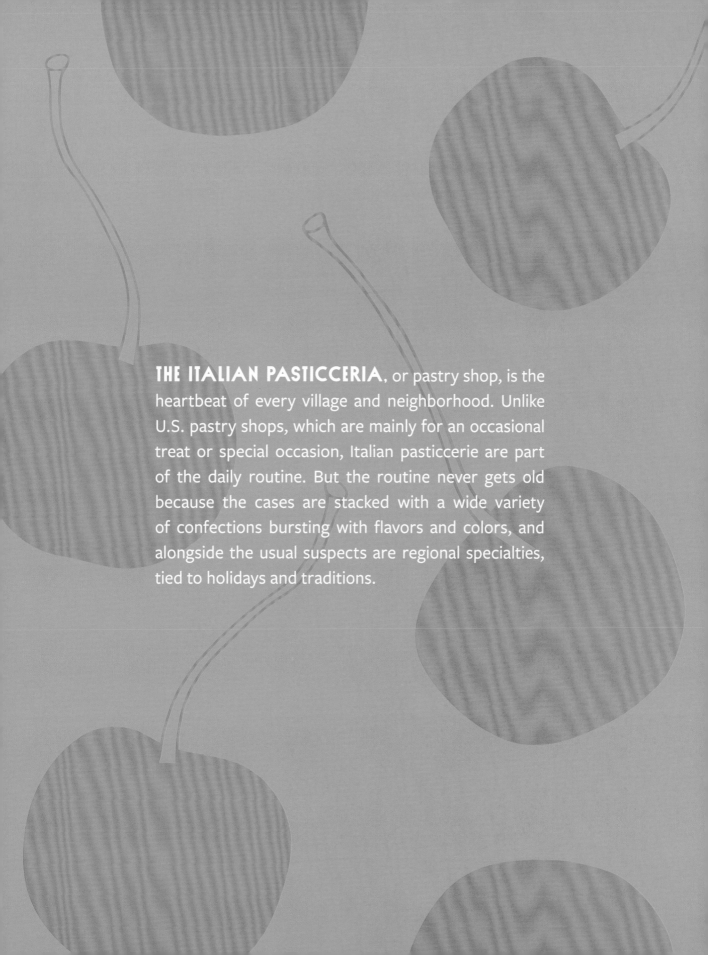

**THE ITALIAN PASTICCERIA**, or pastry shop, is the heartbeat of every village and neighborhood. Unlike U.S. pastry shops, which are mainly for an occasional treat or special occasion, Italian pasticcerie are part of the daily routine. But the routine never gets old because the cases are stacked with a wide variety of confections bursting with flavors and colors, and alongside the usual suspects are regional specialties, tied to holidays and traditions.

# STRUFFOLI

MAKES ONE STRUFFOLI RING

*Most of the Italian sweets that we Americans recognize come from Southern Italy, namely Naples and Sicily. And in the south, almost everything, sweet or savory, happily takes a dip in the deep-fryer. (Not unlike our own Southern cuisine!) Struffoli, sometimes called pignolata, is a classic example. It's a popular dish to make during the winter holidays all the way through Carnevale, Italy's answer to Mardi Gras. These miniature fried dough balls get tossed in warm honey, scented with orange and lemon, and finished with a generous amount of rainbow nonpareils for a perfectly festive touch, no matter the occasion.*

| | | |
|---|---|---|
| Large eggs | 3 | |
| Granulated sugar | 200 grams | 1 cup |
| Unsalted butter, melted | 55 grams | 4 tablespoons |
| Marsala | 30 grams | 2 tablespoons |
| Grated zest of 1 lemon | | |
| Grated zest of 1 orange | | |
| Freshly squeezed orange juice | 30 grams | 2 tablespoons |
| All-purpose flour | 425 grams | 3 cups |
| Baking powder | 3 grams | ½ teaspoon |
| Fine sea salt | 1 gram | ¼ teaspoon |
| Canola oil, for deep-frying | 2 liters | 2 quarts |
| Wildflower honey | 320 grams | 1 cup |
| Rainbow nonpareils, for garnish | | |

In a large bowl, whisk the eggs. Add the sugar, melted butter, Marsala, lemon zest, orange zest, and orange juice and whisk until the sugar is dissolved. Sift in the flour, baking powder, and salt. Use a wooden spoon to stir into a soft dough. Wrap tightly in plastic and set aside to rest at room temperature for 1 hour.

Cut the dough into 10 equal portions and keep covered with plastic while you work on each portion. Dust a work surface with flour. Roll each portion into a 12-inch (30 cm) rope, then cut into twelve 1-inch (2.5 cm) pieces and roll into balls. Continue rolling and cutting all of the dough.

Set a wire rack on a baking sheet. Pour the oil into a large Dutch oven fitted with a deep-fry thermometer and heat to 350°F (177°C).

Working in batches so as not to crowd the oil, fry the struffoli until golden brown, using a spider strainer or large slotted spoon to gently lower them in the oil and stir them around, about 4 minutes. Transfer to the wire rack to drain.

Carefully remove the oil and clean the Dutch oven. Add the honey and bring to a boil over medium-high heat. Let cook for 3 to 4 minutes until thickened (it will foam as it cooks). Remove from the heat and add the fried struffoli. Toss to coat completely. Use a spider strainer to let the excess honey drip off, then transfer to a serving plate, piling the struffoli into a ring shape using hands dipped in cold water to shape as needed. Decorate with nonpareils and serve.

Leftover struffoli simply does not exist, nor should it.

# ZEPPOLE DI SAN GIUSEPPE

**MAKES 6 ZEPPOLE**

*My full name is Renato Giuseppe Poliafito. It's incredibly Italian, and as a child I was tortured with mispronunciations and teasing (always by kids named things like Mike, Chris, or Tom). For a brief time, I tried going by Joe (the Anglicization of Giuseppe), but my Regular Joe fantasy didn't stick. It wasn't until much later that I realized my name was pretty fantastic, and wholly unique. The feast of San Giuseppe is in mid-March, around the time I was born, hence my middle name. These delicious confections, comprising a simple choux pastry sandwiching pastry cream, with a cherry on top, are a traditional treat for Saint Joey, and I guess, by extension, me, too. And after all I've been through, I deserve it.*

| | | |
|---|---|---|
| Unsalted butter | 115 grams | 8 tablespoons |
| Granulated sugar | 8 grams | 2 teaspoons |
| Fine sea salt | 1 gram | ¼ teaspoon |
| All-purpose flour | 140 grams | 1 cup |
| Large eggs | 4 | |
| Pastry Cream (page 268), for filling | | |
| Powdered sugar and Amarena cherries, for serving | | |

Preheat the oven to 375°F (190°C) and set a rack in the center. Line a baking sheet with parchment paper. Use a 3-inch (8 cm) biscuit cutter or a drinking glass to trace six 3-inch (8 cm) circles evenly spaced across the parchment. Flip the parchment over so the ink is visible through the paper.

In a medium saucepan, combine the butter, sugar, salt, and 225 grams (1 cup) water over high heat. Bring to a boil, then reduce the heat to low. Add the flour and use a wooden spoon to stir vigorously until the dough forms a smooth ball. Continue stirring for about 2 minutes until the dough begins to leave a dry film on the bottom of the saucepan or the dough registers 175°F (80°C) on an instant read thermometer inserted into the center.

Transfer the dough to a stand mixer fitted with the paddle and beat on medium speed for about 1 minute to cool the dough slightly. Add the eggs one at a time, fully incorporating before adding the next one. The finished dough should be smooth and shiny. Dip the paddle into the dough and lift it out; the dough should hang in a heavy V shape as it falls off the paddle.

Transfer the dough to a piping bag fitted with a large star tip. Pipe the dough in thick circles on the prepared baking sheet, following the traced circles, leaving a 1-inch (2.5 cm) hole in the center of each.

Bake, without opening the oven door, until lightly golden, about 25 minutes. After 25 minutes, you can open the door to check on them and continue to bake for an additional 5 minutes, if needed. Transfer to a wire rack to cool completely.

Slice the cooled zeppole in half horizontally and remove the tops. Pipe a thick layer of pastry cream over the bottom halves. Gently press the top halves on and pipe a small amount of pastry cream in the center holes. Dust with powdered sugar and garnish with a cherry before serving.

The zeppole can be stored in an airtight container in the refrigerator for up to 1 day.

# PANFORTE SCURO

MAKES ONE 9-INCH (23 CM) PANFORTE

*This dense, nutty, fruity, spicy, and delightful treat is a Northern Italian holiday staple that dates back to the Middle Ages. There are so many varieties and styles of panforte, but I prefer the scuro ("dark") variety, which adds a nice amount of cocoa powder to the mix. The blueprint for this recipe comes via my friend, fellow Italian, and talented baker in her own right, Jennifer Tafuri. Most modern recipes omit the ground pepper, but I love it for the little unexpected zing and bite in an otherwise honey-sweet dessert. Feel free to have some fun here, swapping in the dried fruit, nuts, and spices you like the most. Customization is encouraged!*

| | | |
|---|---|---|
| All-purpose flour | 100 grams | ⅔ cup |
| Good-quality cocoa powder, plus more for coating the pan | 8 grams | 4 teaspoons |
| Ground cinnamon | 3 grams | 1 teaspoon |
| Ground ginger | 2 grams | ½ teaspoon |
| Pinch of ground cloves | | |
| Fine sea salt | 1 gram | ¼ teaspoon |
| Ground white pepper or ground black pepper | 1 gram | ¼ teaspoon |
| Grated zest of 1 orange | | |
| Dried figs, quartered (1¼ cups) | 150 grams | 5 ounces |
| Dried prunes, diced (1 cup) | 150 grams | 5 ounces |
| Dried apricots, diced (¾ cup) | 125 grams | 4½ ounces |
| Blanched almonds, toasted and chopped | 140 grams | 1 cup |
| Skinned hazelnuts, toasted and chopped | 140 grams | 1 cup |
| Granulated sugar | 150 grams | ¾ cup |
| Wildflower honey | 210 grams | ⅔ cup |
| Powdered sugar, for garnish | | |

Preheat the oven to 300°F (150°C) and set a rack in the center.

Coat a 9-inch (23 cm) springform pan with cooking spray, line with a parchment round, and dust with cocoa powder, knocking out any excess.

In a large bowl, whisk the flour, cocoa powder, cinnamon, ginger, cloves, salt, pepper, and orange zest. Stir in the figs, prunes, apricots, almonds, and hazelnuts.

In a small saucepan, combine the sugar and honey. Bring to a boil over medium heat, stirring until the sugar is completely dissolved. Insert a candy thermometer and let boil until the temperature reaches 238° to 240°F (114° to 115°C). Immediately pour the honey mixture into the bowl with the dry ingredients and use a rubber spatula to stir until fully combined. Transfer into the prepared pan and spread into an even layer.

Transfer to the oven and bake for approximately 45 minutes or until firm to the touch. Cool completely in the pan. Remove from the springform sides and invert onto a serving plate. Lightly dust with powdered sugar before serving.

The panforte can be wrapped tightly and stored in an airtight container at room temperature for up to 2 weeks.

# COCOA RICOTTA ZEPPOLE WITH TAHINI GLAZE

**MAKES ABOUT 20 ZEPPOLE**

*In the past few years, fried zeppole have been popping up everywhere. (If you're wondering why these look different from Zeppole di San Giuseppe, page 148, the short answer is Italians are nothing if not inconsistent.) When you are of a certain age—not necessarily me, just speaking generally here—it's funny to see things from your childhood come back in style again. Zeppole have been an Italian street fair and bazaar staple for generations. Originally fried on demand, stuffed in a brown paper bag, and shaken up with a generous amount of powdered sugar, these days they are found on fancier restaurants' menus along with a dipping sauce. These slightly elevated, ricotta-enriched cousins are a little denser and more luxurious, with a cocoa-based dough and coated in a vanilla and tahini glaze. Think of them as sophisticated Dunkin' chocolate-glazed Munchkins.*

### FOR THE GLAZE

| | | |
|---|---|---|
| Powdered sugar, sifted, plus more as needed | 120 grams | 1 cup |
| Whole milk, plus more as needed | 30 grams | 2 tablespoons |
| Tahini, well stirred | 30 grams | 2 tablespoons |
| Pure vanilla extract | 5 grams | 1 teaspoon |
| Pinch of fine sea salt | | |

### FOR THE ZEPPOLE

| | | |
|---|---|---|
| Cocoa powder | 12 grams | 2 tablespoons |
| Boiling water | 30 grams | 2 tablespoons |
| All-purpose flour | 110 grams | ¾ cup |
| Granulated sugar | 50 grams | ¼ cup |
| Baking powder | 10 grams | 2 teaspoons |
| Fine sea salt | 2 grams | ½ teaspoon |
| Fresh Ricotta (page 272) or good-quality store-bought ricotta cheese, drained overnight | 250 grams | 9 ounces/1 cup |
| Large eggs | 2 | |
| Pure vanilla extract | 5 grams | 1 teaspoon |
| Canola oil, for deep-frying | 2 liters | 2 quarts |
| Sesame seeds, for garnish | | |

**Make the glaze** ▶ In a large bowl, whisk the powdered sugar, milk, tahini, vanilla, and salt until smooth. If the mixture is too thick, add more milk 1 teaspoon at a time to reach a viscous but pourable consistency. If your glaze is too loose, add more powdered sugar 1 teaspoon at a time.

**Make the zeppole** ▶ In a small bowl, whisk the cocoa powder and boiling water to make a paste. In a medium bowl, sift the flour, granulated sugar, baking powder, and salt. ▶▶▶

In a stand mixer fitted with the paddle, combine the drained ricotta and eggs. Beat on medium speed until incorporated. Add the cocoa paste and vanilla and mix until combined. Remove the bowl from the mixer and fold in the flour mixture until combined.

Set a wire rack in a baking sheet. Line another baking sheet with paper towels. Pour the canola oil into a large Dutch oven with a deep-fry thermometer attached. Heat the oil over medium heat until it reaches 375°F (190°C). If the oil dips too low in temp, the zeppole will absorb the oil and be soggy and greasy, so be sure to adjust the heat as needed to maintain a steady temperature.

Working in batches so as not to overcrowd the pot or the temperature will drop too quickly, use a 2-tablespoon cookie scoop (1 ounce) to carefully place a few zeppole at a time into the hot oil and fry, using a spider strainer or slotted spoon to flip frequently, until they are puffy and dark brown, about 3 minutes. Transfer to the paper towels to drain.

Use tongs to toss the warm zeppole in the glaze, completely coating. Place the glazed zeppole on the wire rack and immediately sprinkle with sesame seeds. Let set for 30 minutes, then transfer to a serving platter.

The zeppole are best when eaten within a few hours of frying.

Naples, Campania, Italy

# CHOCOLATE PIZZELLE

**MAKES ABOUT 34 PIZZELLE**

*Jessie Sheehan, an avid baker, cookbook author, and all-around vibrant, wonderful friend, once gifted me a pizzelle maker. Not an electric one, but an old-school, metal, medieval torture device to be used over an open flame. It's up to you how you want to make these, but I do recommend leaning on electricity. A slightly more modern take on a recipe that originated all the way back in the eighth century, pizzelle are like a proto-waffle, but thin and crispy like a cookie, with an intricate pattern from the pizzelle maker. You can certainly go with a more classic flavor profile—anise, lemon, and cinnamon are the most common—by omitting the cocoa and espresso powders, upping the flour by 35 grams (¼ cup), and swapping out the vanilla extract with 10 grams (2 teaspoons) of flavoring. All that matters with these popular holiday treats is you make them in abundance.*

| | | |
|---|---|---|
| Large eggs | 3 | |
| Granulated sugar | 250 grams | 1¼ cups |
| Cocoa powder | 25 grams | ¼ cup |
| Baking powder | 10 grams | 2 teaspoons |
| Pure vanilla extract | 10 grams | 2 teaspoons |
| Instant espresso powder | 1 gram | 1 teaspoon |
| Fine sea salt | 2 grams | ½ teaspoon |
| All-purpose flour | 250 grams | 1¾ cups |
| Unsalted butter, melted | 115 grams | 8 tablespoons |
| Powdered sugar, for serving | | |

**SPECIAL EQUIPMENT**
Electric pizzelle maker

Preheat an electric pizzelle maker to medium heat.

In a large bowl, whisk the eggs and granulated sugar until combined. Add the cocoa powder, baking powder, vanilla, espresso powder, and salt and whisk to combine. Add the flour and use a rubber spatula to incorporate, then stir in the melted butter.

Lightly spritz the pizzelle maker with cooking spray. Scoop 1 rounded tablespoon of batter into each mold and press the top down. (Adjust the amount to what works in your pizzelle maker, as needed.) Use a fork to remove the cooked pizzelle to a wire rack to cool; they will be a little floppy at first but firm up as they rest. Continue with the remaining batter, spraying the pizzelle maker with more cooking spray as needed.

Let the pizzelle sit at room temperature for 30 minutes. Dust the cooled pizzelle with powdered sugar before serving.

The pizzelle can be layered with parchment paper and stored in an airtight container at room temperature for up to 2 weeks.

# RUM BABÀ

**MAKES 12 BABÀ**

*You're probably wondering: Wait! I thought the baba au rhum was a French pastry! Well, it technically is, but Italians have appropriated this dessert over the centuries and have laid claim to it as well, just ask any Neapolitan. As a matter of fact, my dad used to take me to the local Italian bakery every Sunday, where I'd practically inhale a rum babà and, most of the time, chase it with a second. It wasn't until much later that I realized my enthusiasm for these yeast-risen, cream-filled delights had something to do with the generous amount of rum saturating them. Turns out I was getting drunk off of those weekend treats, then spending the rest of the day giddily happy and jacked on sugar, before waking up slightly hungover to get ready for another Monday of first grade. So, yes, perhaps I was a functioning alcoholic at the age of six, but I'd like to believe I've turned my life around. Or maybe I've just been chasing that high ever since.*

### FOR THE BABÀ

| | | |
|---|---|---|
| Whole milk, at room temperature | 55 grams | ¼ cup |
| Granulated sugar | 50 grams | ¼ cup |
| Envelope active dry yeast | 7 grams | 2¼ teaspoons |
| All-purpose flour | 320 grams | 2¼ cups |
| Large eggs | 4 | |
| Fine sea salt | 2 grams | ½ teaspoon |
| Unsalted butter, at room temperature | 170 grams | 12 tablespoons |

### FOR THE SYRUP

| | | |
|---|---|---|
| Granulated sugar | 300 grams | 1½ cups |
| Dark rum | 335 grams | 1½ cups |
| Zest strips of 1 orange | | |
| Cinnamon stick | 1 | |
| Whole cloves | 4 | |
| Basic Whipped Cream (page 271) or Pastry Cream (page 268), and Amarena cherries, for serving | | |

### SPECIAL EQUIPMENT

| | |
|---|---|
| Babà molds or two 6-cup popover pans | 12 |

**Make the babà** ▶ In a stand mixer fitted with the dough hook, combine the milk, sugar, and yeast. Mix on low speed until combined. Let sit for about 5 minutes until the yeast foams and is fragrant. Add the flour, eggs, and salt and mix on low speed for about 5 minutes to combine. Increase the speed to medium and mix for about 10 minutes until smooth and elastic. Add the butter in pieces, letting each piece mix in before adding the next. Continue mixing for about 8 minutes until the dough is shiny, elastic, and pulling away from the sides of the bowl.

Lightly coat a large bowl with cooking spray and transfer the dough to the bowl. Cover tightly with plastic wrap and let rise until doubled in size, about 2 hours. ▶ ▶ ▶

Punch the dough down, cover, and let rise again for 1 more hour.

Lightly coat 12 babà molds or the 12 cups of 2 popover pans with cooking spray. Divide the dough into 12 equal portions (about 70 grams each). Form each piece into a ball by cupping your hand over it and using your thumb and pinky to shape while rolling. Set one in each mold. Let rise, uncovered, until the dough is cresting over the top of the cups, about 1 hour.

During this final rise, preheat the oven to 375°F (190°C) and set a rack in the center.

**Meanwhile, make the syrup** ▶ In a medium saucepan, combine the sugar, rum, orange zest strips, cinnamon stick, cloves, and 225 grams (1 cup) water. Simmer over medium heat until the sugar is completely dissolved, about 2 to 4 minutes. Remove from the heat and set aside to let the flavors develop.

Bake the babà until golden brown on top, 20 to 25 minutes. Let cool in the pans for about 30 minutes, then transfer to a wire rack to cool completely, about 1 hour.

Reheat the syrup over low heat, until hot, then remove from the heat. One by one, submerge each babà in the syrup, turning with tongs to fully soak. Return to the wire rack while soaking the remainder. Reserve the syrup. (The soaked babà can be stored in an airtight container in the refrigerator for up to 5 days. Bring to room temperature before serving.)

To serve, split each babà lengthwise top to bottom to open, without cutting all the way through. Spoon the reserved syrup over the inside to soak, then you can choose your own adventure: fill with either whipped cream (page 271) or pastry cream (page 268), and top with an Amarena cherry. Serve immediately.

Custonaci, Sicily, Italy

# TORRONE

MAKES 24 BARS

*I think Shakespeare said it best: A nougat by any other name would taste as sweet. Enter the torrone, a nut-filled confection that all Italians, tip to toe, know intimately. Torrone is a popular gift to give in Italy, mixed with all types of nuts and candied fruits, or infused with citrus or berries. Torrone comes in more brittle varieties, but I love a soft, chewy pull to mine, encased in a dark chocolate shell.*

| | | |
|---|---|---|
| Large egg whites | 3 | |
| Powdered sugar | 60 grams | ½ cup |
| Fine sea salt | 2 grams | ½ teaspoon |
| Wildflower honey | 640 grams | 2 cups |
| Granulated sugar | 400 grams | 2 cups |
| Pure vanilla extract | 5 grams | 1 teaspoon |
| Blanched almonds | 140 grams | 1 cup |
| Unsalted pistachios | 120 grams | 1 cup |
| Dark chocolate, preferably Valrhona Caraïbe, chopped | 680 grams | 24 ounces |

Coat a 9 by 13-inch (23 by 33 cm) baking pan with cooking spray and line with parchment, creating a sling with a 2-inch (5 cm) overhang on two sides. Coat again with more cooking spray.

In a stand mixer fitted with the whisk, beat the egg whites on medium speed until soft peaks form. Add the powdered sugar and salt and continue beating on medium speed until thick, glossy medium peaks form.

In a large saucepan fitted with a candy thermometer, combine the honey and sugar. Cook without stirring over medium heat, allowing the mixture to simmer until it reaches 315°F (157°C). Immediately remove from the heat and let cool for 2 minutes.

Return the mixer to medium speed. Very slowly pour the honey mixture into the egg whites. Try to pour the honey down the side of the bowl so it doesn't splatter as the whisk runs. Add the vanilla. Continue beating until it is fully incorporated and develops into a thick and fluffy meringue that sticks to the whisk, about 4 minutes. Remove the bowl and use a rubber spatula coated with cooking spray to fold in the almonds and pistachios.

Transfer the meringue to the prepared baking pan and spread to the edges. Spray a piece of parchment with cooking spray, place the parchment, sprayed side down, on top of the torrone and use your hands to pat the torrone into an even layer. Lift the parchment, respray, and set on the surface of the torrone. Let set at room temperature until firm but still pliable, about 3 hours.

Peel off the parchment and use the sling to lift the torrone onto a cutting board. Cut the torrone in half lengthwise and then crosswise to create 4 rectangles. Cut each one into 6 strips 1 inch (2.5 cm) wide, for 24 pieces total.

Set a wire rack in a baking sheet. ▶▶▶

Fill a medium saucepan with 2 inches (5 cm) of water and bring to a simmer over medium heat. Set a medium shallow heatproof bowl over the saucepan, making sure the bowl doesn't touch the water. Add about two-thirds of the chocolate to the bowl and stir frequently as it melts. Check periodically with a candy thermometer or digital thermometer until the chocolate reaches 120°F (49°C). Remove from the heat and stir in the remaining third of the chocolate in two parts, letting the first part melt before stirring in the second.

Continue stirring until the chocolate cools to about 82°F (28°C), then set it back over the simmering water (adding more water to the saucepan if needed). Reheat, continuing to stir, until the chocolate reaches 90°F (32°C). Remove the bowl from the heat.

Working one at a time, dip the torrone in the chocolate, using a fork to rotate until fully covered. Transfer to the wire rack to set while coating the remainder. Let the chocolate set for about 20 minutes before serving.

The torrone can be layered with parchment paper and stored in an airtight container at room temperature for up to 2 weeks.

Ortigia, Sicily, Italy

# MINNE DI SANT'AGATA

MAKES 8 MINNE

*The story of Sant'Agata is insanely tragic, but in happier news, she got to be the patron saint of Catania (and of nurses, breast cancer, and volcanic eruptions). This pastry is ubiquitous in Italy in February, with the celebration of Agata, as well as a popular fixture of Sicilian pastry shops year-round. It's not a coincidence that these look like breasts—there are quite a few breast-shaped desserts found throughout Italy—and for anyone with a strong enough constitution to read it, the story of Agata will explain these ones in particular. This breast cake originated in Catania, where my parents are from, and definitely deserves a place in this book. In an attempt to not be quite so literal, I've placed an Amarena cherry on the inside of the pastry instead of the traditional Maraschino on top, and swapped out the ricotta filling with a classic pastry cream, effectively marrying the minne with another Italian favorite from Puglia, the pasticciotti, which could lead me to the same fate as dear Agata next time I set foot in Catania, but I'm willing to risk it.*

| | | |
|---|---|---|
| Pasta Frolla (page 283) | | |
| Pastry Cream (page 268) | | |
| Amarena cherries | 8 | |
| Egg whites | 4 | |
| Pinch of fine sea salt | | |
| Powdered sugar, sifted, plus more as needed | 540 grams | 4½ cups |
| Fresh lemon juice, plus more as needed | 15 grams | 1 tablespoon |
| Red food gel | | |

SPECIAL EQUIPMENT

| | |
|---|---|
| Three-inch (8 cm) hemisphere silicone molds | 10 |

**Make the pasta frolla and pastry cream and refrigerate as directed.**

Preheat the oven to 350°F (180°C) and set a rack in the center. Set the hemisphere molds on a baking sheet. Line a baking sheet with parchment paper.

Remove the pasta frolla from the fridge and roll it out on a lightly floured surface to about ⅛ inch (3 mm) thick. Use a 4-inch (10 cm) round cutter to cut 10 rounds from the dough and place one in each mold. Gently press to line the mold evenly, trimming off any excess. Return the scraps to the leftover dough and reroll until ⅛ inch (3 mm) thick. Use a 3-inch (8 cm) cookie cutter and cut 10 more rounds from the dough. Place the smaller rounds on the parchment-lined baking sheet, cover with plastic wrap, and refrigerate while filling the molds.

Remove the pastry cream from the refrigerator and fill each mold with about 75 grams of the filling (about ¾ of the way up). Place 1 cherry into the center of the cream, pressing down gently so the cherry is submerged. Remove the frolla rounds from the refrigerator (reserve the lined baking sheet for later) ▶▶▶

Naples, Campania, Italy

and, using the tip of your finger, wet the edge of each round with water and place them, wet-side down, on top of each dome, pressing down along the rim to enclose the filling.

Bake until the pastry is golden brown, about 30 minutes, rotating halfway through. Remove from the oven and let cool completely in the molds, about 1 hour.

In a stand mixer fitted with the whisk, combine the egg whites and salt. Beat on medium-high speed until soft peaks form, about 3 minutes. Reduce the speed to low and sift in about 480 grams (4 cups) of the powdered sugar, followed by the lemon juice. Continue to whisk until the mixture has a thick but pourable consistency, adding more powdered sugar or lemon juice as needed.

Remove about 100 grams (½ cup) of the icing to a small bowl. Stir in a drop of red food gel and then stir in the remaining powdered sugar until you have achieved a stiff icing. Transfer the pink icing to a piping bag with a small tip. Pour the remaining white icing into a measuring cup or any vessel with a pour spout.

Place a wire rack over the lined baking sheet. Carefully unmold the cakes and invert them, dome-side up, onto the rack. Slowly pour the white icing over each dome, starting in the center and letting it run down, making sure each pastry is completely covered. Let sit for 5 minutes, until set. Pipe a little pink icing on the center of each dome, in whatever shape you see fit, just as an accent. Transfer the cakes to a serving platter. Refrigerate for about 1 hour to set before serving.

The minne can be stored in an airtight container in the refrigerator for up to 2 days.

# CANNOLI CROCCANTE

**MAKES 12 CANNOLI**

*Making the traditional cannoli found in Italian American bakeries is, to put it lightly, not the easiest task. The dough is tough to get just right and then it needs to be wrapped around a mold and deep-fried. (Many bakeries buy pre-made shells, but you didn't hear it from me.) A couple summers ago, I stumbled across these cannoli croccante in Naples, and it was one of those magic "a-ha!" moments that sometimes happen in a foreign country. I'd finally found a cannoli that's easier to make, at the bakery or at home. The shell is essentially a lace cookie, studded with chopped nuts and bound together with sugar and a little flour, then rolled onto a cannoli mold when fresh out of the oven. I fill these with sweet ricotta, but Nutella folded into some pastry cream is also welcome in the piping bag.*

### FOR THE CANNOLI

| | | |
|---|---|---|
| Unsalted butter | 55 grams | 4 tablespoons |
| Light brown sugar | 75 grams | 6 packed tablespoons |
| Fresh orange juice | 30 grams | 2 tablespoons |
| Light corn syrup | 50 grams | 2½ tablespoons |
| All-purpose flour | 30 grams | 3 tablespoons |
| Walnuts, finely chopped | 120 grams | 1 rounded cup |

### FOR THE FILLING

| | | |
|---|---|---|
| Fresh Ricotta (page 272), or good-quality ricotta cheese, drained overnight | 455 grams | 16 ounces/2 cups |
| Powdered sugar | 70 grams | ½ cup |
| Pure vanilla extract | 5 grams | 1 teaspoon |
| Grated orange zest | 2 grams | 1 teaspoon |
| Mini semisweet chocolate chips | 60 grams | ¼ cup |

### SPECIAL EQUIPMENT

| | |
|---|---|
| Cannoli molds | 12 |

**Make the cannoli** ▶ Preheat the oven to 350°F (180°C). Line two baking sheets with silicone baking mats or parchment paper.

In a small saucepan, melt the butter over medium heat. Add the brown sugar, orange juice, and corn syrup, and stir once to submerge the sugar. Bring the mixture to a simmer and cook until thick, 3 to 5 minutes. Stir in the flour and walnuts. Remove from the heat and let the dough cool until still slightly warm, about 30 minutes.

Scoop 22 grams (1 tablespoon) of dough, and using your hands, roll the dough into a ball and place onto the baking sheet. Add 5 more scoops of dough for a total of 6 balls of dough, spacing them evenly.

Bake for 5 minutes, then rotate the baking sheet.

As soon as the first batch goes into the oven, prep the second baking ▶▶▶

sheet with 6 balls of dough. When you rotate the first batch, add the second baking sheet to the oven, making a sort of cannoli shell assembly line.

When the first batch spreads and starts to crisp, another 5 minutes, remove from the oven and cool on the baking sheet for 3 minutes. Timing is important here, so working quickly, roll each cookie around a cannoli mold and let set for 10 minutes. If the cookie hardened too quickly before you could roll it around the mold, just pop it back in the oven for no more than 1 minute to soften so you can easily roll. Once set, remove the shells from the molds and set them seam-side down on a cooling rack to cool completely.

Repeat this process with the second batch.

**While the shells cool, make the filling** ▶ In a medium bowl, combine the ricotta, powdered sugar, vanilla, and orange zest. Whisk until fully combined. Add the chocolate chips and fold to incorporate. Transfer to a piping bag fitted with a large star tip and refrigerate for 30 minutes.

Pipe the filling into both sides of each cannoli shell, starting from the center and working outward. Arrange the filled cannoli on a plate and serve.

The unfilled cannoli shells and filling can be stored separately in airtight containers in the refrigerator for up to 24 hours. Fill just before serving.

Castellammare del Golfo, Sicily, Italy

Siena, Tuscany, Italy

# 6

# CAKES + TORTAS

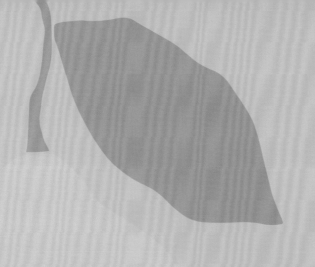

**AMERICAN CAKES ARE HUGE**, multilayer affairs, covered in decorations and rich frostings, while classic Italian tortas tend to be more rustic, simple, and based in traditions and local flavors. One isn't necessarily better and both could learn a lot from each other. So this chapter marries traditions from both countries for slices that are bold in flavor, big in aesthetics, and anything but traditional!

# APPLE TORTA

MAKES ONE 10-INCH (25 CM) CAKE

*If you live in the Northeast, you know that apple picking is an annual marker of fall. (And prime social media content.) Outdoorsy is not a word I or anyone else would associate with me, so I prefer to just visit a nearby orchard, make my purchase, and drag home enough bushels of apples to keep the doctor away for months. In my attempt to get through them all, this simple apple cake came to be a fall favorite at the café. It's a single layer cake, reminiscent of the Italian torta di mele, that really allows the apple flavor to shine through.*

| | | |
|---|---|---|
| Honeycrisp or Granny Smith apples (about 600 grams), peeled | 3 | |
| All-purpose flour | 285 grams | 2 cups |
| Baking soda | 8 grams | 1¼ teaspoons |
| Fine sea salt | 4 grams | 1 teaspoon |
| Ground cinnamon | 3 grams | 1 teaspoon |
| Granulated sugar | 200 grams | 1 cup |
| Dark brown sugar | 100 grams | ½ cup packed |
| Canola oil | 130 grams | ⅔ cup |
| Large eggs, at room temperature | 3 | |
| Pure vanilla extract | 5 grams | 1 teaspoon |
| Sour cream | 150 grams | ⅔ cup |

Preheat the oven to 350°F (180°C) and set a rack in the center. Coat a 10-inch (25 cm) cake pan with cooking spray and line with a parchment round.

Grate 2 of the apples over a bowl, reserving the juices. Thinly slice the third apple.

In a medium bowl, sift the flour, baking soda, salt, and cinnamon. In a stand mixer fitted with the paddle, combine the granulated sugar, dark brown sugar, and oil. Beat on low speed until combined. Add in the eggs one at a time, followed by the vanilla, scraping down the bowl as needed. Add the flour mixture in three parts, alternating with the sour cream, beginning and ending with the flour mixture. Scrape down the sides of the bowl as needed. Mix until no streaks of flour remain. Remove the bowl from the mixer and fold in the grated apple and all the reserved juice.

Transfer to the prepared pan and smooth into an even layer. Top with the thinly sliced apple, creating two overlapping concentric circles or decorate however you'd like.

Bake until a cake tester inserted in the center comes out clean, 80 to 90 minutes, rotating the pan halfway through. Let cool completely in the pan. Release from the pan and slice and serve.

This torta can be covered and stored at room temperature for up to 3 days.

# RICOTTA POLENTA TORTA

**MAKES ONE 9-INCH (23 CM) CAKE**

*This gluten-free polenta and almond cake, spiked with lemon and fluffed with ricotta and sour cream, practically melts in your mouth and should be your go-to for a simple, unfussy dessert on summer nights. We dust ours with a little powdered sugar, but plating with some fresh macerated fruit or Basic Whipped Cream (page 271) would be equally lovely.*

| | | |
|---|---|---|
| Fresh Ricotta (page 272) or good-quality ricotta cheese, drained overnight | 230 grams | 11 ounces/1 cup |
| Sour cream | 60 grams | ¼ cup |
| Fresh lemon juice | 120 grams | ½ cup |
| Pure vanilla extract | 5 grams | 1 teaspoon |
| Almond flour | 225 grams | 2 cups |
| Finely ground polenta | 80 grams | ½ cup |
| Baking powder | 5 grams | 1 teaspoon |
| Fine sea salt | 4 grams | 1 teaspoon |
| Granulated sugar | 200 grams | 1 cup |
| Unsalted butter, at room temperature | 180 grams | 13 tablespoons |
| Grated lemon zest | 3 grams | 1½ teaspoons |
| Large eggs, at room temperature, separated | 5 | |
| Powdered sugar, for garnish | | |

Preheat the oven to 350°F (180°C) and set a rack in the center. Generously coat a 9-inch (23 cm) springform pan with cooking spray.

In a large bowl, whisk the ricotta, sour cream, lemon juice, and vanilla. In a separate bowl, combine the almond flour, polenta, baking powder, and salt.

In a stand mixer fitted with the paddle attachment, combine the granulated sugar and butter. Beat on high speed until light and fluffy, about 3 minutes. Mix in the lemon zest. Add the egg yolks and mix well, scraping down the sides as needed. Add the ricotta mixture and beat to combine. Note: the mixture will look broken and that's okay! With the mixer on low speed, add in the polenta mixture and mix until well combined. Transfer the batter to a large bowl.

Wash and dry the stand mixer bowl, then return to the stand mixer and snap on the whisk. Beat the egg whites on high speed until medium-stiff peaks form, about 5 to 8 minutes. Add half of the whites to the bowl with the batter and fold in. Fold in the remaining egg whites until just a few streaks remain. Transfer the batter into the prepared pan, smoothing the top.

Bake until the cake is golden brown and a tester inserted into the center comes out with a few crumbs, 45 to 50 minutes, rotating the pan halfway through, until the cake is light golden brown on the edges. Cool completely in the cake pan before releasing the springform.

Dust the top of the cake with powdered sugar just before serving.

This cake can be covered and refrigerated for up to 3 days.

# TORTA DI GRANO SARACENO

**MAKES ONE 9-INCH (23 CM) CAKE**

*This rustic torta is textbook cucina povera, peasant cooking that forms the base of Italy's most famous recipes. Originating from the alpine region of Tyrol in the extreme north of Italy, it's a perfect example of using what you have on hand. A simple cake made from nut and buckwheat flours (hence, gluten-free) has a warm, rich flavor that elevates the torta into something special. Split in half, filled with jam (red currant is traditional, but raspberry is also a favorite), and finished with a simple dusting of powdered sugar (or freeze-dried raspberry powder for a stunning and slightly tart touch), it's more than the sum of its parts.*

| | | |
|---|---|---|
| Buckwheat flour, plus more for dusting | 160 grams | 1⅓ cups |
| Almond flour | 150 grams | 1½ cups |
| Baking powder | 10 grams | 2 teaspoons |
| Fine sea salt | 1 gram | ¼ teaspoon |
| Unsalted butter, at room temperature | 240 grams | 17 tablespoons |
| Granulated sugar | 250 grams | 1¼ cups |
| Large eggs, at room temperature, separated | 2 | |
| Sour cream | 115 grams | ½ cup |
| Pure vanilla extract | 5 grams | 1 teaspoon |
| Granny Smith apple, peeled and grated (about 100 grams) | 1 | |
| Grated orange zest | 2 grams | 1 teaspoon |
| Raspberry preserves | 300 grams | 1¾ cups |
| Powdered sugar or powdered freeze-dried raspberries, for garnish (optional) | | |

**NOTE**

Traditionally, it is a combination of buckwheat and hazelnut flours that make up this cake. But I swapped that out for almond flour, as it is an easier (and more affordable) flour to find. However, if you want to re-create the original, swap out for hazelnut flour in equal parts and use red currant jam instead of raspberry preserves.

Preheat the oven to 350°F (180°C) and set a rack in the center. Coat a 9-inch (23 cm) springform pan with cooking spray, line with a parchment round, and dust with buckwheat flour, knocking out any excess.

In a medium bowl, whisk the buckwheat flour, almond flour, baking powder, and salt.

In a stand mixer fitted with the paddle, combine the butter and 200 grams (1 cup) of the granulated sugar. Mix on medium speed until light and fluffy, 3 to 5 minutes. Reduce the speed to low and add the egg yolks one at a time, stopping to scrape the sides as needed, until fully incorporated. Add the sour cream and vanilla and mix on medium speed until the mixture is pale in color, about 2 minutes. Reduce the speed to low and mix in the grated apple and orange zest. Remove the bowl from the mixer and scrape down the sides. Fold in the flour mixture, mixing well to combine. Transfer the batter to a large bowl.

Wash and dry the stand mixer bowl, then return to the stand mixer and snap on the whisk. Beat the egg whites on low until frothy, about 2 minutes. Add the remaining granulated sugar and beat on medium-high speed until stiff peaks form, about 5 minutes. Add one-third of the whites to the bowl with the batter and fold in. Fold in the remaining egg whites in two parts until just a few streaks remain. Pour the batter into the prepared pan, smoothing the top.

Bake until the cake is set and a tester inserted in the center comes out clean, 40 to 45 minutes, rotating halfway through. Cool the cake in the pan for 30 minutes before removing the springform. Transfer to a wire rack to cool completely.

Use a serrated knife to slice the cake horizontally through the middle. Remove the top layer. Dollop the preserves in the center of the bottom layer and use an offset spatula to spread in an even layer, stopping about ½ inch (1 cm) before the edge. Carefully place the top layer on top of the preserves and gently press down until the preserves reach the edge. If desired, dust the top of the cake with powdered sugar and freeze-dried raspberry powder before serving.

This torta can be covered and stored at room temperature for up to 3 days.

# BOSCO NERO

MAKES ONE 10-INCH (25 CM) CAKE

*My husband, Sven, is from Germany, a country, like Italy, where people practically live for something sweet. In my attempt to marry Italian and German culture—in life and in the kitchen—I wanted to create a dessert that captured the essence of a Black Forest cake with the rustic, deconstructed approach of an Italian, single-layer torta. Enter the Bosco Nero, a deeply dark, devil's food cake topped with a light and airy cream and homemade cherry jam. In a rush, the cake can be made with Basic Whipped Cream (page 271) and Amarena cherries spooned from the jar. But I always think it's worth going the extra mile for the ones you love.*

| | | |
|---|---|---|
| Pastry Cream (page 268) | 275 grams | 1 cup |
| All-purpose flour | 250 grams | 1¾ cups |
| Good-quality cocoa powder | 70 grams | ¾ cup |
| Baking soda | 8 grams | 1¼ teaspoons |
| Fine sea salt | 2 grams | ½ teaspoon |
| Canola oil | 150 grams | ¾ cup |
| Granulated sugar | 350 grams | 1¾ cups |
| Large eggs, at room temperature | 3 | |
| Pure vanilla extract | 5 grams | 1 teaspoon |
| Buttermilk | 460 grams | 2 cups |
| Heavy cream, cold | 230 grams | 1 cup |
| Cherry Jam (recipe follows) or a jar of Amarena cherries in syrup | | |
| Mini chocolate chips, for garnish | | |

**Make the pastry cream and refrigerate as directed.**

Preheat the oven to 350°F (180°C) and set a rack in the center. Coat a 10-inch (25 cm) round cake pan with cooking spray and line with a parchment round.

In a medium bowl, sift together the flour, cocoa, baking soda, and salt.

In a stand mixer fitted with the paddle, combine the oil and sugar. Beat on low speed, until fully combined, about 1 minute. Add the eggs, one at a time, and the vanilla, stopping to scrape down the sides as needed. Add the flour mixture in three parts, alternating with the buttermilk, beginning and ending with the flour mixture. Mix until no streaks of flour remain. Pour the batter into the prepared cake pan.

Bake until a cake tester comes out clean, 30 to 40 minutes, rotating the pan halfway through. Cool completely in the pan.

Once the cake has cooled, remove 275 grams (1 cup) of the pastry cream from the refrigerator and transfer into a large bowl. Whisk until smooth and creamy, about 2 minutes. In a stand mixer fitted with the whisk, beat the heavy cream on medium-high speed until stiff peaks form, about 4 minutes. Fold one-third of the whipped cream into the pastry cream, until combined, then fold in the remaining whipped cream in two parts.  ▶▶▶

Remove the cooled cake from the pan and place on a cake stand or serving plate and top with the chilled cream. Frost the cake with an offset spatula, pushing the cream to the edges in an even layer. You want all the cream to sit on top of the cake and not go over the edge. Leave some peaks and valleys on top so the cherry jam has places to pool and collect.

Scoop the cherry jam with a 1-tablespoon measure and dot it on top of the cream, evenly dispersed, so each slice will have a helping of jam. If using Amarena cherries in syrup, dollop 2 to 3 cherries in their syrup on the cream so each slice will get a helping. Finish with a rim of mini chocolate chips and serve.

This cake can be covered and refrigerated for up to 2 days.

# CHERRY JAM

### MAKES 750 GRAMS (2 CUPS)

| | | |
|---|---|---|
| Pitted sweet cherries, fresh or frozen | 455 grams | 1 pound |
| Granulated sugar | 300 grams | 1½ cups |
| Grated zest and juice of 1 lemon | | |
| Amaretto liqueur | 15 grams | 1 tablespoon |

In a large saucepan, combine the cherries, sugar, lemon zest, and lemon juice. Cook over low heat, stirring occasionally, until the sugar dissolves, 8 to 10 minutes. Increase the heat to medium and let the mixture come to a rolling boil. Continue to boil, stirring constantly, for 2 minutes. Reduce the heat to low and let the jam simmer, stirring occasionally so the fruit doesn't scorch or stick to the bottom of the pan, until the jam reaches 220°F (104°C) on a thermometer, 20 to 30 minutes. Remove from the heat and stir in the amaretto. Transfer the jam to a 1-pint mason jar, uncovered, to cool completely. Once cool, you can use to top the Bosco Nero. Otherwise, seal the jar and refrigerate.

The jam can be refrigerated for up to 2 weeks.

# ALMOND TORTA WITH ROASTED PLUMS

MAKES ONE 10-INCH (25 CM) CAKE

*This almond cake exemplifies the rustic simplicity of Italian desserts. The roasted plums are a perfect balance to saturate the cake with flavor and make it visually stunning, but honestly, this works with almost any fruit. I've tossed in strawberries, cherries, blueberries, and peaches, all with similar success. We have served this cake in its many forms at the café since day one. It's one of my absolute favorites, and I am sure it will be one of yours as well.*

## FOR THE CAKE

| | | |
|---|---|---|
| Granulated sugar | 300 grams | 1½ cups |
| Sliced almonds | 75 grams | ¾ cup |
| All-purpose flour | 215 grams | 1½ cups |
| Baking powder | 5 grams | 1 teaspoon |
| Fine sea salt | 1 gram | ¼ teaspoon |
| Unsalted butter, cubed and at room temperature | 170 grams | 12 tablespoons |
| Large eggs, at room temperature | 2 | |
| Large egg yolks, at room temperature | 2 | |
| Pure vanilla extract | 5 grams | 1 teaspoon |
| Almond extract | 3 grams | ½ teaspoon |

## FOR THE TOPPING

| | | |
|---|---|---|
| Roasted Plums (recipe follows) | 450 grams | about 5 |
| Sliced almonds | 30 grams | ¼ cup |
| Powdered sugar, for garnish | | |

NOTE

If using fresh cherries, blueberries, or other berries for topping, skip the roasting, use 300 grams (about 10 ounces), and sprinkle them evenly over the batter.

**Make the cake** ▶ Preheat the oven to 350°F (180°C) and set a rack in the center. Coat a 10-inch (25 cm) cake pan with cooking spray and line with a parchment round.

In a food processor, combine the granulated sugar and almonds. Process until the nuts are finely ground, about 1 minute. Add the flour, baking powder, and salt and pulse about 4 times to combine. Add the cubed butter and pulse about 6 times until the mixture resembles coarse sand. Add the whole eggs, egg yolks, vanilla, and almond extract and process until smooth, about 2 minutes, stopping to scrape the sides as needed.

Transfer the batter to the prepared cake pan and smooth the top. Arrange the roasted plums, skin-side down, evenly over the surface of the cake. Feel free to create a pattern with the plum slices or place randomly for a more rustic affair. Drizzle a little of the roasting liquid over the plums and sprinkle the sliced almonds over the torta and plums.

Bake until a cake tester inserted into the center comes out with a few crumbs, 60 to 70 minutes, rotating the pan halfway through. Let cool completely in the pan.

To release, run a small offset spatula or paring knife along the edge of the pan before inverting onto a wire rack and then flipping onto a serving ▶ ▶ ▶

plate, so the plums are facing up. Dust with powdered sugar before serving.

This cake can be stored in an airtight container at room temperature for up to 3 days.

# ROASTED PLUMS

**MAKES 950 GRAMS (1 QUART)**

*I'm suggesting roasting a little more than you need for the Almond Torta (page 183). The leftover fruit can top your favorite ice cream or be enjoyed on its own with some toasted sliced almonds and a sprinkling of turbinado sugar.*

| | | |
|---|---|---|
| Raspberry preserves | 160 grams | ½ cup |
| Pinch of fine sea salt | | |
| Plums (about 8), quartered | 900 grams | 2 pounds |

**NOTE**

I also recommend Italian prune plums, if you can find them, for their sweet, zingy flavor, but any type of plum or stone fruit will work here. Just keep a careful eye on roasting time, depending on their size and ripeness.

Preheat the oven to 400°F (200°C) and set a rack in the center. Line a baking sheet with parchment paper.

In a large bowl, whisk together the preserves, salt, and 75 grams (⅓ cup) water. Add the plums and toss until evenly coated. Arrange the plums, cut-side up, on the prepared pan and roast until they are just tender, 20 to 25 minutes. Remove from the oven and let cool completely before using.

New York Cheesecake with Berry Topping (page 188) and Italian Ricotta Cheesecake

# ITALIAN RICOTTA CHEESECAKE

**MAKES ONE 8-INCH (20 CM) CHEESECAKE**

*Oh, the majesty of the cheesecake! I could write odes, ballads, and sonnets about it. Most cultures have their own version, and for a very good reason: It's delicious. This torta di ricotta—crustless, and scented with orange—was a staple in my home. I wanted to stay mostly true to the original, but made a few small tweaks, including the addition of mascarpone to give it a tangier flavor and silkier texture than ricotta alone. Its American cousin is on the next page, and I encourage you to add both to your repertoire.*

| | | |
|---|---|---|
| Cornstarch | 18 grams | 2 tablespoons |
| Granulated sugar | 200 grams | 1 cup |
| Large eggs, at room temperature, separated | 3 | |
| Fresh Ricotta (page 272) or good-quality ricotta cheese, drained overnight | 460 grams | 16 ounces/2 cups |
| Mascarpone or sour cream | 220 grams | 1 cup |
| Pure vanilla extract | 10 grams | 2 teaspoons |
| Almond extract | 1 gram | ¼ teaspoon |
| Grated zest of 2 oranges | | |

Preheat the oven to 500°F (260°C) and set a rack in the center. Line an 8-inch (20 cm) cake pan with parchment paper letting it stick out of the top. It won't be smooth and it shouldn't be, it'll add to the rustic feel of the cake. Coat thoroughly with cooking spray.

In a small bowl, whisk the cornstarch with 100 grams (½ cup) of the sugar.

In a stand mixer fitted with the whisk, beat the egg yolks, then stream in the cornstarch mixture. Beat on medium-high until pale and thick, 3 to 5 minutes. Add the ricotta, mascarpone, vanilla, almond extract, and orange zest. Beat until combined, then pour the mixture into a large bowl.

Wash and dry the stand mixer bowl and whisk and return to the stand mixer. Beat the egg whites on medium speed until frothy, about 2 minutes. Add the remaining sugar and beat on high to form glossy stiff peaks, 3 to 4 minutes. Scoop one-third of the egg whites into the ricotta mixture and fold to combine until you can barely see any white streaks. Continue adding the egg whites in two more parts until the batter is fully incorporated.

Pour the filling into the prepared cake pan and smooth the top.

Place the cake pan on a baking sheet and slide it into the oven. Bake for 10 minutes. Reduce the oven temperature to 350°F (180°C) and bake until dark golden brown and uniformly wobbly across the surface, another 30 to 40 minutes, rotating halfway through. If cake is becoming too dark, tent with some foil.

Let the cheesecake cool to room temperature, then lightly cover in plastic wrap and refrigerate overnight, until fully set.

Before serving, use the parchment to lift the cheesecake out of the pan, peel the parchment away, and slice.

This cake can be covered and refrigerated for up to 3 days.

# NEW YORK CHEESECAKE WITH BERRY TOPPING

MAKES ONE 9-INCH (23 CM) CHEESECAKE

*There was never any question in my mind that the classic NY-style cheese-cake needed to be in this book alongside its cugino italiano (see Italian Ricotta Cheesecake, page 187). This version was born from other styles of cheesecakes, brought over by European immigrants, and is the result of melding ideas and using the ingredients available. It has now become a signature of the city, as well as a global export. I think this cheesecake recipe should be everyone's go-to. It's a simple, reliable preparation that is dense, creamy, and shot through with the tang of both cream cheese and mascarpone (my favorite flavor and texture booster in both cheesecakes). After it's cooled and topped with fresh berries? Fuhgeddaboudit.*

### FOR THE CRUST

| | | |
|---|---|---|
| Graham cracker crumbs | 250 grams | 2½ cups |
| Granulated sugar | 25 grams | 2 tablespoons |
| Fine sea salt | 1 gram | ¼ teaspoon |
| Unsalted butter, melted and cooled | 85 grams | 6 tablespoons |

### FOR THE FILLING

| | | |
|---|---|---|
| Cream cheese, at room temperature | 680 grams | 24 ounces |
| Mascarpone | 450 grams | 2 cups |
| Granulated sugar | 300 grams | 1½ cups |
| Fine sea salt | 2 grams | ½ teaspoon |
| Large eggs, at room temperature | 6 | |
| Fresh lemon juice | 15 grams | 1 tablespoon |
| Pure vanilla extract | 30 grams | 2 tablespoons |
| Heavy cream | 155 grams | ⅔ cup |

### FOR SERVING

Berry Topping (recipe follows)

**Make the crust** ▶ Preheat the oven to 350°F (180°C) and set a rack in the center. Coat a 9-inch (23 cm) springform pan with cooking spray. Stack three 18-inch (46 cm) sheets of foil and fold the edges to form one thick sheet. Place the springform pan in the center and fold the foil up and around the sides to ensure no water will enter the pan.

In a large bowl, whisk the graham cracker crumbs, sugar, and salt. Pour in the melted butter and mix with your hands until combined. Press evenly onto the bottom and halfway up the sides of the prepared pan.

Bake until golden brown, 6 to 8 minutes. Set aside to cool.

**Make the filling** ▶ In a stand mixer fitted with the paddle, beat the cream cheese on medium-high speed until smooth, about 3 minutes. Add the ▶▶▶

mascarpone, sugar, and salt. Beat on medium speed until smooth, stopping to scrape down the sides as needed.

In a small bowl, whisk the eggs vigorously. Reduce the speed of the stand mixer to low and pour the eggs through a fine-mesh sieve into the mixer bowl. Add the lemon juice and vanilla to the mixer bowl, then slowly pour in the heavy cream. Scrape down the sides and bottom.

Pour the cheesecake batter over the crust, filling all the way to the top. Set the springform in a large roasting pan and place in the oven, leaving the door open.

Pour hot tap water in the roasting pan to come halfway up the sides of the springform to create a water bath, close the door, and bake until the cheesecake is set but still slightly wobbly, 2 to 2½ hours, carefully rotating the pan halfway through.

Remove from the oven and let the springform cool in the water bath for 30 minutes, then transfer to a wire rack to cool completely. Loosely cover with plastic wrap and refrigerate for at least 4 hours, or preferably overnight, until fully chilled and set.

When ready to serve, release the springform and spoon the berry topping over the cake.

This cake can be covered and refrigerated for up to 3 days.

# BERRY TOPPING

## MAKES 450 GRAMS (3 CUPS)

*This topping uses strawberries, blueberries, and raspberries, but any mix of berries, or even cherries, will play well in this mix. It's perfect for topping cakes, serving over ice cream, or nestled in a bowl with freshly whipped cream for a simple dessert.*

| | | |
|---|---|---|
| Strawberries, fresh or frozen, trimmed | 155 grams | 1½ cups |
| Blueberries, fresh or frozen | 130 grams | 1 cup |
| Raspberries, fresh or frozen | 110 grams | 1 cup |
| Granulated sugar | 75 grams | ¼ cup |
| Fresh lemon juice | 5 grams | 1 teaspoon |

In a large saucepan, combine 105 grams (1 cup) of the strawberries, 65 grams (½ cup) of the blueberries, 55 grams (½ cup) of the raspberries, the sugar, and lemon juice. Bring to a simmer over medium heat and cook until the berries soften and thicken into a liquid, about 5 minutes. Remove from the heat and stir in the remaining strawberries, blueberries, and raspberries. Cool completely in the saucepan, then transfer to an airtight container and refrigerate until ready to use.

The berry topping can be refrigerated for up to 3 days.

# SPUMONI LOAF

**MAKES 1 LOAF CAKE**

*Spumoni is a traditional Southern Italian dessert, a multilayered stack of gelato (usually cherry, pistachio, and chocolate) with chopped fruit and nuts, then cut into slices. Rainbow cookies—a classically Italian American dessert ubiquitous in U.S. bakeries but almost nonexistent in Italy—comprise a soft stack of different colors of almond cake, layered with jam, and covered in chocolate. This recipe pulls from the best of both. Built at the scale of a spumoni, the almond cake is joined by chocolate, cherry, and pistachio. The layers are sandwiched with a raspberry jam, then topped with a shimmery dark chocolate glaze. This tricolor cake has a few steps, but it's made to impress.*

### FOR THE LAYERS

| | | |
|---|---|---|
| All-purpose flour | 285 grams | 2 cups |
| Baking powder | 5 grams | 1 teaspoon |
| Fine sea salt | 1 gram | ¼ teaspoon |
| Almond paste, coarsely chopped | 225 grams | 8 ounces |
| Granulated sugar | 200 grams | 1 cup |
| Unsalted butter, at room temperature | 335 grams | 24 tablespoons |
| Large eggs, at room temperature, separated | 4 | |
| Whole milk | 75 grams | ⅓ cup |
| Almond extract | 10 grams | 2 teaspoons |
| Pure vanilla extract | 5 grams | 1 teaspoon |
| Cocoa powder, sifted | 20 grams | 3 tablespoons |
| Boiling water | 30 grams | 2 tablespoons |
| Mini chocolate chips | 20 grams | 2 tablespoons |
| Pistachio extract | 1 gram | ¼ teaspoon |
| Green food gel | | |
| Unsalted pistachios, toasted and roughly chopped | 40 grams | ¼ cup |
| Red food gel | | |
| Cherry preserves | 65 grams | 3 tablespoons |

### FOR THE ASSEMBLY

| | | |
|---|---|---|
| Raspberry preserves | 130 grams | 6 tablespoons |
| Dark chocolate, chopped | 170 grams | 6 ounces |
| Heavy cream | 175 grams | ¾ cup |
| Light corn syrup | 105 grams | ⅓ cup |
| Pure vanilla extract | 5 grams | 1 teaspoon |
| Pinch of fine sea salt | | |
| Chopped pistachios, for garnish | 20 grams | 2 tablespoons |
| Maraschino cherries, for garnish | 3 | |

**Make the layers** ▶ Preheat the oven to 325°F (160°C) and set a rack in the center. Coat three identical 9 by 5-inch (23 by 13) loaf pans with   ▶▶▶

cooking spray and line each with a parchment sling, leaving about 1 inch (2.5 cm) of parchment overhang along the length of the pan.

In a medium bowl, whisk the flour, baking powder, and salt.

In a stand mixer fitted with the paddle, beat the almond paste and sugar at medium speed until the almond paste is in pea-sized pieces. Add the butter and beat on medium-high speed until smooth, about 5 minutes. Add the egg yolks one at a time, stopping to scrape the sides as needed. Add the milk, almond extract, and vanilla and mix until combined. Reduce the speed to low and add the flour mixture in two parts, mixing until each one is combined. Transfer the batter to a large bowl.

Clean and dry the mixer bowl. Return to the stand mixer and snap on the whisk. Beat the egg whites on medium speed to medium-stiff peaks, about 4 minutes. Add one-third of the beaten whites to the batter and fold to combine. Add the remaining egg whites in two parts, folding until no streaks remain.

Evenly divide the batter into three medium bowls (about 425 grams or 1¾ cups per bowl). In a small bowl, mix the cocoa powder and boiling water together to form a paste. Add to one bowl of batter, along with the chocolate chips, and fold to combine. To the second bowl of batter, add the pistachio extract, 2 drops of green food gel, and pistachios and fold until combined. In the last bowl, add 1 drop of red food gel and the cherry preserves and fold until combined. Transfer each batter to its own loaf pan and spread in an even layer.

Bake the layers until baked through and springy when touched, 40 to 50 minutes, rotating the pans halfway through. (The flavors may be done at slightly different times, so check each individually.) Transfer the pans to a wire rack to cool for 20 minutes. Remove each cake from the pan using the parchment sling, carefully remove the parchment, and set on the wire rack to cool completely, about 1 hour.

**Assemble the cake** ▶ Trim the top of each layer with a serrated knife to create a level surface. Place a sheet of plastic wrap on the counter. Place the pistachio layer in the center of the wrap and make sure there is enough plastic to cover the entire cake. Spread 65 grams (3 tablespoons) of the raspberry preserves on top in an even layer. Place the cherry layer on top, lining up the sides. Spread the remaining preserves on top. Top with the chocolate layer, lining up the sides, and wrap the cake tightly. Place the cake in a clean loaf pan and place in the refrigerator to set, at least 4 hours or overnight.

Line a baking sheet with parchment and set a wire rack on top. Remove the cake from the pan, unwrap, and place on a cutting board. If the edges are angled or uneven, use a serrated knife and cut straight down on all sides. Remove any excess crumbs and transfer the spumoni to the wire rack, flipping so the pistachio is the top layer. Return to the refrigerator while you make the glaze.

To make the glaze, place the chopped chocolate in a heatproof ▶▶▶

medium bowl (preferably with a pour spout). In a medium saucepan, bring the heavy cream and corn syrup to a boil over medium heat, stirring frequently. Remove from the heat and stir in the vanilla and salt. Pour the cream mixture over the chopped chocolate and stir until the chocolate has completely melted. Set aside to cool for 30 minutes, until slightly thickened.

Remove the cake from the refrigerator and, working quickly, pour the glaze over each side, allowing it to coat the layers all the way to the bottom of the cake. Pour the rest of the glaze over the top of the cake. Using an offset spatula, smooth the top and push the extra glaze toward the edges, allowing it to run down the sides. Then smooth the sides of the cake until the entire cake is covered in a nice, even layer. Top the cake with 3 small piles of chopped pistachios, like little nests, lined down the center. Top each of those nests with a cherry. Return to the refrigerator to set for 1 hour.

To serve, use an offset spatula to transfer the cake to a platter. Allow it to sit at room temperature for about 10 minutes before slicing.

This cake can be covered and refrigerated for up to 5 days.

# CARROT CAKE

**MAKES ONE 10-INCH (25 CM) CAKE**

*Ginger Fisher Baldwin has been my savior more times than I can count. She started as a baker at the original Red Hook location of Baked and quickly rose through the ranks. When we opened a second location in Manhattan, we left her in charge of things back in Brooklyn while we had our hands full with our new shop. She eventually moved on to other projects, but when the time came for me to embark on my solo project, which eventually became Ciao, Gloria, I asked her if she'd join me. She said yes right away and was my culinary partner in developing the menu into what it is today. She has again moved on to other projects, but I owe her the sun and moon, and I am forever grateful for her expertise and friendship. She developed this recipe for our opening menu and it reminds me of her every time I cut a slice for a customer. While carrot cake is a very popular cake stateside, it's grown in popularity in Italy in recent years. This is our imagining of the cake, made with a more "nonna" approach. It's a single layer, nut-free cake that is almost equal parts cake and frosting (a ratio I firmly stand behind), and I can say, wholeheartedly, that this is the best carrot cake I have ever tasted.*

### FOR THE CAKE

| | | |
|---|---|---|
| All-purpose flour, plus more for dusting | 215 grams | 1½ cups |
| Baking soda | 9 grams | 1½ teaspoons |
| Baking powder | 4 grams | 1 teaspoon |
| Ground cinnamon | 3 grams | 1 teaspoon |
| Fine sea salt | 2 grams | ½ teaspoon |
| Ground ginger | 2 grams | ½ teaspoon |
| Ground nutmeg | 1 gram | ¼ teaspoon |
| Freshly grated carrots | 325 grams | 2½ cups |
| Sweetened shredded coconut | 80 grams | ¾ cup |
| Golden raisins | 80 grams | ½ cup |
| Dark brown sugar | 150 grams | ¾ cup packed |
| Granulated sugar | 150 grams | ¾ cup |
| Canola oil | 150 grams | ¾ cup |
| Large eggs, at room temperature | 3 | |

### FOR THE FROSTING

| | | |
|---|---|---|
| Mascarpone, cold | 230 grams | 1 cup |
| Heavy cream, cold | 230 grams | 1 cup |
| Pure vanilla extract | 5 grams | 1 teaspoon |
| Pinch of fine sea salt | | |
| Powdered sugar, sifted | 120 grams | 1 cup |
| Toasted coconut flakes, for garnish | 15 grams | ¼ cup |

**Make the cake** ▶ Preheat the oven to 350°F (180°C) and set a rack in the center. Coat a 10-inch (25 cm) round cake pan with nonstick spray, line with a parchment round, and dust with flour, knocking out any excess.

In a medium bowl, whisk together the flour, baking soda, baking ▶▶▶

powder, cinnamon, salt, ginger, and nutmeg. In a separate bowl, stir together the carrots, coconut, and raisins.

In a stand mixer fitted with the paddle, beat both sugars and the oil on low until combined. Add the eggs one at a time, stopping to scrape the sides as needed. Add the flour mixture in two parts until just combined. Add the carrot mixture and mix well. Transfer the batter to the prepared pan.

Bake until a cake tester inserted into the center comes out clean, 40 to 50 minutes, rotating the pan halfway through. Let the cake cool in the pan for 30 minutes before turning out onto a wire rack to cool completely, about 1 hour.

**While the cake cools, make the frosting** ▶ In a stand mixer fitted with the whisk, combine the mascarpone, cream, vanilla, and salt. Whip on medium speed until completely smooth, 2 to 3 minutes. Sift in the powdered sugar and whip until stiff peaks form and the frosting is smooth and spreadable, about 5 minutes.

Transfer the cooled cake to a stand or serving plate and top with the frosting. Use an offset spatula to push the frosting to the edges in an even layer, covering the top but leaving the sides clean. Finish with a border of coconut flakes.

This cake can be covered and refrigerated for up to 3 days.

# PISTACHIO LEMON CAKE

**MAKES ONE 8-INCH (20 CM) LAYER CAKE**

*Pistachios are synonymous with Sicily and Sicilians will tell you that their island produces the finest, case closed. My parents' town is not that far from Bronte, the pistachio capital of Sicily, if not the world, where every shop, bakery, and café celebrates this nut, in foods both sweet and savory. On my last trip to Sicily, I spent the day buzzing around visiting different relatives (who all live within a three-block radius of each other) and, as I was saying my good-byes, one cousin ran off and a few seconds later, reappeared with a bag of vacuum-packed pistachios. "For you to take home and bake with! These are from our farm." This cake, enriched with pistachio cream spread (available online and at most Italian markets), accented with sharp lemon, and finished with chopped pistachios, is a tribute to all the flavors of my Italian home in the height of summer.*

## FOR THE CAKE

| | | |
|---|---|---|
| All-purpose flour, plus more for dusting | 425 grams | 3 cups |
| Granulated sugar | 400 grams | 2 cups |
| Baking powder | 15 grams | 1 tablespoon |
| Fine sea salt | 2 grams | ½ teaspoon |
| Unsalted butter, cubed and at room temperature | 195 grams | 14 tablespoons |
| Whole milk, at room temperature | 380 grams | 1⅔ cups |
| Large egg yolks, at room temperature | 3 | |
| Pure vanilla extract | 5 grams | 1 teaspoon |
| Almond extract | 1 gram | ¼ teaspoon |
| Pistachio cream spread | 20 grams | 1 tablespoon |
| Large egg whites, at room temperature | 5 | |
| Unsalted pistachios, toasted and roughly chopped | 50 grams | ½ cup |

## FOR THE FILLING

| | | |
|---|---|---|
| Unsalted butter, at room temperature | 85 grams | 6 tablespoons |
| Powdered sugar | 60 grams | ½ cup |
| Pinch of fine sea salt | | |
| Mascarpone | 115 grams | ½ cup |
| Pistachio cream spread | 60 grams | 3 tablespoons |

## FOR THE FROSTING

| | | |
|---|---|---|
| Double recipe Italian Buttercream (page 267) | | |
| Grated lemon zest | 4 grams | 1 tablespoon |
| Fresh lemon juice | 55 grams | 3 tablespoons |

**Make the cake** ▶ Preheat the oven to 350°F (180°C) and set a rack in the center. Coat two 8-inch (20 cm) round cake pans with cooking spray, line with parchment rounds, and dust with flour, knocking out any excess.

In a stand mixer fitted with the paddle, mix the flour, sugar, baking ▶▶▶

powder, and salt on low speed. Add the butter, one piece at a time and mix until it resembles coarse sand. In a small bowl, whisk the milk and egg yolks. Add half the milk mixture to the mixer and mix on medium speed for 30 seconds. Stop to scrape down the sides, then add the remaining milk mixture and mix on medium speed until smooth and fluffy, about 1 minute. Add the vanilla extract, almond extract, and pistachio spread and mix until just combined. Transfer the batter to a large bowl.

Wash and dry the stand mixer bowl, then return to the stand mixer and snap on the whisk. Beat the egg whites on high speed until medium peaks form, about 3 minutes. Add half of the whites to the bowl with the batter and fold in. Add the chopped pistachios and remaining egg whites and fold until just a few streaks remain. Divide the batter between the prepared pans.

Bake until a cake tester comes out clean, 40 to 50 minutes, rotating the pans halfway through. Cool in the pans for 30 minutes, then turn out onto a wire rack to cool completely.

Make the filling ▶ In a stand mixer with the paddle, mix the butter until smooth. Sift the powdered sugar and add to the mixer, followed by the salt, scraping down the bowl as needed.

Add in the mascarpone and mix until incorporated. Add in the pistachio spread and mix until the filling begins to thicken and emulsify, at least 30 to 45 seconds. Use immediately or refrigerate until ready to use. (If cold, let the filling soften at room temperature before spreading.)

Just before assembling, make the frosting ▶ In a stand mixer fitted with the whisk, beat the buttercream on low speed. Add the lemon zest and lemon juice and beat until smooth and incorporated, about 3 minutes.

To assemble the cake, use a serrated knife to trim off the tops of both cake layers, creating an even surface. Place one cake layer, cut-side up, on a turntable cake stand or serving plate. Fit a piping bag with a large round tip. Put about 85 grams (½ cup) of buttercream in the bag and pipe a border around the edge of the cake to help contain the filling. Spoon all of the filling in the center of the cake layer. Use a small offset spatula to spread in an even layer out to the buttercream border.

Place the second cake layer, cut-side down, on top of the filling and frosting. Top the cake with 170 grams (1 cup) of the buttercream, spreading a thin layer on the top and sides of the cake as a "crumb coat." Place the cake in the refrigerator for 15 to 20 minutes to set.

Use the remaining frosting to frost the sides and top of the cake. Any remaining pistachios, buttercream, and filling can be used to accent the top of the cake (as seen in the photo).

This cake can be covered and refrigerated for up to 3 days.

Capri, Campania, Italy

# CHOCOLATE HAZELNUT CAKE

**MAKES ONE 8-INCH (20 CM) LAYER CAKE**

*For those of you not yet trapped in the cult, Ferrero Rocher chocolates—created in 1982 by the Italian confectioner Michele Ferrero—are made up of a hazelnut ganache, covered in chopped hazelnuts, with a crispy chocolate shell. My German mother-in-law gifts us a box every Christmas, and Sven and I devour them within hours (sometimes minutes) of receiving them. So, as a chocolate-obsessed bakery owner, I pulled from what I love when creating our signature chocolate cake. Dark chocolate layers sandwich a filling that is deeply inspired by the crunchy, hazelnutty chocolate of a Ferrero Rocher. Topped with a smooth chocolate Italian buttercream with a nip of Frangelico for good measure, it's a bona fide winner.*

### FOR THE GANACHE

| | | |
|---|---|---|
| Milk chocolate, preferably Valrhona Azélia, chopped | 225 grams | 8 ounces |
| Heavy cream | 155 grams | ⅔ cup |
| Light corn syrup | 20 grams | 1 tablespoon |
| Unsalted butter | 15 grams | 1 tablespoon |
| Fine sea salt | 1 gram | ¼ teaspoon |
| Toasted hazelnuts, chopped | 200 grams | 1⅓ cup |

### FOR THE CAKE

| | | |
|---|---|---|
| All-purpose flour | 285 grams | 2 cups |
| Good-quality cocoa powder | 95 grams | 1 cup |
| Baking soda | 12 grams | 2 teaspoons |
| Fine sea salt | 2 grams | ½ teaspoon |
| Canola oil | 160 grams | ¾ cup plus 1 tablespoon |
| Granulated sugar | 450 grams | 2¼ cups |
| Large eggs, at room temperature | 4 | |
| Pure vanilla extract | 15 grams | 1 tablespoon |
| Buttermilk | 575 grams | 2½ cups |

### FOR THE FROSTING

| | | |
|---|---|---|
| Italian Buttercream (page 267) | | |
| Dark chocolate, preferably Valrhona Caraïbe, melted and cooled | 100 grams | 3½ ounces |
| Frangelico (optional) | 15 grams | 1 tablespoon |

**Make the ganache** ▸ Place the chocolate in a heatproof medium bowl. In a small saucepan, combine the heavy cream, corn syrup, butter, and salt and bring to a boil over medium heat. Pour over the chocolate and mix until the chocolate is melted and smooth. Fold in 150 grams (1 cup) of the hazelnuts (reserving the remainder to top the finished cake). Cover with plastic wrap and refrigerate for at least 2 hours or overnight. Note: Before using, let the ganache return to room temperature. This will make it easier to spread on the cake. ▸▸▸

**Meanwhile, make the cake** ▶ Preheat the oven to 350°F (180°C) and set a rack in the center. Coat two 8-inch (20 cm) round cake pans with cooking spray and line with parchment rounds.

In a medium bowl, sift the flour, cocoa, baking soda, and salt.

In a stand mixer fitted with the paddle, combine the oil and sugar and beat on low speed until combined. Add the eggs one at a time, stopping to scrape the sides. Add the vanilla and mix to combine. Add the flour mixture in three parts, alternating with the buttermilk, beginning and ending with the flour mixture. Divide the batter between the prepared pans.

Bake until a cake tester comes out clean, 40 to 50 minutes, rotating the pans front to back halfway through. Let cool in the pans for 30 minutes, then turn out onto a wire rack to cool completely, about 1 hour.

**Just before assembling, make the frosting** ▶ In a stand mixer fitted with the whisk, beat the buttercream on low speed. Slowly add the cooled chocolate. Beat until smooth and incorporated, about 3 minutes. Add the Frangelico (if using) and mix until incorporated.

To assemble the cake, use a serrated knife to trim off the tops of both cake layers, creating an even surface. Place one cake layer, cut-side up, on a turntable cake stand or serving plate. Spoon all of the ganache in the center of the cake layer. Use a small offset spatula to spread in an even layer to the edges.

Place the second cake layer, cut-side down, on top of the ganache. Top the cake with 170 grams (1 cup) of the buttercream, spreading a thin layer on the top and sides of the cake as a "crumb coat." Place the cake in the refrigerator for 15 to 20 minutes to set.

Use the remaining frosting to frost the sides and top of the cake in any manner of your choosing.

Sprinkle the remaining hazelnuts on top of the cake to decorate.

This cake can be covered and refrigerated for up to 3 days.

# VELLUTO ROSSO

**MAKES ONE 8-INCH (20 CM) LAYER CAKE**

*There was a time when red velvet really took over the American imagination, when you couldn't swing a fork without hitting someone eating a red velvet cupcake—or cinnamon roll, or pancake. It's become an emblem of American dessert in other countries, even Italy, where classic American-style desserts—like brownies, chocolate chip cookies, and cheesecake—have come into fashion. So this recipe is a take on the classically American cake, as seen through an Italian lens. It's slightly darker in color and more chocolate-forward. A thin layer of raspberry preserves and a combo of cream cheese and mascarpone frosting gives this cake an addictive tang, but leaves a creamier and more sophisticated finish. We serve it at the bakery in February, under the pseudonym Velluto Rosso, to celebrate Valentine's Day, but it's a perfectly stunning and delicious cake to serve year-round.*

### FOR THE CAKE

| | | |
|---|---|---|
| Cake flour for the pan | | |
| Boiling water | 115 grams | ½ cup |
| Good-quality cocoa powder | 50 grams | ½ cup |
| Red food coloring | | 1½ tablespoons |
| Buttermilk, at room temperature | 305 grams | 1⅓ cups |
| Cake flour | 390 grams | 3¼ cups |
| Fine sea salt | 6 grams | 1 teaspoon |
| Granulated sugar | 400 grams | 2 cups |
| Unsalted butter, at room temperature | 225 grams | 16 tablespoons |
| Large eggs | 3 | |
| Pure vanilla extract | 10 grams | 2 teaspoons |
| Distilled white vinegar | 20 grams | 1 tablespoon plus 1 teaspoon |
| Baking soda | 6 grams | 2 teaspoons |

### FOR THE FROSTING

| | | |
|---|---|---|
| Unsalted butter, at room temperature | 225 grams | 16 tablespoons |
| Cream cheese, at room temperature | 450 grams | 16 ounces |
| Powdered sugar, sifted | 360 grams | 3 cups |
| Fine sea salt | | ⅛ teaspoon |
| Whole milk, plus more if needed | 45 grams | 3 tablespoons |
| Vanilla extract | 10 grams | 2 teaspoons |
| Mascarpone | 450 grams | 16 ounces |

### FOR ASSEMBLY

| | | |
|---|---|---|
| Raspberry preserves | 85 grams | ¼ cup |
| Alchermes (optional) | 5 grams | 1 teaspoon |

**Make the cake** ▶ Preheat the oven to 350°F (180°C) and set a rack in the center. Coat two 8-inch (20 cm) round cake pans with cooking spray, line with parchment rounds, and dust with flour, knocking out any excess. ▶▶▶

In a medium bowl, combine the boiling water, cocoa powder, and food coloring. Whisk to combine, then whisk in the buttermilk. In a separate medium bowl, sift the cake flour and salt.

In a stand mixer fitted with the paddle, combine the granulated sugar and butter and beat on medium-high speed until light and fluffy, about 5 minutes. Reduce the speed to low and add the eggs one at a time, stopping to scrape the sides as needed. Add the vanilla and mix until combined. Add the flour mixture in three parts, alternating with the buttermilk mixture, beginning and ending with the flour mixture. Mix until no streaks of flour remain. In a small bowl, whisk the vinegar and baking soda, then immediately fold into the batter. Divide the batter between the prepared pans.

Bake until a cake tester comes out clean, 45 to 55 minutes, rotating the pans halfway through. Let cool in the pans for 30 minutes, then turn out onto a wire rack to cool completely, about 1 hour.

**Just before assembling the cake, make the frosting** ▶ In a stand mixer fitted with the whisk, whip the butter until smooth. With the mixer on medium speed, add the cream cheese little by little and mix until smooth and fluffy, scraping down the bowl as needed. Add the powdered sugar and salt, in two additions, and mix on low speed until well combined.

With the mixer running on low speed, gradually add the milk and vanilla and whip until the frosting is smooth and glossy.

Lastly, add the mascarpone, scraping down the sides of the bowl as needed. Whip on medium speed until the frosting thickens, which should only take a few seconds. If the frosting seems too thick to spread, add a little milk 1 tablespoon at a time to loosen.

**Assemble the cake** ▶ Use a serrated knife to trim off the tops of both cake layers (see note about optional decoration), creating an even surface. Place one cake layer, cut-side up, on a turntable cake stand or serving plate. In a small bowl, mix the raspberry preserves with the alchermes liqueur (if using). Use a small offset spatula to spread the raspberry preserves over the top of the cake. Fit a piping bag with a large round tip. Put about 250 grams (1½ cups) of frosting in the bag and pipe in a circular motion, starting at the edges and working into the center.

Place the second cake layer, cut-side down, on top of the frosting. Top the cake with 170 grams (1 cup) of the frosting, spreading a thin layer on the top and sides of the cake as a "crumb coat." Place the cake in the refrigerator for 15 to 20 minutes to set.

Use the remaining frosting to frost the sides and top of the cake, in however manner you'd like. Then chill for another 15 minutes to set.

This cake can be covered and refrigerated for up to 2 days. Bring to room temperature before enjoying.

# APEROL SPRITZ CAKE

## MAKES ONE 8-INCH (20 CM) LAYER CAKE

*Here in the U.S., I am not much of a drinker. I'll have the occasional cocktail, a couple of sips of wine, a celebratory Prosecco, but not much beyond that. But when I'm in Italy, I can't resist the pull of a nightly Aperol spritz. Served nice and cold during aperitivo, along with a host of snacks to prime you for dinner, it's a drink I can really get behind. The main ingredient, Aperol, is an aperitif infused with sweet fruit and bitter herbs for a syrupy, complex bottle of alcohol. Mixed with Prosecco, a splash of club soda, garnished with a slice of orange (and very traditionally, a green olive), the result is a drink that has the gorgeous orangey-reddish hue of a Mediterranean sunset. So of course I wanted to translate these flavors into a layer cake. (Don't worry, I omitted the olive!) Here, orange-scented vanilla cake is layered with an orange and Aperol curd and then topped with Prosecco buttercream, with a simple ombré decor to match the beauty of the drink.*

### FOR THE CAKE

| | | |
|---|---|---|
| All-purpose flour, plus more for dusting | 445 grams | 3¼ cups |
| Granulated sugar | 450 grams | 2¼ cups |
| Baking powder | 15 grams | 1 tablespoon |
| Fine sea salt | 2 grams | ½ teaspoon |
| Grated orange zest (from 2 oranges) | 10 grams | 2 tablespoons |
| Unsalted butter, cubed and at room temperature | 180 grams | 13 tablespoons |
| Whole milk, at room temperature | 400 grams | 1½ cups |
| Pure vanilla extract | 15 grams | 1 tablespoon |
| Large egg yolks, at room temperature | 3 | |
| Large egg whites, at room temperature | 5 | |

### FOR ASSEMBLY

| | | |
|---|---|---|
| Double recipe Italian Buttercream (page 267) | | |
| Prosecco | 170 grams | ¾ cup |
| Aperol Simple Syrup (recipe below) | | ½ cup |
| Orange and Aperol Curd (recipe follows) | 260 grams | 1 cup |
| Orange food gel | | |
| Red food gel | | |

**Make the cake** ▶ Preheat the oven to 350°F (180°C) and set a rack in the center. Coat two 8-inch (20 cm) round cake pans with cooking spray, line with parchment rounds, and dust with flour, knocking out any excess.

In a stand mixer fitted with the paddle, combine the flour, sugar, baking powder, salt, and orange zest. With the mixer on low, add the butter, one piece at a time and mix until it resembles coarse sand. In a small bowl, whisk the milk, vanilla, and egg yolks. Add half the milk mixture and mix on medium speed for 30 seconds. Stop to scrape down the sides, then add the remaining ▶▶▶

milk mixture and mix on medium speed until smooth and fluffy, about 1 minute. Transfer the batter to a large bowl.

Wash and dry the stand mixer bowl, then return to the stand mixer and snap on the whisk. Beat the egg whites on high speed until medium peaks form, about 3 minutes. Add half of the whites to the bowl with the batter and fold in, then add the remaining egg whites and fold until just a few streaks remain. Divide the batter between the prepared pans.

Bake until a cake tester inserted in the center comes out clean, 30 to 40 minutes, rotating the pans halfway through. Transfer the pans to a wire rack and let cool for 20 minutes. Invert the cakes, remove the parchment, and let cool completely before assembling.

**To assemble** ▶ In a stand mixer fitted with the whisk, beat the buttercream on low speed. Slowly add the Prosecco and beat until smooth and incorporated, about 2 minutes.

Use a serrated knife to trim off the tops of both cake layers, creating an even surface. Place one cake layer, cut-side up, on a turntable cake stand or serving plate. Brush the top of the cake generously with the syrup. Fit a piping bag with a large round tip. Put about 85 grams (½ cup) of the buttercream frosting in the bag and pipe a border around the edge of the cake to help contain the curd. Spoon the curd in the center of the cake layer. Use a small offset spatula to spread in an even layer out to the frosting border.

Place the second cake layer, cut-side down, on top of the curd. Brush with the remaining syrup and top with 170 grams (1 cup) of the frosting, spreading a thin layer on the top and sides of the cake as a "crumb coat." Place the cake in the refrigerator for 15 to 20 minutes to set.

Divide the remaining frosting among three small bowls (about 325 grams each), then remove 1 tablespoon of frosting from each of the first two bowls and add them to the third bowl. (The third bowl will be for the top of the cake.) To the first bowl, add 5 drops of orange gel and 2 drops of red gel and mix well. To the second bowl, add 4 drops of orange gel and mix well. To the third bowl, add 1 drop of orange gel and mix well.

Starting at the bottom of the cake, use an offset spatula to apply the darkest orange frosting to the cake in a band along the bottom third. Wipe the spatula clean and apply the medium orange frosting in a band along the middle third. Wipe the spatula once again and apply the light orange frosting to the final third and top surface of the cake. Wipe the spatula clean and start smoothing the edges of the cake, while turning the turntable, so the colors start blending into one another. Wipe the spatula clean again and, while turning the turntable, start bringing in the frosting from the top edges toward the center of the cake.

Once the sides and top are smooth, wipe the spatula once again and start adding a textured swoop to the top of the cake ▶ Start at the edge furthest from you and press the tip of the spatula gently into the buttercream at a slight angle. Move the spatula from edge to edge, working your way across and toward you until you've reached the edge of the cake closest to you.

This cake can be covered and refrigerated for up to 3 days.

## APEROL SIMPLE SYRUP

| | | |
|---|---|---|
| Granulated sugar | 100 grams | ½ cup |
| Aperol | 55 grams | ¼ cup |

In a small saucepan, combine the Aperol, sugar, and 65 grams (¼ cup) of water. Simmer over medium heat and stir until the sugar is dissolved. Set aside to cool.

## ORANGE AND APEROL CURD

MAKES 580 GRAMS (1¾ CUPS)

*In addition to making a great cake filling, this curd is delightful mixed into yogurt or spread onto a slice of toast.*

| | | |
|---|---|---|
| Granulated sugar | 135 grams | ⅔ cup |
| Cornstarch | 3 grams | 1 teaspoon |
| Large egg yolks | 6 | |
| Large egg | 1 | |
| Grated orange zest (from 1 orange) | 5 grams | 1 tablespoon |
| Fresh orange juice | 120 grams | ½ cup |
| Grated lemon zest | 1 gram | ½ teaspoon |
| Fresh lemon juice | 5 grams | 1 teaspoon |
| Pinch of fine sea salt | | |
| Aperol | 30 grams | 2 tablespoons |
| Unsalted butter, cubed | 115 grams | 8 tablespoons |

In a medium saucepan, whisk the sugar and cornstarch to combine. Whisk in the egg yolks, whole egg, orange zest, orange juice, lemon zest, lemon juice, and salt. Set over low heat, stirring constantly with a silicone spatula, and scraping the sides as needed. Cook until the mixture is thick and bubbling, about 10 minutes. Remove from the heat. Whisk in the Aperol, then add the butter one piece at a time, whisking until smooth.

Set a fine-mesh sieve over a medium bowl. Strain the curd to remove any lumps and remaining zest. Press plastic wrap directly on the surface of the curd. Refrigerate for at least 4 hours or overnight, until set.

# CANNOLI CAKE

MAKES ONE 10-INCH (25 CM) CAKE

*When asked to name a classic Italian dessert, most people in Italy and the U.S. would probably say cannoli, proving the influence it has had on both Italian and Italian American culture. Cannoli are so deeply woven into the fabric of desserts and so symbolic of both countries, a crunchy, creamy bridge between two worlds made through immigration. The flavors of a cannoli are so sweetly intoxicating that I needed to find a way to enjoy them on a larger scale. Enter the cannoli cake! A cinnamon-infused, brown sugar cake gets studded with candied orange and chocolate chips, then topped with a whipped ricotta frosting. This cake really fulfills my cravings in a much more snackable form.*

### FOR THE CAKE

| | | |
|---|---|---|
| Dark brown sugar | 300 grams | 1½ packed cups |
| Unsalted butter, melted and cooled | 140 grams | 10 tablespoons |
| Large eggs, at room temperature | 2 | |
| Pure vanilla extract | 10 grams | 2 teaspoons |
| All-purpose flour, plus more for dusting | 285 grams | 2 cups |
| Baking powder | 10 grams | 2 teaspoons |
| Baking soda | 6 grams | 1 teaspoon |
| Fine sea salt | 2 grams | ½ teaspoon |
| Ground cinnamon | 6 grams | 2 teaspoons |
| Buttermilk | 285 grams | 1¼ cups |
| Mini chocolate chips | 110 grams | ½ cup |
| Candied orange, diced | 65 grams | ½ cup |

### FOR THE FROSTING

| | | |
|---|---|---|
| Ricotta | 120 grams | ½ cup |
| Orange juice | 15 grams | 1 tablespoon |
| Pure vanilla extract | 2 grams | ½ teaspoon |
| Pinch of fine sea salt | | |
| Powdered sugar | 150 grams | 1¼ cup |
| Heavy cream, cold | 230 grams | 1 cup |
| Mini chocolate chips | 55 grams | ¼ cup |
| Unsalted pistachios, toasted and roughly chopped, for garnish | 25 grams | ¼ cup |

**Make the cake** ▶ Preheat the oven to 350°F (180°C) and set a rack in the center. Coat a 10-inch (25 cm) round cake pan with nonstick spray, line with a parchment round, and dust with flour, knocking out any excess.

In a stand mixer fitted with the paddle, beat the brown sugar and butter on low speed until combined. Add the eggs one at a time, stopping to scrape the sides as needed. Add the vanilla and mix until well combined. In a medium bowl, sift the flour, baking powder, baking soda, salt, and cinnamon. Add the flour to the mixer bowl in two parts, alternating with the buttermilk, beginning and ending with the flour mixture. Mix on low until no streaks of flour remain. Use a rubber spatula to fold in the chocolate chips and candied orange. ▶▶▶

Transfer the batter into the prepared pan and smooth the top. Bake for 45 to 50 minutes, rotating halfway, until a cake tester inserted into the center comes out clean. Let the cake cool in the pan for 30 minutes before turning out onto a wire rack and cooling completely, about 1 hour.

**While the cake cools, make the frosting** ▶ In a stand mixer fitted with the whisk, combine the ricotta, orange juice, vanilla, and salt. Whip on low speed until just combined. Sift in the powdered sugar and whisk to combine. Stream in the cream and whip on medium-high speed until the frosting is thickened and spreadable, about 5 minutes. Use a rubber spatula to fold in the chocolate chips.

Scoop all the frosting on top of the cooled cake and use an offset spatula to spread to the edges in an even layer. Finish with a rim of pistachios. Serve immediately or refrigerate until ready to serve.

This cake can be covered and refrigerated for up to 3 days.

# BANANA NUTELLA SNACK CAKE

MAKES ONE 9 BY 13-INCH (23 BY 33 CM) CAKE

*In a previous life, at a previous bakery, we baked cupcakes. Lots and lots of cupcakes, all different flavors, toppings, gimmicks, endless combinations. It was all a bit maddening. But it was the heyday of the cupcake, and I had bills to pay, so I endured. Today, new life, new bakery, no cupcakes. Instead, I set my gaze on the snack cake (a simple, square, single-layer cake perfect for snacking), something, in my eyes, just as delicious as a cupcake, but better for my sanity. We settled on a moist banana cake base topped with a Nutella-infused mascarpone buttercream as our introductory flavor. It was an instant hit and is almost always on the menu. (We've tried other flavors, but the crowd made their demands!) It's an easy recipe to make and the combo of banana, hazelnut, and chocolate is an eternal winner. Will it be enough for you to say good-bye to the cupcake and hello to the snack cake? Let's find out!*

## FOR THE CAKE

| | | |
|---|---|---|
| Cake flour | 330 grams | 2¾ cups |
| Baking powder | 6 grams | 1¼ teaspoons |
| Baking soda | 6 grams | 1 teaspoon |
| Fine sea salt | 4 grams | ¾ teaspoon |
| Unsalted butter, at room temperature | 170 grams | 12 tablespoons |
| Granulated sugar | 400 grams | 2 cups |
| Large eggs, at room temperature | 2 | |
| Mashed overripe bananas (3 to 4 bananas) | 360 grams | 1½ cups |
| Pure vanilla extract | 10 grams | 2 teaspoons |
| Buttermilk | 135 grams | ½ cup |

## FOR THE FROSTING

| | | |
|---|---|---|
| Unsalted butter, at room temperature | 225 grams | 16 tablespoons |
| Nutella | 210 grams | ¾ cup |
| Pinch of fine sea salt | | |
| Powdered sugar | 240 grams | 2 cups |
| Mascarpone, cold | 230 grams | 1 cup |
| Heavy cream, cold | 60 grams | ¼ cup |

**Make the cake** ▶ Preheat the oven to 350°F (180°C) and set a rack in the center. Coat a 9 by 13-inch (23 by 33 cm) baking pan with cooking spray and line with parchment, creating a sling with a 2-inch (5 cm) overhang on two sides.

In a medium bowl, sift the cake flour, baking powder, baking soda, and salt.

In a stand mixer fitted with the paddle, combine the butter and granulated sugar and beat on high until light and fluffy, about 5 minutes. Add the eggs one at a time on low speed, scraping down the sides as needed. Mix in the bananas and vanilla until combined. Add the flour mixture in three parts, alternating with the buttermilk, beginning and ending with the flour mixture. Mix until no streaks of flour remain and the batter looks fluffy. Transfer the batter to the prepared pan and spread into an even layer. ▶ ▶ ▶

Ciao, Gloria,
Prospect Heights, Brooklyn

Bake until a cake tester inserted in the center comes out clean, 40 to 45 minutes, rotating the pan front to back halfway through. Cool completely in the pan, then remove from the pan using the parchment sling and transfer to a cutting board.

**Make the frosting** ▶ In a stand mixer fitted with the paddle, combine the butter, Nutella, and salt. Beat on low speed until smooth and no lumps of butter remain. Sift in the powdered sugar and mix until combined. Change to the whisk attachment and add the mascarpone and heavy cream. Whip on medium-high, until thick and airy, about 2 to 3 minutes.

Scoop the frosting onto the cake, then use an offset spatula to smooth to the edges. Slice into 12 squares before serving.

This cake can be covered and refrigerated for up to 2 days.

# CASSATA

MAKES ONE 9-INCH (23 CM) CAKE

Cassata is a Sicilian specialty, made with sponge cake, ricotta filling, marzipan topping, and gilded with candied fruit. I have wrestled with the idea of updating this ancient, celebrated dessert, this absolute icon of baroque garishness. Would I be run out of town by an angry mob? Or would I be hoisted on shoulders for bringing a beloved cake into the twenty-first century? Like most Sicilian desserts, this is on the sweet side of the spectrum, basically sugar on sugar on sugar. But the charm is just how ostentatious and kitschy it is, like a drag queen showing up unexpectedly to Sunday dinner (I mean, I'd love that). So I wanted to stay true to the original (because who wants to be burned at the stake?), but made a few small tweaks that will hopefully keep the villagers at bay. I'll be honest, this cake is a commitment, both of ingredients and time, so it's best saved for the most special of occasions. Do yourself a favor and spread the work out over two days, and the eventual reward will be a sweet one.

### FOR THE PISTACHIO MARZIPAN

| | | |
|---|---|---|
| Unsalted pistachios | 85 grams | ¾ cup |
| Almond flour | 75 grams | ¾ cup |
| Granulated sugar | 150 grams | ¾ cup |
| Fresh lemon juice | 15 grams | 1 tablespoon |
| Light corn syrup | 20 grams | 1 tablespoon |
| Pistachio extract (optional) | 2 grams | ¼ teaspoon |
| Powdered sugar, for kneading | | |
| Green food gel | | |

### FOR THE MARSALA SYRUP

| | | |
|---|---|---|
| Granulated sugar | 50 grams | ¼ cup |
| Marsala | 55 grams | ¼ cup |

### FOR THE RICOTTA FILLING

| | | |
|---|---|---|
| Fresh Ricotta (page 272) or good-quality ricotta cheese, drained overnight | 500 grams | 2 cups |
| Powdered sugar, sifted | 240 grams | 2 cups |
| Pure vanilla extract | 10 grams | 2 teaspoons |
| Grated lemon zest | 2 grams | 1 teaspoon |
| Semisweet mini chocolate chips | 60 grams | ⅓ cup |

### FOR THE CAKE

Pan di Spagna (page 222)

**NOTE**

Make the pan di spagna up to 2 days in advance. Wrap tightly in plastic and store at room temperature.

### FOR THE GLAZE

| | | |
|---|---|---|
| Powdered sugar, plus more as needed | 180 grams | 1½ cups |
| Fresh lemon juice, plus more as needed | 20 grams | 1½ tablespoons |

| | | |
|---|---|---|
| **Large egg white** | 1 | |
| **Powdered sugar, sifted** | 160 grams | 1⅓ cups |
| **Candied fruits, such as orange, citron, zucca, or cherries** | | |

SPECIAL EQUIPMENT

**9-inch (23 cm) deep-dish pie plate**

ANOTHER NOTE

Marzipan can also be left at room temperature in a cool, dry place for up to 3 days. If using store-bought marzipan, portion out 300 grams, add 1 drop of green food gel, and knead until uniform in color and consistency.

YET ANOTHER NOTE

The cooled Marsala syrup can be stored in an airtight container in the refrigerator for up to 1 week. Bring to room temperature before using.

**Make the marzipan** ▶ Line a baking sheet with parchment paper.

In a food processor, process the pistachios to a fine flour, 4 to 5 minutes. Add the almond flour and pulse about 4 times to combine.

In a medium saucepan, combine the granulated sugar, lemon juice, corn syrup, and about 30 grams (2 tablespoons) water. Cook over low heat, stirring frequently, until the sugar has dissolved completely. Remove from the heat, add the nut flour to the sugar mixture, and stir until it comes together. Spread the mixture onto the prepared baking sheet and let cool for 1 hour.

Once cooled, start kneading until the marzipan is smooth and uniform, using a little powdered sugar as needed. Add 1 drop of green food gel and knead until the marzipan is uniformly green. Place on a sheet of plastic wrap and use the plastic to shape the marzipan into a log. Wrap tightly and refrigerate.

**Make the Marsala syrup** ▶ In a small saucepan, combine the granulated sugar, Marsala, and 115 grams (½ cup) water. Stir over medium heat until the sugar is completely dissolved. Remove from the heat to cool.

**Make the ricotta filling** ▶ On the day of assembly, set a fine-mesh sieve over a medium bowl. Use a rubber spatula to push the ricotta through the sieve and into the bowl. Add the powdered sugar, vanilla, and lemon zest. Whisk until fully combined. Fold in the chocolate chips. Cover with plastic wrap and refrigerate until ready to use.

**Assemble the cake** ▶ Line the pie plate with plastic wrap, leaving enough overhang to eventually wrap the top of the cake.

Use a serrated knife to trim the pan di spagna, removing all of the dark outer crust. Level the top of the cake and once trimmed, slice the layer horizontally, making two even layers each about ¾ inch (2 cm) thick.

On a lightly floured surface, roll out the marzipan to a roughly 5 by 12-inch (13 by 30 cm) rectangle about ¼ inch (6 mm) thick. Cut lengthwise down the center to create two 2½ by 12-inch (6 by 30 cm) strips. Carefully line the sides of the pie plate with the strips, joining the ends and sealing them together. Trim off any extra marzipan so that there is about a ½-inch (1 cm) overhang.

Trim one of the cake layers to fit the base of the pie plate, and then generously brush the layer with the syrup. Spoon the chilled ricotta filling ▶ ▶ ▶

over the cake, using an offset spatula to smooth it out. Generously brush the other cake layer with Marsala syrup and then place it on top of the ricotta, syrup side down. Trim off any excess, and gently press down and then cover with the overhanging plastic wrap. Weigh down the cake with a plate and refrigerate for 3 hours, until set.

**Just before removing the cassata from the refrigerator, make the glaze** ▶ In a small bowl, whisk the powdered sugar and lemon juice. Whisk to a thick but pourable consistency, adding more lemon juice 1 teaspoon at a time, as needed. If it becomes too thin, add a little more powdered sugar to get it to the perfect consistency.

Unwrap the cassata and invert the cake onto a serving platter. Brush off any flour that may still be on the marzipan. Gently press the center of the sponge to indent a space for the glaze to pool and slowly pour the glaze over the top of the cassata. Pour until the glaze just reaches the edges of the marzipan without spilling over. Return to the refrigerator for at least 1 hour, until set.

**Decorate the cake** ▶ In a stand mixer fitted with the whisk, beat the egg white on medium speed until frothy, about 1 minute. Gradually add the powdered sugar until incorporated, then increase the speed to high and whisk until thick, fluffy, and slightly shiny. Transfer to a piping bag with a small round tip. Decorate the top and sides of the cake with icing and candied fruit, in whatever manner comes to mind when you think "baroque." Return to the refrigerator to let the icing set for 30 minutes before serving.

This cassata can be covered and refrigerated for up to 3 days.  ▶▶▶

# PAN DI SPAGNA

**MAKES ONE 10-INCH (25 CM) CAKE**

*Pan di spagna is the Italian answer to sponge cake. This buttery version, spiked with honey and Marsala, is the only recipe I use. It was originally created by my friend and very talented baker, the late Gina DePalma, and appears in her book,* Dolce Italiano.

| | | |
|---|---|---|
| Cake flour, plus more for dusting | 240 grams | 2 cups |
| Baking powder | 8 grams | 1½ teaspoons |
| Fine sea salt | 4 grams | 1 teaspoon |
| Large eggs, separated, at room temperature | 8 | |
| Granulated sugar | 250 grams | 1¼ cups |
| Wildflower honey | 40 grams | 2 tablespoons |
| Marsala | 15 grams | 1 tablespoon |
| Pure vanilla extract | 5 grams | 1 teaspoon |
| Unsalted butter, melted and cooled | 115 grams | 8 tablespoons |
| Cream of tartar | 1 gram | ¼ teaspoon |

Preheat the oven to 325°F (160°C) and set a rack in the center. Coat a 10-inch (25 cm) round cake pan with cooking spray, line with a parchment round, and dust with flour, knocking out any excess.

In a medium bowl, sift the cake flour, baking powder, and salt.

In a stand mixer fitted with the whisk, combine the egg yolks, sugar, and honey and beat at medium speed until very pale and fluffy and doubled in volume, 5 to 8 minutes. Reduce the speed to low and add the Marsala, vanilla, and melted butter until combined. Transfer the mixture to a large bowl and fold in the flour mixture until almost combined, with a few streaks of flour remaining.

Wash and dry the mixer bowl and whisk and return to the stand mixer. Beat the egg whites on medium speed until frothy, about 2 minutes. Add the cream of tartar and beat on high speed to form stiff peaks, 3 to 4 minutes. Scoop one-third of the egg whites into the batter and fold to combine until you can barely see any white streaks. Fold in the remaining egg whites in two parts until the batter is very light. Pour the batter into the prepared pan and smooth the top.

Bake until golden and a cake tester inserted in the center comes out clean, 30 to 40 minutes, rotating the pan front to back halfway through. Let the cake cool for 5 minutes in the pan, then invert onto a wire rack to cool completely.

The pan di spagna can be wrapped in plastic and stored at room temperature for up to 4 days.

# TORTA CAPRESE

MAKES ONE 9-INCH (23 CM) CAKE

*This is a cake of many names and variations, found all over Italy. But all roads seem to lead back to the torta caprese, originating on the famous vacation island of Capri, right off of the Amalfi Coast. This gluten-free almond flour cake is a close relative to the flourless chocolate cake or the Sachertorte. It has a dense and moist interior, almost fudgy, with a pleasingly crunchy exterior. And even though the ingredient list is short, it's deceptively rich with a deep chocolatey flavor. It's traditionally served with a dusting of cocoa powder, but a scoop of gelato (see pages 233–235) or pile of Basic Whipped Cream (page 271) would be more than welcome.*

| | | |
|---|---|---|
| Dark chocolate, chopped | 225 grams | 8 ounces |
| Unsalted butter | 225 grams | 16 tablespoons |
| Granulated sugar | 225 grams | 1¼ cups |
| Almond flour | 225 grams | 2¼ cups |
| Fine sea salt | 2 grams | ½ teaspoon |
| Large eggs, separated, at room temperature | 5 | |
| Pure vanilla extract | 5 grams | 1 teaspoon |
| Cocoa powder, for garnish | | |

Preheat the oven to 350°F (180°C) and set a rack in the center. Coat a 9-inch (23 cm) springform pan with cooking spray and line with a parchment round.

Fill a medium saucepan with 1 inch (2.5 cm) water and bring to a simmer over medium heat. Set a heatproof medium bowl over the saucepan, making sure the bowl doesn't touch the water. Add the chopped dark chocolate and butter to the bowl and use a silicone spatula to stir occasionally as the chocolate melts. Remove the bowl from the saucepan. Whisk in the sugar, almond flour, and salt and let cool for 10 minutes. Whisk in the egg yolks and vanilla until the batter is smooth.

In a stand mixer fitted with the whisk, beat the egg whites on medium speed to medium-stiff peaks, about 5 minutes. Scoop about one-third of the egg whites into the batter and fold to loosen. Add the remaining egg whites in two parts, gently folding until just incorporated. Transfer the batter to the prepared cake pan.

Bake until a cake tester comes out mostly clean with a few crumbs, 30 to 40 minutes, rotating the pan front to back halfway through. The cake will look puffed up and feel firm to the touch. Let cool completely in the pan, about 2 hours. Remove the springform and transfer to a cake stand or serving plate. Dust with cocoa powder before slicing.

The torta can be covered and stored at room temperature for up to 2 days.

# AMARETTO CHOCOLATE BUNDT

**MAKES 1 BUNDT CAKE**

*I love chocolate cake in its myriad forms, be it cup, snacking, layer, loaf, or, in this instance, Bundt. This is a fantastically tender and deeply chocolatey cake, and another one of my favorite recipes from Ciao, Gloria. The addition of Amaretto, the supremely sweet almond liqueur, in both the cake and glaze also make this a delightfully boozy affair. (If we're laying all our cards on the table, I capital L love Amaretto.) Combining these two ingredients makes total, blissful sense. Of course, I highly recommend a good-quality cocoa powder and dark chocolate chip, as they are the stars here. The Amaretto just aids in the drama.*

### FOR THE CAKE

| | | |
|---|---|---|
| Good-quality cocoa powder, plus more for dusting | 50 grams | ½ cup |
| Dark chocolate, chopped | 140 grams | 5 ounces |
| Hot coffee | 140 grams | ⅔ cup |
| Sour cream | 175 grams | ¾ cup |
| All-purpose flour | 215 grams | 1½ cups |
| Fine sea salt | 2 grams | ½ teaspoon |
| Baking soda | 6 grams | 1 teaspoon |
| Unsalted butter, at room temperature | 140 grams | 10 tablespoons |
| Dark brown sugar | 310 grams | 1½ cups packed, plus 1 tablespoon packed |
| Large eggs, at room temperature | 5 | |
| Pure vanilla extract | 15 grams | 1 tablespoon |
| Amaretto | 30 grams | 2 tablespoons |
| Mini chocolate chips | 110 grams | ½ cup |

### FOR THE CHOCOLATE GLAZE

| | | |
|---|---|---|
| Unsalted butter | 115 grams | 8 tablespoons |
| Good-quality cocoa powder | 65 grams | ⅔ cup |
| Corn syrup | 15 grams | 1 tablespoon |
| Amaretto | 15 grams | 1 tablespoon |
| Pure vanilla extract | 10 grams | 2 teaspoons |
| Powdered sugar | 200 grams | 1⅔ cups |
| Heavy cream | 30 grams | 2 tablespoons |

**Make the cake** ▶ Preheat the oven to 350°F (180°C) and set a rack in the center. Thoroughly coat a 12-cup Bundt pan with cooking spray. Dust with cocoa powder and knock out the excess.

In a medium bowl, combine the cocoa powder and dark chocolate. Pour the hot coffee into the bowl and whisk gently until the mixture is smooth. Let cool completely, about 30 minutes. Whisk in the sour cream.

In a separate medium bowl, whisk the flour, salt, and baking soda.

In a stand mixer fitted with the paddle, beat the butter and brown sugar at medium-high speed until light and fluffy, about 5 minutes. Reduce the   ▶ ▶ ▶

speed to low and add the eggs one at a time, stopping to scrape the sides as needed. Add the vanilla and Amaretto and mix until combined. Add the flour mixture in three parts, alternating with the chocolate mixture, beginning and ending with the flour mixture. Mix until no streaks of flour remain. Remove the bowl from the mixer and fold in the chocolate chips. The batter should be fluffy and aerated. Transfer the batter to the prepared pan, smoothing the top.

Bake until a cake tester comes out mostly clean with a few crumbs, 45 to 55 minutes, rotating the pan halfway through. Let cool for about 30 minutes in the pan before unmolding onto a wire rack to cool completely, about 2 hours.

When the cake is cooled, make the glaze ▶ Fill a medium saucepan with 1 inch (2.5 cm) of water and bring to a simmer over medium heat. Set a heatproof medium bowl over the saucepan, making sure the bowl doesn't touch the water. Add the butter, cocoa powder, and corn syrup and stir with a rubber spatula. Add the Amaretto and vanilla. Add the powdered sugar and stir so no lumps remain. The glaze will be glossy and a bit stiff. Add the heavy cream, 1 tablespoon at a time, until it has a thick but pourable consistency. Remove from the heat and use immediately or let cool, cover, and store in the fridge. The glaze will keep for about 5 days.

Transfer the cake to a serving plate. Gently pour the glaze over the Bundt and nudge it with a spoon or offset spatula down the sides, if needed, making sure it doesn't drip completely off the sides. Once the glaze has set, slice and serve.

This Bundt can be covered and stored at room temperature for up to 3 days.

Scopello, Sicily, Italy

# 7

# SPOONS

**ITALIANS LOVE SPOON DESSERTS** (exactly what it sounds like, desserts meant to be eaten with a spoon). Where we in the U.S. might think of spoonable treats as a little simple and child-friendly—like ice cream, pudding, and Jell-O—the Italians approach them with a sophisticated flair. Every trattoria dessert menu seems to be formed around desserts that are cool, refreshing, and very spoonable. Give your fork the night off!

*Clockwise from bottom left:*
**Zabaglione Gelato** (page 234),
**Pistachio Granita** (page 236),
**Fior di Latte Gelato** (page 233),
**Almond Granita** (page 236),
**Amarena Gelato** (page 234),
**Cioccolato Nero Gelato** (center, page 235),
**Lemon Rosemary Granita** (page 237),
and **Blackberry Sage Granita** (page 237)

# GELATO FOUR WAYS

**EACH MAKES 2 PINTS**

*I was five years old on my first visit to my parents' village in Sicily. My cousin Rosalba joined me for play dates and strolls in the park, an early evening tradition in Italy. There was a little gelateria near the park and the night I had my first scoop was the moment I reached nirvana. The creamy, nuanced richness was so different from the basic flavors available in American grocery stores at the time (this was before brands like Ben & Jerry's took hold). Over the years I have probably tried every flavor in every shop here, there, and everywhere. So when it came time to pick a gelato recipe for the book, I couldn't land on just one because there are so many to choose from. So I'm giving you four. The gold standard of any gelato shop is their fior di latte (literally "flower of milk"), as there is no other flavor besides milk and cream. So in making this one, go for the highest quality milk and cream you can—it's simple, but sublime. Zabaglione, a Marsala-infused custard, isn't always the easiest flavor to find (it's a little old-fashioned, a little nonno, like a rum raisin might be in the U.S.), but it's always been one of my favorites. Amarena cherries are a perfect burst of flavor studded throughout a vanilla base. And the cioccolato nero version uses black cocoa, for a deep color and a slight bitterness offset with chopped shards of milk chocolate.*

**NOTE**

The gelato can be stored in an airtight container in the freezer for up to 2 weeks.

**SPECIAL EQUIPMENT**

Ice cream maker

## FIOR DI LATTE GELATO

| | | |
|---|---|---|
| Granulated sugar | 200 grams | 1 cup |
| Cornstarch | 18 grams | 2 tablespoons |
| Fine sea salt | 1 gram | ¼ teaspoon |
| Whole milk | 455 grams | 2 cups |
| Heavy cream | 230 grams | 1 cup |

In a large bowl, combine the sugar, cornstarch, and salt. Whisk until combined. In a large saucepan fitted with a thermometer, combine the milk and cream. Set over low heat, stirring often so the bottom doesn't scorch, until the mixture reaches 170°F (76°C). Slowly pour the warm milk mixture into the sugar and cornstarch mixture, whisking constantly, until the sugar is dissolved.

Pour the mixture back into the saucepan and set over low heat. Cook, stirring constantly, until the mixture reaches 185°F (85°C) and is nicely thick. Pour the mixture through a fine-mesh sieve into a clean large bowl, cover with a kitchen towel, and let cool to room temperature, about 1 hour.

Cover tightly with plastic wrap and refrigerate until very cold, at least 4 hours or up to 24 hours.

Pour the mixture through a fine-mesh sieve into the frozen bowl of an ice cream maker. Churn according to the manufacturer's instructions. Transfer the gelato to two 1-pint containers or a 1-quart container and freeze for at least 2 hours before serving.  ▶ ▶ ▶

## ZABAGLIONE GELATO

| | | |
|---|---|---|
| Granulated sugar | 200 grams | 1 cup |
| Large egg yolks | 4 | |
| Marsala | 40 grams | 3 tablespoons |
| Fine sea salt | 1 gram | ¼ teaspoon |
| Whole milk | 455 grams | 2 cups |
| Heavy cream | 230 grams | 1 cup |

In a large bowl, combine the sugar and egg yolks. Whisk until combined. Whisk in the Marsala and salt. In a large saucepan fitted with a thermometer, combine the milk and cream. Set over low heat, stirring often so the bottom doesn't scorch, until the mixture reaches 170°F (76°C). Slowly pour the warm milk mixture into the egg mixture, whisking constantly, until the sugar is dissolved.

Pour the mixture back into the saucepan and set over low heat. Cook, stirring constantly, until the mixture reaches 185°F (85°C) and is nicely thick. Pour the mixture through a fine-mesh sieve into a clean large bowl, cover with a kitchen towel, and let cool to room temperature, about 1 hour.

Cover tightly with plastic wrap and refrigerate until very cold, at least 4 hours or up to 24 hours.

Pour the mixture through a fine-mesh sieve into the frozen bowl of an ice cream maker. Churn according to the manufacturer's instructions. Transfer the gelato to two 1-pint containers or a 1-quart container and freeze for at least 2 hours before serving.

## AMARENA GELATO

| | | |
|---|---|---|
| Granulated sugar | 200 grams | 1 cup |
| Large egg yolks | 4 | |
| Pure vanilla extract | 45 grams | 3 tablespoons |
| Fine sea salt | 1 gram | ¼ teaspoon |
| Whole milk | 455 grams | 2 cups |
| Heavy cream | 230 grams | 1 cup |
| Amarena cherries, drained | 230 grams | 8 ounces |

In a large bowl, combine the sugar and egg yolks. Whisk until combined. Whisk in the vanilla and salt. In a large saucepan fitted with a thermometer, combine the milk and cream. Set over low heat, stirring often so the bottom doesn't scorch, until the mixture reaches 170°F (76°C). Slowly pour the warm milk mixture into the egg mixture, whisking constantly, until the sugar is dissolved.

Pour the mixture back into the saucepan and set over low heat. Cook, stirring constantly, until the mixture reaches 185°F (85°C) and is nicely thick. Pour the mixture through a fine-mesh sieve into a clean large bowl, cover with a kitchen towel, and let cool to room temperature, about 1 hour.

Cover tightly with plastic wrap and refrigerate until very cold, at least 4 hours or up to 24 hours.

Pour the mixture through a fine-mesh sieve into the frozen bowl of an ice cream maker. Churn according to the manufacturer's instructions. When the gelato is ready, add the cherries and churn until just combined, about 1 minute. Transfer the gelato to two 1-pint containers or a 1-quart container and freeze for at least 2 hours before serving.

# CIOCCOLATO NERO GELATO

| | | |
|---|---|---|
| Granulated sugar | 200 grams | 1 cup |
| Black cocoa powder | 25 grams | ¼ cup |
| Large egg yolks | 4 | |
| Fine sea salt | 1 gram | ¼ teaspoon |
| Whole milk | 455 grams | 2 cups |
| Heavy cream | 230 grams | 1 cup |
| Milk chocolate, preferably Valrhona Azélia, chopped | 115 grams | 4 ounces |

In a large bowl, combine the sugar and cocoa powder. Whisk until combined. Whisk in the egg yolks and salt. In a large saucepan fitted with a thermometer, combine the milk and cream. Set over low heat, stirring often so the bottom doesn't scorch, until the mixture reaches 170°F (76°C). Slowly pour the warm milk mixture into the egg mixture, whisking constantly, until the sugar is dissolved.

Pour the mixture back into the saucepan and set over low heat. Cook, stirring constantly, until the mixture reaches 185°F (85°C) and is nicely thick. Pour the mixture through a fine-mesh sieve into a clean large bowl, cover with a kitchen towel, and let cool to room temperature, about 1 hour.

Cover tightly with plastic wrap and refrigerate until very cold, at least 4 hours or up to 24 hours.

Pour the mixture through a fine-mesh sieve into the frozen bowl of an ice cream maker. Churn according to the manufacturer's instructions. When the gelato is ready, add the chopped milk chocolate and churn until just combined, about 1 minute. Transfer the gelato to two 1-pint containers or a 1-quart container and freeze for at least 2 hours before serving.

# GRANITA FOUR WAYS

**EACH MAKES 2 QUARTS**

*The Sicilian sun is ablaze in the summer months—most months, really—so starting your day with a fresh brioche bun and a flavored granita, meant to be spooned in icy piles over the bread, isn't so much idyllic as it is necessary. Sicilians have been serving this for centuries, originally with snow collected from the island's mountains, lightly flavored with citrus and honey. Once ice on demand became possible, the offerings boomed. My granita of choice is almond—nutty, sweet, and filling—but I've also included a rich and creamy pistachio, blackberry accented with warm sage, and lemon with just enough woodsy rosemary. Whether enjoying for dessert or dessert-for-breakfast—with a fresh brioche (see Brioche con Tuppo, page 19)—you'll be transported to a warm Sicilian vacation.*

**NOTE**

The granita can be stored in an airtight container in the freezer for up to 1 week.

## ALMOND GRANITA

| | | |
|---|---|---|
| Whole milk | 340 grams | 1½ cups |
| Almond paste | 130 grams | 4½ ounces |
| Granulated sugar | 100 grams | ½ cup |
| Slivered almonds | 55 grams | ½ cup |
| Almond extract | 5 grams | 1 teaspoon |

In a blender, combine the milk, almond paste, sugar, slivered almonds, almond extract, and 225 grams (1 cup) water. Blend on high until smooth. Set a fine-mesh sieve over an 8 by 8-inch (20 by 20 cm) baking pan and pour the mixture through. Press on the solids with a rubber spatula to release any remaining liquid, then discard the solids.

Press plastic wrap on the surface of the mixture and freeze until icy, about 2 hours.

Use a fork to scrape into a loose mixture, then freeze for another 2 hours before scraping again. Repeat the process one more time to create a granita with small icy pieces. Keep frozen until ready to serve.

## PISTACHIO GRANITA

| | | |
|---|---|---|
| Whole milk | 340 grams | 1½ cups |
| Pistachio paste or pistachio cream | 155 grams | 5½ ounces |
| Granulated sugar | 100 grams | ½ cup |
| Unsalted pistachios | 70 grams | ½ cup |
| Pistachio extract or almond extract | 5 grams | 1 teaspoon |

In a blender, combine the milk, pistachio paste, sugar, pistachios, pistachio extract, and 225 grams (1 cup) water. Blend on high until smooth. Set a fine-mesh sieve over an 8 by 8-inch (20 by 20 cm) baking pan and pour the mixture through. Press on the solids with a rubber spatula to release any remaining liquid, then discard the solids.

Press plastic wrap on the surface of the mixture and freeze until icy, about 2 hours.

Use a fork to scrape into a loose mixture, then freeze for another 2 hours before scraping again. Repeat the process one more time to create a granita with small icy pieces. Keep frozen until ready to serve.

## BLACKBERRY SAGE GRANITA

| | | |
|---|---|---|
| Blackberries | 340 grams | 12 ounces |
| Granulated sugar | 100 grams | ½ cup |
| Fresh sage leaves | 4 grams | ¼ cup |

NOTE

If you are lucky enough to find mulberries (the arid cousin to the blackberry and the version of granita you'll find all over Sicily), use them instead!

In a blender, combine the blackberries, sugar, sage, and 340 grams (1½ cups) water. Blend on high until smooth. Set a fine-mesh sieve over an 8 by 8-inch (20 by 20 cm) baking pan and pour the mixture through. Press on the solids with a rubber spatula to release any remaining liquid, then discard the solids.

Press plastic wrap on the surface of the mixture and freeze until icy, about 2 hours.

Use a fork to scrape into a loose mixture, then freeze for another 2 hours before scraping again. Repeat the process one more time to create a granita with small icy pieces. Keep frozen until ready to serve.

## LEMON ROSEMARY GRANITA

| | | |
|---|---|---|
| Granulated sugar | 200 grams | 1 cup |
| Fresh rosemary leaves | 2 grams | 2 tablespoons |
| Strips of zest from 1 lemon | | |
| Fresh lemon juice (from 5 to 6 lemons) | 240 grams | 1 cup |

In a small saucepan, bring the sugar and 225 grams (1 cup) water to a boil over medium heat until the sugar is completely dissolved. Add the rosemary and lemon zest strips and let the mixture steep until cooled to room temperature, about 1 hour.

Stir in the lemon juice. Set a fine-mesh sieve over an 8 by 8-inch (20 by 20 cm) baking pan and pour the mixture through. Press on the solids with a rubber spatula to release any remaining liquid, then discard the solids.

Press plastic wrap on the surface of the mixture and freeze until icy, about 2 hours.

Use a fork to scrape into a loose mixture, then freeze for another 2 hours before scraping again. Repeat the process one more time to create a granita with small icy pieces. Keep frozen until ready to serve.

# PEACHES AND CREAM SEMIFREDDO

MAKES ONE 9-INCH (23 CM) SEMIFREDDO

*Biting into a ripe summer peach can be transportive, and I don't just feel that way because of* Call Me by Your Name. *Peach season in Italy means every gelateria and granita cart will be pushing sweet pesca treats, and this peaches and cream semifreddo is my ode to that time of year. Here, peaches are cooked down to release their sweetness and folded into a custardy, creamy base. Semifreddo, as its name literally means, is only half-frozen, to something like the texture of an ice cream cake. It's cool and refreshing, especially topped with even more peaches for the best kind of seasonal celebration.*

### FOR THE SEMIFREDDO

| | | |
|---|---|---|
| Diced peaches (4 to 5 peaches) | 300 grams | 3½ cups |
| Granulated sugar | 65 grams, plus 100 grams | 5 tablespoons, plus ½ cup |
| Fresh lemon juice | 5 grams | 1 teaspoon |
| Large eggs | 2 | |
| Large egg yolks | 3 | |
| Heavy cream, cold | 345 grams | 1½ cups |
| Elderflower syrup (optional) | 12 grams | 2 tablespoons |

### FOR THE TOPPING

| | | |
|---|---|---|
| Sliced peaches (1 to 2 peaches) | 85 grams | ½ cup |
| Granulated sugar | 25 grams | 2 tablespoons |
| Fresh lemon juice | 5 grams | 1 teaspoon |

**Make the semifreddo** ▶ Line a 9 by 5-inch (23 by 13 cm) loaf pan with plastic wrap, leaving about 3 inches (8 cm) of overhang on all sides. Set in the freezer to chill.

In a medium saucepan, combine the peaches, 65 grams (5 tablespoons) of the sugar, and the lemon juice. Cook over medium-low heat, stirring often, until the sugar dissolves and the mixture starts to bubble. Continue to cook, stirring occasionally, until the peaches release their juices and the mixture begins to thicken, about 10 minutes. Transfer to a medium bowl to cool for 30 minutes. Cover with plastic wrap and refrigerate for 2 hours until chilled.

Fill a medium saucepan with 2 inches (5 cm) of water and bring to a simmer over medium heat. Set a heatproof medium bowl over the saucepan, making sure the bowl doesn't touch the water. Add the eggs and egg yolks and remaining sugar and whisk constantly until the mixture is pale and thick, 5 to 8 minutes. It should fall off the whisk in slow ribbons and suspend on the surface for a few seconds. Remove the bowl from the saucepan and set aside to cool for 30 minutes. Cover with plastic wrap and refrigerate for 1 hour until chilled.

When the yolk mixture is fully chilled, in a stand mixer fitted with the whisk, beat the heavy cream and elderflower syrup (if using) over medium speed until stiff peaks form, about 5 minutes. Fold the whipped cream into the yolk ▶▶▶

mixture in three parts, until no streaks remain. Add one-third of the cooled peaches and fold to combine.

Transfer the mixture into the frozen loaf pan, then spoon the remaining peach mixture over the top. Cover with the plastic overhang, pressing onto the surface of the peaches. Freeze for 4 hours or overnight.

**While the semifreddo is freezing, make the topping** ▶ In a small saucepan, combine the peaches, sugar, and lemon juice. Set over low heat, stirring constantly, until the sugar dissolves and starts to bubble, about 2 minutes. Transfer to a small bowl to cool for 30 minutes, then cover with plastic wrap and refrigerate for at least 2 hours or until the semifreddo is ready.

Uncover the semifreddo and invert onto a serving plate. Discard the plastic wrap. Spoon the chilled peach topping over the semifreddo before serving.

The semifreddo can be wrapped in plastic and stored in the freezer for up to 1 week.

# CREMA DI CAFFÈ

SERVES 4

*Crema di caffè didn't hit my radar until a recent trip to Italy. I was at an over-sized supermarket in Tuscany, buying some ingredients for dinner when I decided an espresso was in order. Fortunately, there was a coffee bar inside the supermarket—this is Italy, after all—and I noticed one of those frozen beverage machines filled with a thick, tan liquid. It was dispensed into a small espresso cup with a quick shaving of chocolate on top and a demitasse spoon on the side. And it was perfect. Creamy, light, a little sweet, and a total joy.*

| | | |
|---|---|---|
| Heavy cream, cold | 240 grams | 1 cup plus 2 tablespoons |
| Espresso powder | 6 grams | 1 tablespoon |
| Powdered sugar | 40 grams | ⅓ cup |
| Dark chocolate bar, at room temperature, for serving | | |

In a small bowl, combine 10 grams (2 tablespoons) of the heavy cream and the espresso powder. Microwave on high for 30 seconds. Transfer to the refrigerator to cool completely, about 15 minutes.

In a large bowl, using a handheld mixer, beat the remaining heavy cream and sugar to soft peaks. With the mixer running, slowly pour in the espresso mixture and continue mixing to slightly firmer peaks that droop over easily.

Divide the mixture among four demitasse glasses or small bowls.

Use a vegetable peeler to shave curls from the dark chocolate bar. Shave along the edge for small curls or along the flat surface for wider curls. Garnish the cream with the chocolate curls before serving.

Crema di caffè should be enjoyed immediately.

# MALTED TIRAMISÙ

**MAKES ONE 9 BY 13-INCH (23 BY 33 CM) TIRAMISÙ**

*The kitchen was my mom's domain, and her domain alone. Because I was the youngest of three, she was a bit worn down by the time I came into the picture, so I was allowed to hang around as a quiet spectator and, every now and then, invited to participate. One of the first desserts I ever made with her was a tiramisù. I remember dipping the savoiardi into espresso and whipping eggs into mascarpone. I also remember eating at least half of it by the next morning. I've made many iterations of the classic, but this one, shot through with malted milk powder, is a real riff on both Italian and American culture. The nutty, toasty flavor of malt plays so well with espresso, somehow boosting everything around it. Topping it with crushed Whoppers is maybe a little extra, but if you ask me, it's absolutely necessary.*

| | | |
|---|---|---|
| Brewed espresso (or 340 grams/1½ cups boiling water plus 3 grams/2 teaspoons instant espresso powder) | 340 grams | 1½ cups |
| Granulated sugar | 40 grams, plus 100 grams | 3 tablespoons, plus ½ cup |
| Malted milk powder | 105 grams | ¾ cup |
| Rum | 30 grams | 2 tablespoons |
| Large eggs, separated | 5 | |
| Mascarpone | 455 grams | 2 cups |
| Pure vanilla extract | 5 grams | 1 teaspoon |
| Fine sea salt | 1 gram | ¼ teaspoon |
| Savoiardi (page 280) or store-bought ladyfingers (see Note) | 48 | |
| Cocoa powder, for dusting | | |
| Malted milk balls, such as Whoppers, lightly crushed, for garnish | 70 grams | ½ cup |

**NOTE**

If you aren't in the mood to make your own savoiardi (what kind of animal are you?!), you can run to the grocery store and grab a couple packs of ladyfingers. You'll need two 7-ounce (200-gram) packages.

In a large shallow bowl, whisk the espresso and 40 grams (3 tablespoons) of the sugar until the sugar is dissolved. Add 35 grams (¼ cup) of the malted milk powder and the rum and whisk until dissolved.

In a stand mixer fitted with the whisk, combine the egg yolks, remaining sugar, and remaining malted milk powder. Beat on high speed until the mixture thickens and turns pale, about 5 minutes. Switch to the paddle and add the mascarpone, vanilla, and salt. Beat on medium speed until the mixture is combined. Transfer to a large bowl.

Clean and dry the mixer bowl and whisk. Return to the stand mixer and beat the egg whites on medium-high speed until stiff peaks form, 3 to 5 minutes. Gently fold the egg whites into the mascarpone mixture in two parts, folding until just incorporated.

Dip the savoiardi into the coffee mixture until saturated, 1 to 2 seconds on each side. Arrange a single layer of them in a 9 by 13-inch (23 by 33 cm) baking pan. Top with one-third of the mascarpone mixture, spreading it toward the edge in an even layer. Repeat this step two more times until you have used up all the cookies and cream. ▶ ▶ ▶

Top the tiramisù with a dusting of cocoa powder, then cover loosely with plastic wrap and refrigerate for at least 4 hours or overnight. The longer it rests, the better the flavors will be.

When ready to serve, top the tiramisù with the malt balls.

The tiramisù can be wrapped with plastic and stored in the refrigerator for up to 3 days.

Palermo, Sicily, Italy

# BUDINO BIONDO

MAKES 6 BUDINOS

*Blonde chocolate is just white chocolate in disguise, slightly caramelized to give it a golden color and a toasted flavor, and easily found online or in specialty baking shops. The budino, Italy's answer to the pudding cup, is the perfect vessel for the rich flavor of this specialty chocolate, and adding a little hit of Grand Marnier gives a boozy citrus note that cuts through the richness. If you'd prefer a stronger chocolate version, simply use a mixture of dark and milk chocolate and add 5 grams (1 tablespoon) of cocoa powder to the egg mixture.*

| | | |
|---|---|---|
| Blonde chocolate, preferably Valrhona's Dulcey, chopped | 225 grams | 8 ounces |
| Unsalted butter, at room temperature | 15 grams | 1 tablespoon |
| Large egg yolks | 6 | |
| Granulated sugar | 50 grams | ¼ cup |
| Heavy cream | 460 grams | 2 cups |
| Fine sea salt | 1 gram | ¼ teaspoon |
| Grand Marnier (optional) | 15 grams | 1 tablespoon |
| Basic Whipped Cream (page 271), for serving | | |

In a large heatproof bowl, combine the chocolate and butter. In a medium saucepan, whisk together the egg yolks, sugar, heavy cream, and salt. Set over low heat and use a wooden spoon to stir constantly until the mixture thickens and coats the back of the spoon, 6 to 8 minutes. Remove from the heat and stir in the Grand Marnier (if using).

Set a fine-mesh sieve over the bowl with the chocolate and pour the custard through. Let the custard melt the chocolate for about 2 minutes before stirring vigorously until the butter and chocolate are incorporated.

Portion the mixture into six 8-ounce glasses. Press plastic wrap directly on the surface of each pudding and refrigerate for at least 2 hours, until chilled.

Top with a scoop of whipped cream before serving.

The budino can be wrapped in plastic and stored in the refrigerator for up to 4 days.

# STRAWBERRY PANNA COTTA

MAKES 4 PANNA COTTA

*Nigella Lawson said it best: Panna cotta should have the quiver of a seventeenth-century courtesan's inner thigh. Panna cotta, literally "cooked cream," is a softly set pudding and a wonderfully blank canvas for any number of flavors mixed in or served on top. This one takes things in a daring direction with a beautiful presentation that is surprisingly easy to execute. But if you want to keep things simple, feel free to pour the panna cotta into small bowls or ramekins to set and finish with warm melted chocolate, gooey caramel, or a spoonful of stewed fruit.*

### FOR THE PANNA COTTA

| | | |
|---|---|---|
| Unflavored gelatin | 5 grams | 2 teaspoons |
| Whole milk | 225 grams | 1 cup |
| Heavy cream | 230 grams | 1 cup |
| Granulated sugar | 50 grams | ¼ cup |
| Vanilla bean paste or | 12 grams | 2 teaspoons |
| pure vanilla extract | 10 grams | 2 teaspoons |

### FOR THE STRAWBERRIES

| | | |
|---|---|---|
| Unflavored gelatin | 5 grams | 2 teaspoons |
| Seedless strawberry jam | 255 grams | 1 cup |
| Sliced strawberries | 170 grams | 1 cup |

**Make the panna cotta ▶** In a muffin tin, set four 8-ounce serving glasses at a 45-degree angle. Stuff the muffin tin with paper towels if needed to hold the glasses in place.

Pour 55 grams (¼ cup) water into a small saucepan and sprinkle the gelatin over the water. Let sit for 2 minutes until the gelatin is hydrated, then bring to a gentle simmer over low heat, whisking to dissolve the gelatin. Remove from the heat as soon as the gelatin is dissolved.

In a medium saucepan, combine the milk, heavy cream, and sugar. Bring to a boil over medium-high heat, whisking constantly so the bottom doesn't scorch. Remove from the heat and whisk in the gelatin mixture and vanilla bean paste.

Pour the mixture into a 3- to 4-cup measuring cup with a pour spout (or use a ladle with a pour spout) and evenly divide the mixture among the four glasses. The mixture should fill half of the glass at a perfect diagonal, almost to the rim. Leaving the glasses where they are, cover each glass with a small square of plastic wrap and transfer the muffin tin to the refrigerator for at least 4 hours or overnight, until the panna cotta is firm.

**Once the panna cotta is firm, prepare the strawberries ▶** Pour 115 grams (½ cup) water into a medium saucepan and sprinkle the gelatin over the water. Let sit for 2 minutes until the gelatin is hydrated, then bring to a gentle simmer over low heat, whisking to dissolve the gelatin. Remove from the heat as soon as the gelatin is dissolved and whisk in the strawberry jam.  ▶ ▶ ▶

Fill a large bowl with plenty of ice, then set a medium bowl in the center. Pour the strawberry mixture into the bowl and chill, stirring often, until it's starting to thicken to a soft gel-like texture, 20 to 30 minutes. Stir in the sliced strawberries.

Remove the panna cotta glasses from the refrigerator and set upright. Pour the strawberry mixture evenly among the glasses, filling in the other half of the glass. Cover again with plastic wrap and refrigerate for at least 2 hours, until set.

The panna cotta can be wrapped in plastic and stored in the refrigerator for up to 2 days.

# ZUPPA INGLESE WITH BLACKBERRIES

**SERVES 4**

*Zuppa inglese, or "English soup," is a traditional dessert from Emilia-Romagna, served in restaurants or made at home for special occasions. Its origins are unclear, but the obvious guess is that it's a riff on the English trifle. The bulk of the effort goes into making a very simple vanilla cream, thickened with egg yolks and a little cornstarch to a pudding-like consistency. Traditionally, sponge cake is used for the layering, but I enjoy the lighter simplicity of ladyfingers soaked in spice-heavy amaro with sweet blackberries to accent. It's a refreshing dessert, especially during the height of summer when berries are at their most plump.*

### FOR THE BERRIES

| | | |
|---|---|---|
| Blackberries | 170 grams | 6 ounces |
| Granulated sugar | 15 grams | 1 tablespoon |

### FOR THE AMARO SIMPLE SYRUP

| | | |
|---|---|---|
| Amaro, such as Faccia Brutto or Amaro Nonino | 65 grams | ¼ cup |
| Granulated sugar | 30 grams | 2 tablespoons |

### FOR THE ZUPPA

| | | |
|---|---|---|
| Granulated sugar | 100 grams | ½ cup |
| Cornstarch | 18 grams | 2 tablespoons |
| Large egg yolks | 4 | |
| Whole milk | 460 grams | 2 cups |
| Heavy cream | 115 grams | ½ cup |
| Pure vanilla extract | 15 grams | 1 tablespoon |
| Pinch of fine sea salt | | |
| Savoiardi (page 280) or store-bought ladyfingers | 8 | |

**Make the berries ▶** In a medium bowl, combine the blackberries and sugar and use a wooden spoon to lightly mash. Set aside to macerate.

**Make the amaro simple syrup ▶** In a small saucepan, combine the amaro, sugar, and 65 grams (¼ cup) water. Stir and set over medium-high heat. Bring to a boil until the sugar dissolves. Transfer to a small, shallow bowl and set aside to cool.

**Make the zuppa ▶** In a medium bowl, whisk together the sugar and cornstarch. Whisk in the egg yolks until combined.

In a medium saucepan, combine the heavy cream and milk. Set over low heat and stir constantly until the mixture comes to a simmer. Slowly pour a little of the hot milk into the egg mixture, whisking constantly. Continue whisking and adding the milk a little at a time until the mixture is combined and smooth. Add the vanilla and salt, and return the warmed mixture to the same saucepan over low heat, whisking constantly, until the mixture comes to a boil and begins to thicken, 2 to 3 minutes. Set a fine mesh sieve over a clean medium bowl and pour the zuppa through, using a silicone spatula to help it pass through. Press plastic wrap directly onto the surface of the cream. Let cool for 30 minutes and then refrigerate for 1 hour, until completely cooled.

**Assemble the zuppa** ▶ Arrange four 12-ounce (355 ml) serving glasses on a work surface. Dip a savoiardi in the amaro syrup, turning to coat on both sides, until saturated, about 1 to 2 seconds per side. Break in half and set on the bottom of a serving glass. Spoon about 85 grams (a rounded ¼ cup) of the zuppa into the glass, then add about 45 grams (a rounded ¼ cup) of the macerated berries. Dip another savoiardi in the amaro before breaking in half and setting on top of the berries. Finish with another 85 grams (rounded ¼ cup) of zuppa. Repeat the process in three more glasses to build three more servings.

    Serve immediately or cover with plastic wrap and refrigerate for up to 2 hours. Assembled zuppa should be enjoyed on the same day. The unassembled custard and berries can be covered in plastic and stored in the refrigerator for up to 2 days.

# BIANCOMANGIARE

SERVES 8

Biancomangiare is the unofficial dessert of the EU—almost every country in Western Europe has some variation on it, like the French blanc-manger or Spanish manjar blanco. It was likely introduced to Europe by Arab traders in the early medieval period and was originally used as a vessel for meat or fish, not unlike those nightmarish 1950s savory Jell-O molds here in the U.S. But by the Baroque period, everyone came to their senses and started serving it as a sweet dessert. This version is lightly flavored with a dash of cinnamon, and a drizzle of honey, so it's worth investing in quality dairy. This can be made in individual molds, which I find really charming in its presentation, but any decorative mold, mini cake pan, or small ramekin will do—or even one large Jell-O mold, just give it additional time to set.

| | | |
|---|---|---|
| Cornstarch | 65 grams | 6 tablespoons |
| Granulated sugar | 150 grams | ¾ cup |
| Whole milk | 480 grams | 2 cups |
| Heavy cream | 460 grams | 2 cups |
| Cinnamon stick | 1 | |
| Wildflower honey, for serving | | |

Coat 8 decorative 120 gram (4- to 5-ounce) molds, mini cake pans, or small ramekins with cooking spray.

In a large saucepan, whisk the cornstarch and sugar. Slowly add milk and whisk to dissolve the cornstarch so there are no lumps. Whisk in the heavy cream and add the cinnamon stick. Set the saucepan over low heat. Whisk constantly, until the mixture just begins to thicken to the point where the whisk leaves streaks behind and the mixture just begins to bubble, about 10 to 15 minutes. Remove the cinnamon stick and immediately remove from the heat.

Pour the mixture into the prepared molds and let cool for 10 minutes. Cover with plastic wrap and refrigerate for at least 4 hours, until fully firm, or up to 24 hours.

To serve, flip the molds to release the biancomangiare. Lightly drizzle each one with honey before serving.

The biancomangiare can be stored in an airtight container in the refrigerator for up to 2 days.

San Gimignano, Tuscany, Italy

# PANETTONE BREAD PUDDING

*Growing up, panettone was a once-a-year event, sliced and served with Prosecco on New Year's Eve. My mom was never one for leftovers, half-eaten anything had no place in our home, so by the next morning any stray panettone was in the trash. When I got older and was living on my own (where leftovers were all that were keeping me alive at times), I came to understand the versatility of left-over bread, especially the sweet afterlife of panettone. Now at Christmastime I purposely buy a second loaf, just to have an excuse to make this bread pudding. Saturated with a rich, eggy custard, shot through with cream and Amaretto, and sliced almonds for a little crunch, there is no better version of bread pudding than this one right here.*

| | | |
|---|---|---|
| 1 loaf panettone, fresh or stale, cut into 1-inch (2.5 cm) cubes | 455 grams | 1 pound |
| Large eggs | 4 | |
| Large egg yolks | 4 | |
| Granulated sugar | 200 grams | 1 cup |
| Heavy cream | 460 grams | 2 cups |
| Whole milk | 455 grams | 2 cups |
| Amaretto | 55 grams | ¼ cup |
| Skin-on sliced almonds | 30 grams | ⅓ cup |
| Basic Whipped Cream (page 271), for serving | | |

Preheat the oven to 350°F (180°C) and set a rack in the center. Coat a 9 by 13-inch (23 by 33 cm) baking dish with cooking spray.

Arrange the panettone cubes in a single layer on a baking sheet. Bake until lightly browned, about 10 minutes. Leave the oven on.

In a large bowl, combine the whole eggs, yolks, and sugar and whisk until combined. Whisk in the heavy cream, milk, and Amaretto. Transfer the toasted panettone cubes to the prepared baking dish and pour the custard over the top. Let sit at room temperature for 15 minutes to allow the bread to saturate.

Sprinkle the sliced almonds over the top and bake until the custard is set and the bread pudding is puffy, about 45 minutes. Cool in the baking dish for about 10 minutes before serving generous scoops topped with whipped cream.

The baked bread pudding can be covered with foil and stored in the refrigerator for up to 3 days.

# DELIZIA AL LIMONE E BASILICO

SERVES 10

Delizia al limone ("lemon delight") is ubiquitous along the Amalfi Coast, where the domed curd-filled cakes are made using prized Amalfi lemons. And this dessert really is a love poem to lemons. Since Amalfi lemons are almost impossible to find in the U.S., use the best lemons you can find (Meyer lemons would make a great substitute). Because every part of the lemon features prominently in the dessert, it's worth buying ones that are organically grown. Traditionally, the dessert is a lemon explosion, but I find another classically Italian ingredient, basil, acts as a perfect partner. Its herby freshness pairs so well with lemon as a background flavor that enhances everything. This is a dessert that transports me to the Italian coast, every time. ▶ ▶ ▶

### FOR THE CURD

| | | |
|---|---|---|
| Unflavored gelatin | 7 grams | 1 tablespoon |
| Granulated sugar | 140 grams | ¾ cup |
| Lemon juice | 115 grams | ½ cup |
| Zest from 1 lemon | | |
| Sprig of basil | 1 | |
| Large egg yolks | 8 | |
| Unsalted butter | 140 grams | 6 tablespoons |
| Limoncello | 30 grams | 2 tablespoons |
| Fine sea salt | 2 grams | ¼ teaspoon |

### FOR THE CAKE

| | | |
|---|---|---|
| Cake flour | 335 grams | 2¼ cups |
| Baking powder | 5 grams | 1 teaspoon |
| Fine sea salt | 4 grams | 1 teaspoon |
| Large eggs, separated | 8 | |
| Granulated sugar | 250 grams | 1¼ cups |
| Pure vanilla extract | 5 grams | 1 teaspoon |
| Grated lemon zest | 6 grams | 1 tablespoon |
| Unsalted butter, melted and cooled | 115 grams | 8 tablespoons |
| Cream of tartar | 1 gram | ¼ teaspoon |

### FOR THE SYRUP

| | | |
|---|---|---|
| Granulated sugar | 100 grams | ½ cup |
| Limoncello | 150 grams | ⅔ cup |
| Strips of zest from 1 lemon | | |
| Sprig basil, with stem | 1 | |

### FOR ASSEMBLY

Basic Whipped Cream (page 271)
Heavy cream, as needed
Baby basil leaves

### SPECIAL EQUIPMENT

Ten 3-inch (8 cm) hemisphere silicone molds

**Make the curd** ▶ In a small bowl, bloom the gelatin in 115 grams (½ cup) cold water. In a medium pot over medium heat, whisk together the sugar, lemon juice, lemon zest, basil, and egg yolks. Continue whisking until the mixture reaches 180°F (80°C) on a thermometer. Remove from the heat, and whisk in the butter, limoncello, salt, and gelatin mixture.

Strain the curd into a medium bowl through a fine mesh strainer. Cover with plastic wrap, making sure the plastic makes contact with the surface of the curd to prevent a skin forming. Let cool for 30 minutes and then transfer to the refrigerator for 1 hour to cool completely.

**Make the cake** ▶ Preheat the oven to 350°F (180°C) and set a rack in the center. Set the dome molds on a baking sheet and coat with nonstick spray.

In a medium bowl, sift the cake flour, baking powder, and salt. In a stand mixer fitted with the whisk, beat the egg yolks and sugar on medium speed until very pale, fluffy, and doubled in volume, 5 to 8 minutes. Add the vanilla, lemon zest, and melted butter and whisk on low to combine. Transfer the mixture to a large bowl and fold in the flour mixture until almost combined, with a few streaks of flour remaining.

Wash and dry the mixer bowl and whisk and return to the stand mixer. Beat the egg whites on medium speed until frothy, about 2 minutes. Add the cream of tartar and beat on high to form stiff peaks, 3 to 4 minutes. Scoop half of the egg whites into the batter and fold to combine until you can barely see any white streaks. Fold in the remaining egg whites until the batter is very light.

Transfer the batter to a large piping bag fitted with a large round tip. Pipe the batter into the prepared molds, almost to the top, then smooth the tops if needed. Bake until golden brown and a cake tester comes out clean, 18 to 20 minutes, rotating halfway through. Let the cakes cool completely in the molds, about 1 hour.

**Meanwhile, make the syrup** ▶ In a small saucepan, combine the sugar, limoncello, lemon zest, basil, and 115 grams (½ cup) water. Bring the mixture to a boil over medium heat until the sugar dissolves. Remove from the heat and let cool completely, about 1 hour. Once cooled, discard the lemon zest and basil.

**Assemble the delizia** ▶ When ready to assemble, remove the curd from the refrigerator and whisk until smooth and fluid. Separate about 60 grams (½ cup) of whipped cream and fold it into the curd until incorporated and no streaks are visible. Reserve the rest of the whipped cream for serving the cakes. Transfer the curd to a large piping bag with a round tip.

Set a wire rack in a baking sheet. Remove the cakes from the molds and place them dome-side down on the rack. Working with one of the cakes at a time, use a serrated knife to trim off the bottom to create an even surface. Then use a paring knife to cut a 1½-inch (4 cm) cavity in the center of the dome, going about 1 inch (2.5 cm) deep and reserving about ½ inch (1 cm) of the very bottom of the removed cake (these will be used to seal up the cakes after filling). Repeat with the remaining cakes.

Using a pastry brush or a squeeze bottle, douse each of the cakes generously with the syrup until saturated. Pipe each cavity with enough curd to fill, then press on the reserved cake base to seal the bottom. Turn the cakes dome-side up, brush the domes with more syrup and transfer the entire baking sheet to the freezer to chill for 30 minutes.

While the cakes are chilling, transfer the leftover curd filling from the piping bag to a large bowl and add heavy cream, 1 tablespoon at a time, and whisk until the lemon cream has achieved a thick but easily pourable consistency.

Remove the cakes from the freezer and carefully pour the lemon cream over each dome, making sure to cover each one completely, and letting the excess cream fall onto the baking sheet. Once each cake is covered, return the baking sheet to the refrigerator to set for 1 hour.

For each serving, place a cake on a plate, add a dollop of whipped cream to the top of the dome, and add a baby basil leaf for garnish.

The delizia can be stored in an airtight container in the refrigerator for up to 3 days.

# TARTUFO

**SERVES 4 TO 6**

*Italians take the tartufo—what we know as the savory truffle—very, very seriously. They are worth their weight in gold, and in the fall and winter months, truffle foraging in the northern regions becomes a sport, with trained dogs, and even pigs, sniffing out the underground fungi. The tartufo is also a popular Italian dessert, but luckily the two only share a name, not a flavor profile. Its rounded, dark brown shape is meant to invoke a truffle, with the delicious treasure just under the surface. This recipe features the classic combo of chocolate and vanilla gelato, but any duo of preferred flavors can work.*

|  | | |
|---|---|---|
| Chocolate gelato (or any flavor) | 400 grams | 1 pint |
| Pitted sweet cherries, fresh or frozen, or drained Amarena cherries, chopped | 115 grams | 1 cup |
| Vanilla gelato (or any flavor) | 400 grams | 1 pint |
| Chocolate wafers (about 10), such as Famous Chocolate Wafers, crushed | 65 grams | |
| Refined coconut oil, melted | 40 grams | 3 tablespoons |
| Semisweet chocolate, preferably Valrhona Guanaja, chopped | 115 grams | 4 ounces |

Line a 4- to 6-cup bowl with plastic wrap, leaving about 3 inches (8 cm) of overhang. Let the chocolate gelato sit at room temperature for about 5 minutes, until slightly softened. Scoop into the prepared bowl and smooth into an even layer, then sprinkle the chopped cherries over the top. Freeze for about 1 hour, uncovered, until firm.

Let the vanilla gelato sit at room temperature for about 5 minutes before scooping into the bowl on top of the chocolate. Smooth into an even layer.

Meanwhile, in a small bowl, combine the crushed wafers and 2 tablespoons of the coconut oil. Mix until combined.

Press the wafer crumbs evenly over the vanilla gelato. Use the overhanging plastic wrap to cover, pressing to adhere the crumbs to the gelato. Freeze for about 2 hours, until fully set, or up to 1 week.

Fill a medium saucepan with 1 inch (2.5 cm) of water and bring to a simmer over medium heat. Set a heatproof medium bowl over the saucepan, making sure the bowl doesn't touch the water. Add the chocolate and remaining coconut oil and cook, stirring occasionally with a silicone spatula, until the chocolate melts. Remove the bowl from the saucepan and stir to make sure the oil is fully incorporated.

Set a wire rack over a baking sheet. Remove the bowl from the freezer, unwrap, and invert the tartufo onto the rack. Discard the plastic wrap. Slowly pour the melted chocolate over the center of the tartufo, letting it run down the sides. Use an offset spatula to transfer the tartufo to a serving plate. Serve immediately or freeze, uncovered, for up to 4 hours.

Let sit at room temperature for about 5 minutes before serving.

The tartufo can be wrapped in plastic and stored in the freezer for up to 1 week.

# 8

# FOUNDATIONS

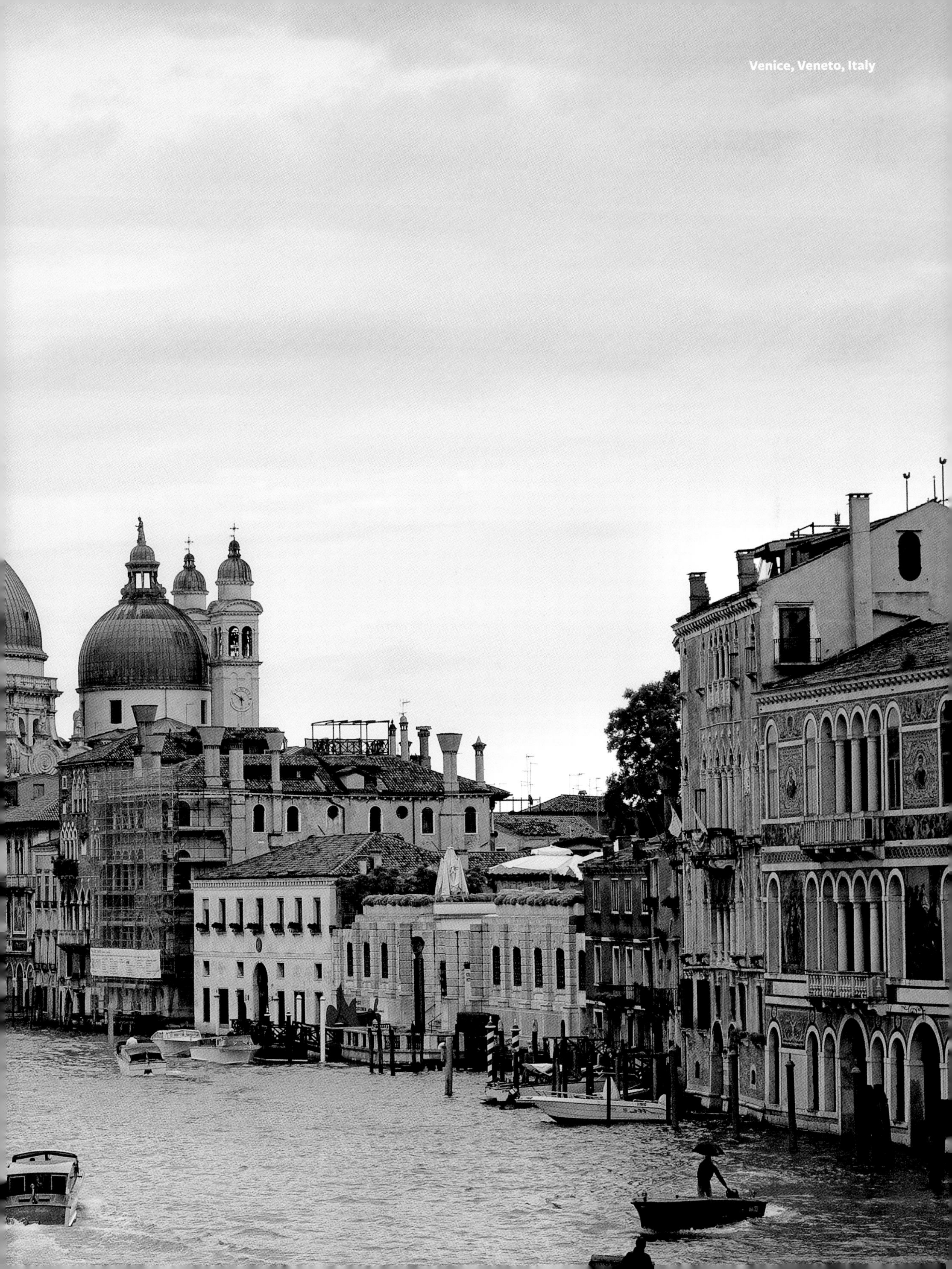

Venice, Veneto, Italy

**MASTERING FOUNDATIONAL TECHNIQUES** is the key to confidence in pastry. These recipes are the building blocks for many things throughout the book, so they're worth a little more time and attention to get right. Included in this chapter are helpful process photos to clarify steps, and everything can be made ahead to break up the baking process into easy steps.

# ITALIAN BUTTERCREAM

**MAKES 500 GRAMS (2¾ CUPS)**

**Used in** ▶ *Mocha Orange Whoopie Pies (page 55), Pistachio Lemon Cake (page 199), Chocolate Hazelnut Cake (page 203), Aperol Spritz Cake (page 209)*

|  | | |
|---|---|---|
| Large egg whites | 3 | |
| Granulated sugar | 150 grams | ¾ cup |
| Unsalted butter, cubed and at room temperature | 335 grams | 24 tablespoons |
| White chocolate, melted | 30 grams | 1 ounce |

In a stand mixer fitted with the whisk, beat the egg whites on medium speed until soft peaks form, about 3 minutes.

In a small saucepan, combine the sugar and 85 grams (6 tablespoons) water and stir once to combine. Set over low heat and bring the mixture to a boil until the syrup has reached 238° to 240°F (114° to 116°C) on a candy thermometer.

With the mixer on low speed, slowly stream the syrup into the egg whites. Once all the syrup is incorporated, increase the speed to high and whip until the steam dissipates and soft, glossy peaks form, 6 to 8 minutes. Add the butter one piece at a time and beat until the buttercream looks thick, fluffy, and spreadable, about 10 minutes. Add the white chocolate and beat until incorporated. Use the buttercream right away or store in the refrigerator until needed.

The buttercream can be stored in an airtight container in the refrigerator for 7 to 10 days. Let sit at room temperature for 15 minutes and whisk to fluff before using.

# PASTRY CREAM

**MAKES 560 GRAMS (2 CUPS)**

*Used in* ▶ *Tricolore Bomboloni (page 15), Crostata della Nonna (page 78), Zeppole di San Giuseppe (page 148), Rum Babà (page 156), Minne di Sant'Agata (page 164), Bosco Nero (page 181)*

| | | |
|---|---|---|
| Whole milk | 455 grams | 2 cups |
| Granulated sugar | 50 grams, plus 65 grams | ¼ cup, plus ⅓ cup |
| Strips of zest from ½ lemon | | |
| Pure vanilla extract | 5 grams | 1 teaspoon |
| Cornstarch | 25 grams | 3 tablespoons |
| Fine sea salt | 1 gram | ¼ teaspoon |
| Large egg yolks | 2 | |
| Large egg | 1 | |
| Unsalted butter | 30 grams | 2 tablespoons |

In a medium saucepan, combine the milk, 50 grams (¼ cup) of the sugar, the lemon zest, and vanilla. Set over medium heat, stirring continuously, until the milk starts to bubble around the edges and the sugar dissolves. Bring it almost to a boil, then remove from the heat.

In a medium bowl, whisk together the remaining sugar, the cornstarch, and salt. Whisk in the yolks and whole egg until well combined. Slowly pour in a little of the hot milk, whisking constantly. Continue whisking and adding the milk a little at a time until the mixture is combined and smooth. Return the mixture to the same saucepan over medium heat, whisking constantly, until the mixture begins to thicken, 2 to 3 minutes.

Remove from the heat, add the butter, and mix until fully incorporated. Set a fine-mesh sieve over a clean medium bowl and pour the pastry cream through, using a rubber spatula to help it pass through. Press plastic wrap directly on the surface of the cream. Let cool for 30 minutes, then refrigerate for 1 hour, until completely cooled.

The pastry cream can be stored in an airtight container in the refrigerator for up to 3 days.

## PISTACHIO PASTRY CREAM

After the pastry cream thickens, remove from the heat and add 80 grams (¼ cup) pistachio spread along with the butter, and mix until fully incorporated.

# BASIC WHIPPED CREAM

**MAKES 290 GRAMS (2 CUPS)**

*Used in* ▶ *Maritozzi (page 27), Espresso Almond Icebox Towers (page 61), Rum Babà (page 156), Budino Biondo (page 246), Panettone Bread Pudding (page 255), Delizia al Limone e Basilico (page 256)*

| | | |
|---|---|---|
| Heavy cream, very cold | 230 grams | 1 cup |
| Pure vanilla extract | 5 grams | 1 teaspoon |
| Powdered sugar | 30 grams | ¼ cup |

In a stand mixer fitted with the whisk, beat the cream and vanilla on medium speed until soft peaks form, about 3 minutes. Add the powdered sugar and continue beating until stiff peaks form, about 2 minutes more.

The whipped cream can be covered and refrigerated for up to 1 day.

## BERRY WHIPPED CREAM

Add 2 tablespoons fruit preserves to the finished cream and beat on low speed until combined, about 30 seconds.

## ESPRESSO WHIPPED CREAM

In a small bowl, whisk together 1 tablespoon of instant espresso powder and 1 tablespoon of boiling water. Set in the refrigerator to cool completely, about 15 minutes. Add the espresso mixture to the finished cream and beat on low speed until combined, about 30 seconds.

# FRESH RICOTTA

**MAKES 1 KILOGRAM (4 CUPS)**

**Used in** ▶ *Pastiera (page 91), Crostini (page 116), Cocoa Ricotta Zeppole with Tahini Glaze (page 151), Cannoli Croccante (page 169), Ricotta Polenta Torta (page 177), Italian Ricotta Cheesecake (page 187), Cassata (page 218)*

| | | |
|---|---|---|
| Pasteurized organic whole milk | 3.75 liters | 1 gallon |
| Pasteurized heavy cream | 115 grams | ½ cup |
| Filtered, non-chlorinated water | 115 grams | ½ cup |
| Vegetable or animal rennet | 1 gram | ½ teaspoon |
| Fine sea salt (optional) | 2 grams | ½ teaspoon |

**NOTE**

Since milk is the main ingredient here, use the best quality you can find for decidedly luxurious results.

In a large heavy pot with a thermometer clipped to the side, combine the milk and heavy cream. Bring to a simmer over medium heat, stirring frequently with a silicone spatula, until the mixture reaches 120°F (49°C). Remove from the heat.

In a small bowl, combine the water and rennet, give a quick stir and add to the warm milk. Stir into the milk and let the mixture sit, undisturbed, for 30 to 40 minutes.

Place a strainer over a medium sized bowl and line the strainer with cheesecloth.

Ladle the curds into the prepared strainer, allowing the whey to seep through into the bowl. Empty the bowl if it begins to get full. Cover the ricotta with the overhanging cheese cloth and let strain until it reaches your preferred consistency, 1 to 2 hours, at room temperature. Stir in the salt (if using).

The ricotta can be stored in an airtight container in the refrigerator for up to 5 days.

# SOURDOUGH STARTER

MAKES 227 GRAMS (1 CUP) USABLE STARTER (ONGOING)

**Used in** ▶ *Sourdough Focaccia Three Ways (page 101)*

| | | |
|---|---|---|
| All-purpose flour, plus more for feeding | 140 grams | 1 cup |
| Whole wheat flour | 115 grams | 1 cup |
| Lukewarm water, plus more for feeding | 230 grams | 1 cup |

**Day 1** ▶ In a 2-quart airtight container, combine the all-purpose flour, whole wheat flour, and water. Stir until no dry patches remain. Cover the container and set in a warm spot (ideally 70° to 80°F or 21° to 27°C) for 24 hours.

**Day 2** ▶ The next day, reserve 115 grams (½ cup) of the starter and discard the rest. Stir in 140 grams (1 cup) all-purpose flour and 115 grams (½ cup) water until no dry patches remain. Re-cover and return to a warm spot for 24 hours.

**Day 3** ▶ On the third day, you should see some bubbles, that the starter has increased in size, and notice a fresh aroma. Reserve 115 grams (½ cup) of the starter and discard the rest. Stir in 140 grams (1 cup) all-purpose flour and 115 grams (½ cup) water until no dry patches remain. Re-cover and return to a warm spot for 12 hours.

Later on the third day, reserve 115 grams (½ cup) of the starter and discard the rest. Stir in 140 grams (1 cup) all-purpose flour and 115 grams (½ cup) water until no dry patches remain. Re-cover and return to a warm spot for 12 hours.

**Days 4 and 5** ▶ Continue discarding and feeding twice a day for 2 more days. By the end of the fifth day the starter should have doubled in volume with lots of bubbles and a yeasty aroma. (If it isn't rising yet, continue the feedings for 2 more days. If it's still not rising, discard and start again.)

Do one last discard and feeding, letting the starter sit for 8 hours. Measure out 230 grams (1 cup) of starter to use.

The starter can be stored in an airtight container in the refrigerator indefinitely, with regular feedings 1 to 2 times a week.

# PIZZA DOUGH

**MAKES 558 GRAMS (1¼ POUNDS)**

*Used in* ▶ *Impanata (page 104), 'Nduja Pizzette (page 106), Caponata Bombas (page 109)*

| | | |
|---|---|---|
| Active dry yeast | 3 grams | 1 teaspoon |
| Warm tap water | 230 grams | 1 cup |
| Fine sea salt | 8 grams | 2 teaspoons |
| All-purpose flour | 320 grams | 2¼ cups |
| Olive oil for the bowl | | |

In a stand mixer fitted with the dough hook, combine the yeast and warm water. Let sit for about 5 minutes, until the yeast is foamy and fragrant. Add the salt and sift in the flour. Mix on low speed until the flour is incorporated, then increase the speed to medium and knead until a smooth, elastic dough forms, about 3 minutes.

Coat a large bowl with olive oil. Transfer the dough to the bowl. Coat a piece of plastic wrap in cooking spray and loosely cover the dough, spray-side down. Refrigerate for at least 24 hours. Let sit at room temperature for 30 minutes before using.

The pizza dough can be covered and stored in the refrigerator for up to 3 days.

# MASTER BRIOCHE

**MAKES 1.2 KILOGRAMS (2½ POUNDS)**

*A PSA about making brioche: Here is a harsh truth, making a true, classic brioche dough puts your mixer through its paces. We have tried to reduce the amount of "hold your mixer down for dear life" moments as much as possible, and still yield a beautiful, buttery bread, but you cannot casually walk away or stare at your phone during this process.*

Used in ▶ *Brioche con Tuppo (page 19), American Cinnamon Rolls (page 20), Sicilian Sticky Buns (page 23), Maritozzi (page 27), Ode to Iris (page 33)*

|  |  |  |
|---|---|---|
| Whole milk, cold | 185 grams | ¾ cup plus 1 tablespoon |
| Active dry yeast | 10 grams | 1 tablespoon |
| Large eggs, cold | 4 | |
| Bread flour | 515 grams | 3½ cups plus 2 tablespoons |
| Granulated sugar | 80 grams | 6 tablespoons |
| Fine sea salt | 12 grams | 1 tablespoon |
| Cold unsalted butter, cubed | 265 grams | 19 tablespoons |

**NOTE**

To check for gluten development, perform what's called a windowpane test: Hold up and stretch a small amount of dough with your hands. It should be elastic enough to be pulled without tearing until it is thin enough to see light through.

In the bowl of a stand mixer, combine the cold milk and yeast. Whisk by hand to dissolve and let sit 2 to 3 minutes.

Place the bowl on the mixer fitted with the dough hook. Mixing on medium-low speed, add the eggs, followed by the bread flour, and mix until the dough comes together and cleans the sides of the bowl, about 3 minutes.

In a small bowl, combine the sugar and salt and add to the mixer. Mix on medium-low speed for 2 more minutes to combine.

Gradually add the cubed butter to the mixer, piece by piece, and continue to mix on low speed for about 10 minutes. Stop the mixer occasionally to scrape down the sides of the bowl. Once the butter is fully incorporated into the dough, mix on medium speed for 15 minutes. After 15 minutes, the dough should appear shiny, loose, and soft.

Turn the mixer up to medium-high speed for 2 to 3 minutes, holding down the mixer if it feels unsteady. The dough should "slap" around as it hits the sides of the bowl. When tested (see Note), the dough should have full gluten development.

Coat a large bowl with cooking spray. Transfer the dough to the bowl. Coat a piece of plastic wrap in cooking spray and loosely cover the dough, coated-side down. Refrigerate for at least 12 hours before using.

The brioche dough can be covered and stored in the refrigerator for up to 2 days.

# SAVOIARDI

**MAKES 48 COOKIES**

*Used in* ▶ *Malted Tiramisù (page 243), Zuppa Inglese with Blackberries (page 250)*

| | | |
|---|---|---|
| All-purpose flour | 200 grams | 1½ cups |
| Cornstarch | 8 grams | 1 tablespoon |
| Baking powder | 5 grams | 1 teaspoon |
| Large eggs, separated | 5 | |
| Granulated sugar, divided | 180 grams | ½ cup |
| Pure vanilla extract | 5 grams | 1 teaspoon |
| Powdered sugar, for dusting | | |

**NOTE**

If making these to use in tiramisù, bake for an additional 2 to 3 minutes so they will better absorb the espresso mixture.

Preheat the oven to 350°F (180°C) and set racks in the upper and lower thirds. Line two baking sheets with parchment paper.

In a medium bowl, combine the flour, cornstarch, and baking powder. Give a quick whisk and set aside.

In a stand mixer fitted with the whisk, beat the egg whites on medium speed until foamy. Reduce the speed to low and gradually add 90 grams (¼ cup) of the granulated sugar. Increase the speed to medium-high and whisk until the mixture is glossy and thick, about 4 minutes. Transfer to a large bowl.

Wash and dry the mixer bowl and whisk. Return to the mixer and add the yolks, vanilla, and remaining granulated sugar to the bowl. Whisk the yolks at medium speed until pale yellow in color, 8 to 10 minutes.

Remove the bowl from the mixer and add one-quarter of the whites to the yolks. Using a rubber spatula, gently fold the whites into the yolks until just combined.

Sift the flour mixture over the egg mixture and gently fold again just until the mixture is incorporated. Gently fold in the remaining whites until just incorporated.

Transfer the batter to a large piping bag fitted with a ½-inch (1 cm) round tip. On one of the prepared baking sheets, pipe the batter in 3½- to 4-inch (9 to 10 cm) logs, leaving about 1 inch (2.5 cm) between them, piping 4 rows of 6 savoiardi on each sheet. Dust with powdered sugar, let rest for 2 to 3 minutes, and then dust again. Repeat with the second baking sheet and remaining batter.

Bake until golden, but still soft to the touch, 12 to 15 minutes, rotating the baking sheet front to back halfway through. Let cool on the baking sheets for 5 minutes, then use an offset spatula to transfer the cookies to a wire rack.

Once the cookies are cooled, transfer them to an airtight container until ready to use.

The savoiardi can be stored in an airtight container at room temperature for up to 2 to 3 weeks.

# PASTA FROLLA

MAKES 748 GRAMS (1 POUND 10 OUNCES)

*Used in* ▶ *Occhi di Bue* (page 69), *Crostata Classica* (page 77), *Crostata della Nonna* (page 78), *Torta del Nonno* (page 79), *Monte Bianco* (page 87), *Pastiera* (page 91), *Minne di Sant'Agata* (page 164)

| | | |
|---|---|---|
| Unsalted butter, at room temperature | 225 grams | 16 tablespoons |
| Powdered sugar | 150 grams | 1¼ cups |
| Grated lemon zest | 2 grams | 1 teaspoon |
| Large egg yolks, at room temperature | 3 | |
| All-purpose flour, plus more for kneading | 320 grams | 2¼ cups |
| Fine sea salt | 1 gram | ¼ teaspoon |

In a stand mixer fitted with the paddle, combine the butter, powdered sugar, and lemon zest and beat on low until combined. Increase the speed to medium and beat until smooth and creamy, about 2 minutes. Reduce the speed to low and add the egg yolks one at a time, scraping down the sides as needed. Stop the mixer and sift in the flour and salt. Mix on low until just combined and the dough begins to form, scraping the sides and bottom to fully mix.

Lightly dust a work surface with flour. Knead the dough, adding additional flour if necessary, until it's uniform and in one piece. Do not overwork the dough; it should come together quickly. Pat the dough into a round and wrap tightly with plastic wrap. Refrigerate for at least 2 hours.

The pasta frolla can be covered and stored in the refrigerator for up to 2 days.

# CHOCOLATE PASTA FROLLA

MAKES 845 GRAMS (1 POUND 15 OUNCES)

| | | |
|---|---|---|
| Cocoa powder | 25 grams | ¼ cup |
| Boiling water | 55 grams | ¼ cup |
| Unsalted butter, at room temperature | 225 grams | 16 tablespoons |
| Powdered sugar | 150 grams | 1¼ cups |
| Large egg yolks, at room temperature | 2 | |
| All-purpose flour, plus more for kneading | 355 grams | 2½ cups |
| Fine sea salt | 1 gram | ¼ teaspoon |

In a small bowl, whisk the cocoa powder and boiling water.

In a stand mixer fitted with the paddle, combine the butter and powdered sugar. Beat on low speed until combined. Increase the speed to medium and beat until smooth and creamy, about 2 minutes. Reduce the speed to low and add the cocoa mixture, mixing until combined. Add the egg yolks one at a time, scraping down the sides as needed. Stop the mixer and sift in the flour and salt. Mix on low until just combined and the dough begins to form, scraping the sides and bottom to fully mix. Continue with the recipe as normal.

rally 200

Roma 42
9059

Rome, Lazio, Italy

# INGREDIENT WEIGHTS

Matching grams to imperial measurements is never an exact art. Throughout the book, I've rounded ingredient weights whenever possible to make the recipes quick and easy. This guide is the true conversions for each ingredient, for the purist bakers or anyone who loves a nerdy reference section. (I count myself in both of those categories.) Certain things, like cornstarch, baking powder, and baking soda have remained exact throughout the book, as they will have a big impact on the final result. Everything else can slide a few grams in either direction and not derail the recipe at all.

| | |
|---:|---|
| **Eggs** | always listed by number instead of weight |
| **All-purpose flour** | 1 cup = 142 grams |
| **Bread flour** | 1 cup = 142 grams |
| **Cake flour** | 1 cup = 120 grams |
| **Almond flour** | 1 cup = 100 grams |
| **Cocoa powder** | 1 cup = 96 grams |
| | |
| **Cornstarch** | 1 tablespoon = 9 grams |
| **Baking powder** | 1 teaspoon = 5 grams |
| **Baking soda** | 1 teaspoon = 6 grams |
| **Fine sea salt** | 1 teaspoon = 4 grams |
| **Ground spices** | 1 teaspoon = 3 grams |
| **Espresso powder** | 1 tablespoon = 4 grams |
| | |
| **Alcohol** | 1 tablespoon = 14 grams |
| **Lemon/orange zest** | 1 tablespoon = 6 grams |
| **Fresh lemon/orange juice** | 1 tablespoon = 15 grams |
| **Pure vanilla extract (and other extracts)** | 1 teaspoon = 5 grams |
| **Vanilla bean paste** | 1 teaspoon = 6 grams |
| **Wildflower honey** | 1 tablespoon = 20 grams |
| **Light corn syrup** | 1 tablespoon = 20 grams |
| **Fruit preserves** | ½ cup = 170 grams |
| **Mini chocolate chips** | 1 cup = 177 grams |
| **Semisweet chocolate chips** | 1 cup = 170 grams |
| **Chocolate bars** | by weight in equivalent ounces |
| | |
| **Granulated sugar** | 1 cup = 200 grams |
| **Powdered sugar** | 1 cup = 120 grams |
| **Dark brown sugar** | 1 packed cup = 198 grams |
| | |
| **Unsalted butter** | 1 tablespoon = 14 grams |
| **Heavy cream** | 1 cup = 230 grams |
| **Buttermilk** | 1 cup = 230 grams |
| **Whole milk** | 1 cup = 227 grams |
| **Ricotta** | 1 cup = 252 grams |
| **Mascarpone** | 1 cup = 230 grams |
| **Sour cream** | 1 cup = 230 grams |
| **Canola oil** | 1 cup = 198 grams |
| **Extra-virgin olive oil** | 1 cup = 200 grams |
| **Water** | 1 cup = 227 grams |

# ACKNOWLEDGMENTS

Allora, after writing four cookbooks, I really thought I would never write another, as the process borders on masochism. Especially when you are running a business simultaneously. Writing a baking book is a bit like writing a chemistry textbook. It needs to be specific, precise, and rooted in science. However, a cookbook must also entertain and engage—through the selection of recipes chosen, the tone in which it is written, and the photography and design of the book itself. It has to tick all those boxes and that's no small feat. This is not something anyone can achieve by themselves. It takes a mighty team of people to make this happen.

First and foremost, thank you to longtime friend, Italian travel companion, and author in his own right, Casey Elsass. Without his initial push, this book would still be a file on my desktop. His regimented and detailed approach to writing and recipe development helped me get to the finish line, three months ahead of schedule, and I will be forever grateful.

"You need to write an Italian baking book!" Those words led me to this point and I couldn't be happier. Alison Fargis, a friend and incredible agent, thanks for being there since my adolescent years at Baked.

To the incredible team who made this book into tangible reality: Kevin Miyazaki, another great travel companion and a most talented photographer. He makes it all seem so effortless and the photos he took of the food, of Italy, of Brooklyn truly capture the mood I was hoping for.

Maeve Sheridan, whose photo studio was our second home for a couple of weeks. Her excitement over this shoot was contagious. And her eye for detail stupendo.

Jesse Szewczyk and Ben Weiner! Two food stylist powerhouses. Thank you for managing a huge shot list and making everything look just so. You are both magicians.

Working on the shoot was one of the most wonderful experiences for me, I hope we get to do it again someday.

Of course, Tom Pold, thank you for coming to bat for this book. Being a part of the Knopf family still leaves me a bit breathless. You have made this whole experience a pleasure. I hope this book makes you and your team proud.

Grazie mille to the army of testers that made these recipes multiple times and asked the hard-hitting questions when confronted with a recipe they had never seen or heard of before: Anna Painter, Agatha Khishchenko, Stephanie Whitten, Dafna Adler, Disco, Tina Zaccardi, Dawn Casale, Chris Benecke, David Bertozzi, Jason Hudson, Alexander Noelle, Topher Chavis, and Anne Innis. And a special shout-out to Brad Thomas Parsons for his guidance on all things amaro and bitters.

In many ways, *Dolci!* is the unofficial Ciao, Gloria cookbook. It stands on its own, but you will find many of its recipes at the café in one form or another. So with that, I'd like to thank my family at Ciao. This "second act" decision to open my own café was like jumping into an abyss. But thankfully, Ginger Fisher Baldwin was there to catch me, rooting me on all the way. Thanks, G., for understanding my vision, helping me create a dessert and pastry menu I am eternally proud of, and for helping me with the development and testing for this book. Pittsburgh, you have a winner.

So much gratitude for Carly Voltero. The real reason Ciao is a busy, bustling café is because of her talent and dedication. She transformed what was intended to be a little bakery with a small savory menu into a breakfast and lunch behemoth that carried us through a pandemic and turned us into what we are today. In many ways, Carly *is* Gloria. She's a powerhouse in the kitchen, one of the most talented people I have ever met, and a riot to be around. Thank you for being a part of this since day one.

Valerie Figueroa, thank you for taking the reins from both Ginger and Carly and leading with them. She is the newest addition to our team and has already proven herself invaluable. She has helped me with last-minute recipe changes and fixes and has kept the kitchen running smoothly while I've been squirreled away in my office putting these pages together.

Thanks to the rest of my small but mighty kitchen, past and future, but most important, present: My cooks, Isrrael, Lucino, Olivia, Catalina, Almeyda, Jesus, Eduardo. What you all do in a single day most people can't achieve in a week. To my bakers! Andy, Stephanie, Arnel, and Natalie. Your talent and joy bring *me* joy!

Misael, Calvin, and Christian: for keeping this café in working order every moment of every day. And to Janet, for helping me with all manner of official office work.

My baristas, the faces of the café, you all make me smile: Daniel, Mei Lu, Sydni, Madison, Heather, Kael. And a special thank-you to Mark Elizabeth Malikowski for being my bestie and the one who can make me laugh at the absurdity of everything, regardless.

To my family and friends, both here and in Italy. My biological and chosen. There are many of you and you know who you are, Thank you for tolerating me at my worst and for answering many obscure questions about the history of Italian desserts.

Sven, you took this journey with me and I'm happy to see where it's taken us. Thank you for dealing with me for two plus decades. XO.

This book is dedicated to my mother, but it's also dedicated to everyone above. None of this would be possible without each of you. And I am grateful for that, every single day.

Capri, Campania, Italy

Naples, Campania, Italy

# INDEX

(Page references in *italics* refer to illustrations.)

Taormina, Sicily, Italy

## A NOTE ABOUT THE AUTHORS

Renato Poliafito is a two-time James Beard nominee and the owner (and manager, and HR department, and handyman, and PR rep) of Ciao, Gloria, a bakery and café with a decidedly Italian accent in Prospect Heights, Brooklyn. This is his fifth cookbook, but he considers *Dolci!* his first "solo album." He enjoys traveling and not traveling in equal measure. In his free time, he is a novice potter and likes to eat sweets (duh). He lives with his husband and potential future dog in Brooklyn.

Casey Elsass is a food writer, recipe developer, and cookbook author living in Brooklyn.

### Also by Renato Poliafito

*Baked: New Frontiers in Baking* (with Matt Lewis)

*Baked Explorations* (with Matt Lewis)

*Baked Elements* (with Matt Lewis)

*Baked Occasions* (with Matt Lewis)

Palermo, Sicily, Italy

## A NOTE ON THE TYPE

The text of this book was set in Freight Text Pro Book, designed by Joshua Darden (b. 1979) and published by GarageFonts in 2005. It was inspired by the "Dutch-taste" school of typeface design and is considered a transitional-style typeface. Legible, stylish, and sturdy, Freight Text was designed to be highly versatile, belonging to a wide-ranging "superfamily" of fonts, including many versions and weights.

*Composed by North Market Street Graphics, Lancaster, Pennsylvania*

*Printed and bound by C&C Offset, China*

*Designed by Anna B. Knighton*

Siena, Tuscany, Italy